Three Years
With the 92d Illinois

THREE YEARS WITH THE 92d ILLINOIS

The Civil War Diary of John M. King

EDITED BY CLAIRE E. SWEDBERG

STACKPOLE
BOOKS

Published by
STACKPOLE BOOKS
5067 Ritter Road
Mechanicsburg, PA 17055
www.stackpolebooks.com

Printed in the United States of America

10 9 8 7 6 5 4 3 2 1

FIRST EDITION

Library of Congress Cataloging-in-Publication Data

King, John M. (John McCandish), b. 1840.
     Three years with the 92nd Illinois: the Civil War diary of John M.
King/edited by Claire E. Swedberg.—1st ed.
        p.   cm.
     Includes bibliographical references and index.
     ISBN 0-8117-1599-X
     1. King, John M. (John McCandish), b. 1840—Diaries. 2. United
States. Army. Illinois Infantry Regiment, 92nd (1862–1865) 3. Illinois—
History—Civil War, 1861–1865—Personal narratives. 4. Unites States—
History—Civil War, 1861–1865—Personal narratives. 5.
Illinois—History—Civil War, 1861–1865—Regimental histories. 6.
Unites States—History—Civil War, 1861–1865—Regimental histories. 7.
Soldiers—Illinois—Rockford—Biography. 8. Rockford (Ill.)—Biography.
I. Swedberg, Claire E. II. Title.
E505.5 92nd 1999
973.7'473'092—dc21
  [B]   98-55166
                                               CIP

CONTENTS

INTRODUCTION

When twenty-two-year-old John McCandish King Jr. enlisted in the Union Army in 1862, he had more education than most young farmers but little life experience beyond the rigors of farm work in Illinois. He had a gift for writing however, a gift he eventually put to use at the printing press of his own newspaper in Illinois.

Born in 1840, John King was the sixth child of John McCandish King and Lucy Boynton. His pioneering father was born in England in 1802, the son of Richard McCandish and Annie Hesketh. Sometime in the first years of the nineteenth century, Richard McCandish died and left Annie to fend for herself against a family of McCandishes, who had disapproved of the marriage. Annie took young John and returned to her own family, soon marrying Walter King. John McCandish King, adopting his new father's name, learned a trade in the woolen factories. In 1823 or '24 he immigrated to the United States and went to work in the mills of New England.

In the 1840s John Sr. and his wife and eight children, including young John M. King Jr., migrated west in two homemade covered wagons loaded with the household goods needed for the large family. In 1846 they settled in Ogle County, Illinois, near the small town of Rockford. Lucy died during a measles epidemic in 1852, leaving twelve-year-old John Jr. and his siblings motherless. Their father soon married Armenia Wadsworth, a widow, who brought her own five children into the household.

Before the Civil War, three of the eldest children left home and married, and four more children were born from the new marriage. John Jr. had grown into a young man by this time and was nearly six feet tall, slender, blond, and blue-eyed.

John King Sr. was a strong abolitionist and raised his family to be the same. When news came in 1860 that South Carolina had seceded John King

Jr. was attending classes at Mount Morris Seminary and working on the farm. News came the following spring of First Bull Run and Lincoln's call for thousands of volunteers.

Local farmers and clerks organized the 92d Illinois Volunteer Infantry following the North's disastrous loss at Second Bull Run in August 1862. This humiliating second loss at the northeastern creek of Virginia served to galvanize young men in the farming country of the Midwest to action. King was one of those men.

So began John's career in the military, of which he chronicles the most fascinating details, with the diligence and astute attention that would eventually serve him as a newsman. He kept a series of diaries with tiny, neatly lettered words, economizing space by omitting unnecessary prepositions and articles. These diaries followed him throughout his campaign southward toward Atlanta, where the Union army made its final drive to squelch the Southern rebellion. From 1862 to 1864 he chronicled everyday life in the South as a member of the Union army and gave vivid accounts of deadly skirmishes and battles, such as Chickamauga and the Battle of Resaca. After a brief stay in the hospital from leg injuries he had sustained while standing picket in the frigid winters, he returned to Illinois in search of an education. He completed a degree at Mount Morris Seminary, which his brother Richard also attended, then considered law school. Instead, he took a job as a schoolteacher, married another teacher named Mary Logsdon, and settled into family life in the midst of postwar prosperity.

Now more involved in politics, especially the cause of the Greenback Party, he sought ways to spread his political views in the agrarian society around him. In 1878, in Rochelle, Illinois, he opened a highly political newspaper named the *Rochelle Telephone,* with his wife, Mary, at his side, along with two apprentice printers and a cook. It was here, in the early 1880s, that John returned to his prized diaries and prepared them for print on a serial basis in his paper, intending more to educate young people than to reflect on glory days with the older veterans. He and Mary printed several hundred issues before the newspaper and their marriage came to an end. Abruptly, after several years of John's dabbling in politics while an increasingly resentful Mary stayed at home working on the newspaper, the two parted ways.

Abandoning his journalistic career and his Civil War diaries, John M. King began a new life in North Dakota. This decision meant that King's view of some of the most famous battles in which he fought, including the burning of Atlanta, never saw print. All we have to illuminate the final activities of the 92d before the war ended is a speech made by 92d Illinois Volunteer Brig. Gen. Smith Atkins twenty years after the war at a veterans reunion.

Based on letters sent home by John and his brother Richard, I have also surmised that John King, who was never wounded in battle, returned to the hospital at the end of the war with an unresolved case of frostbite he had sustained on picket duty and took several months to recuperate before returning to his life in Illinois.

I have chosen to make few editorial changes to the text of King's original work. Some archaic spelling remains, as well as King's own choice of spelling for proper names such as Chicamauga, which is commonly spelled Chickamauga.

The most unpleasant references emerge in the author's commentary regarding slaves and former slaves, which were referred to by Northerners and Southerners alike at the time as "niggers" and "darkies." Though the titles are considered derogatory today, King's use of them was not intended to be. It is likely that this Northerner, who had little knowledge of African-Americans before his tour in the South, intended to be the model of tolerance, and believed himself to be of the most liberal views regarding slavery. I therefore ask the reader to try, as I did, to overlook what, by today's standards, seem to be racist and derogatory references to the African-Americans of that time.

I expect history to prove King's diary most valuable in his commentary about politics within the military, the day-to-day ordeals of the Union army in the South, and the personal views of battles that have traditionally been told from the officers' perspectives. Often quick to judge and quick to condemn, he tells frequently humorous stories of the actions of and repercussions to officers we thought we already knew, such as Gordon Granger, "Old Pap" Thomas, and even General Sherman. King also presents some of the views of Southern slave owners and retells their stories with surprising objectivity. Ultimately, John M. King, with his wry style, has narrated one portion of the Civil War as no one else has.

CHAPTER 1

Everyone Seemed to be Enlisting
June 1862 – January 1863

JANUARY 1, 1863, DANVILLE, KENTUCKY

This morning as I sat on an empty cracker box in my bell tent musing over the fact that this is New Years Day and conjecturing what they are doing at home way up in Illinois, the history of the past year of 1862 was running like a panorama before me. Some of the events come vivid while others more dim. I remembered how I had promised the good folks at home that I would write and tell them all the news, our joys and sorrows, our sickness and health, our pleasures and hardships. And if it ever became my good fortune to return home when this cruel war is over, then I would sit by the old fireside and relate it all in detail.

It is now nearly five months since we enlisted and some of the events are already growing dim in my memory. What will be the condition of my recollections by the time the war is over? I resolved then at once to purchase this diary. Leaving the tent I strolled out upon the regimental grounds and soon found a peddler. Yankee peddlers can be found anywhere. It is said of Bonaparte that once in the middle of a great eastern desert he met an Irishman with a pack on his back peddling. He then declared that an Irishman could be found in any part of the known world. So it is with our Yankee peddlers. I soon found one and purchased a diary for this new year of 1863. It is four inches long by two and a half wide and contains pages for each day of the year, an almanac, rates of postage, memoranda leaves, cash leaves, and a place to carry your girl's photograph. Nearly every unmarried man has a girl that receives most of his letters and as a rule the soldier has her photograph. It is nothing unusual to see two or three soldiers around a camp fire or on picket comparing photographs to see who has the best-looking girl. On one of these comparing occasions a fellow told me, "My girl is not handsome, but awful good." So a place in a diary to carry a photograph made it very saleable.

As my diary was not purchased until five months after enlisting, it becomes necessary to use all the fly leaves and memoranda leaves in order to give the past five months' events. They must be condensed at that.[1]

On the 27th of June, 1862, I had spoken my boyish piece at the annual exhibition of the Mt. Morris Seminary[2] near my home in Byron, Illinois. I then left the old "Standstone," as we used to call it, and went into the harvest field to fight life's usual battles. The soft skin on my hands had begun to chafe and blister in the hot sun from handling the long coarse straw of a very heavy crop. While I was working very hard there a horse and buggy came in the field and the driver steered straight for me. It was Eugene Everts,[3] a young man of about twenty, an old neighbor of mine I had known from childhood. He lived in the town of Marion, Ogle County, Illinois, while I was working in White Rock.

The Battle of Bull Run[4] had been fought about the first of August, 1862, our forces were badly beaten and thousands of our men had become panic stricken, thrown down their guns, and fled. Some of the hostile papers declared that some may be running yet. The loss of this battle created great excitement all over the country, both North and South. The excitement was intensified when on the heels of the disaster at Bull Run came the call for *six hundred thousand* [John's emphasis] more troops. Could so many troops be raised and could they be armed and equipped was the general topic at the time.

It was during this period of excitement that Eugene, in horse and buggy, came into the harvest field. The reaper soon came around to join us and bands gathered to hear the latest war news. Eugene told us that everybody was going to war. One company was being raised in Byron under the captaincy of W. W. Dennis.[5] He said all the boys of my acquaintance in the townships of Marion and Byron were enlisting in Dennis' company. Eugene told us that Dennis was a smart man, brave, good, sober, and upright. He said that I must enlist at once, sign his paper, get into his rig, and help recruit others. All of which I did.

In fact, everyone seemed to be enlisting. I rode several days in company with Eugene and got some recruits. Every time we got one we would drive straight to Byron to swear him in. It made no difference if it was twenty miles away, the country was full of recruiting officers and if you got a man to promise and left him, some other recruiting officer would come along and persuade him to join some other company.

There had been a day appointed for all the boys to meet in Byron, bring in their recruits, and have a general training. Of course I went as a recruit and as assistant recruiting officer. Two loads of us, sixteen in all, went into Byron from the south side of Rock River. Everyone of the number was a member in good standing of a Good Templars Society.[6]

The captain met us at the ferry. My first introduction to Captain Dennis presented a medium-sized man weighing about 140 pounds, wiry, dark haired, and of nervous temperament, a man that could neither lie still, sit still, nor stand still. He was easily disturbed and inclined to be passionate. After an introduction and the shake of the hand all around we were invited, or ordered, to fall in and march up to the hotel. On the way up there the captain remarked that it was so hot that we would need something to drink "to cool off with." Some of the boys began to jest about Good Templars and temperance pledges when the captain remarked that "temperance is well enough for women in times of peace but soldiers cannot be bothered now with temperance pledges."

As soon as we arrived at the hotel, the captain ordered the bar tender to "set em up." And of course he did. To my astonishment everybody drank and Captain Dennis ridiculed me when I refused. I think I would have drunk had it not been for the rather unfavorable impression I received of the captain on our first meeting and also the fact that I could never bear the taste of lager beer. The captain treated a couple of times and then some of the boys treated. The drinks went round in rapid succession. Some of the boys had never drunk before in their lives. The captain then ordered us into line for drill. It was an awkward squad. The boys were all talking, and the captain was constantly crying out "Attention, no talking in the ranks!" But the boys would only repeat the orders and kept right on with their silly gabble, stumbling along like a "Kentucky nig" in a dark forest.

The sun shone out very hot and the captain brought his awkward squad into the shade of Saint John Mix's store for a rest. Most of the boys lay down on the ground and rolled and gabbled worse than ever. In the course of a little the captain commanded us to fall in line. About one-half of the boys staggered into a zig-zag line and the other half could not get on to their feet. Most of those who could not get on their feet were boys who had been well raised and had never drunk beer before. The captain did not appear to be

much affected with what he had drunk. As soon as he saw the real condition of those boys he seemed a little surprised. Turning to me he ordered
me to get our team at once and get the boys in and, turning to another fellow who was the soberest of that load, he ordered him to get the other team
ready. With the assistance of some of the town people those boys were
loaded into wagons just as a butcher would load a dead hog into his wagon.
I started ahead and the other driver was ordered to follow. We crossed the
river in safety, most of the boys being too drunk to fall off the wagon. We
got along nicely until the road forked, when the other load turned to the
right and with a drunken yell, rushed down the road at full speed, passing
over hill and dale, across the bridges and through woods, while each one
that could hold his head up yelled at the horses to go faster. They were soon
out of sight. I afterward learned that none were seriously hurt.

In the load I had, two of the boys were dead drunk in the bottom of
the wagon box. One of the number I know to a certainty had never tasted
liquor before in his life. His parents were among the more respected of the
neighborhood and I was determined not to take him home to his parents in
that condition. I resolved to drive on back roads and timber roads until I got
near home, and keep the boys near a timber brook to sober them off before
letting them go home. Then when sober, if they wished to hide their
drunkenness, they could do so, or if they wished to expose it they might do
that. I had all shades of drunkenness in my load, some could only lie, others
sit up, but one could do neither. The liquor seemed to make him doubly
strong and active. He would jump and yell as though he were Black Hawk[7]
preparing for war. He would jump into the air when we were under headway and land on his feet five or ten feet from the wagon. He would run a
little way, give a yell, another jump, and land among the other drunks in the
wagon. When we got to the brook in the timber a vigorous rubbing and
application of water brought a state of soberness. Some of the boys felt badly
over what had happened. We all agreed to keep it a profound secret, and
very strong pledges were made. The boys all kept their pledge in good faith.

The other load took a special delight in demonstrating to everybody
how awful drunk they were. They told everybody, while drunk and while
sober, that our load was drunker than they were. They gave the names of all
our load and since they all told the same story, they were believed. This
caused a great deal of unspoken remorse in the bosom of at least one of the
boys, for he has never acted like himself since. Leaving home under those
shameful circumstances, he acted dull and gloomy ever after. I am of the

opinion that these circumstances brought on the sickness that hastened his subsequent death.

JANUARY 2, 1863, DANVILLE, KENTUCKY

On one of my trips to Byron to take the names of recruits, I found the captain had left town and gone to Oregon, [Illinois]. I had the names of four recruits who were taken before a justice and sworn in to the service of the United States. The swearing-in process, by a justice of the peace, we afterwards learned was a mere farce. It had no binding effect beyond the mere pledging of the recruit to go to war. But every recruit was "sworn in," and he went through the process of signing his name to a big oath and the document was pretended to be put on file, either in Oregon, Springfield, or Washington.

Well, when I got to Byron I found that Captain Dennis had gone to Oregon and some one came to tell me that he had left special word that if any more recruiting papers came in late that day they must be sent direct to Oregon. So away I went for Oregon with my papers. On my arrival about three o'clock in the afternoon, I found it to be a general recruiting and training day for two other companies organized there, one under Major Woodcock,[8] the other under Major Dutcher.[9] The town was full of people.

I met one of the Byron boys on the street as I drove in and the first thing he asked me was whether I had got any recruiting papers.

On being answered in the affirmative, he was very anxious to take them direct to the captain who was in a great hurry for them. I volunteered to go to the captain with him, but he hesitated and equivocated so I began to suspect that something was wrong and positively refused to let him have the papers. I met Captain Weld[10] who had a short time previous resigned his position in the 34th Illinois Infantry because of ill health. He called me to one side and requested me to sit down by him in the shade of the building. I had known the captain from my boyhood for when he was a "big boy" and I a "little boy," we had attended the same school together. Captain Weld, like the good man that he was, then gave a little history of the day's doings and some good advice. I did not act in accordance with it but had occasion to regret it later. He told me that Captain Dennis had been carousing in saloons all day, drinking with the worst type of men that Ogle County produced. He said the last time he saw Dennis on the street he was so drunk he could not walk without locking arms with another man, and at this moment was lying dead drunk in some part of the town, hid away by his friends.

"My advice to you," he told me, "is to go to war just the same, but by no means put yourself in the hands of a drunken captain. The trials and hardships of camp life are hard at best, but with a drunken captain it is a hundred fold worse."

Captain Weld continued to give me advice that ought to have been heeded. I should have enlisted in another company but on reflection I decided to stand along with those I had persuaded to enlist. I resolved to let their hardships be my hardships. We had enlisted from the same neighborhood together, and we would fight it out together.

After considerable search I found the captain in his room at the hotel, lying on the bed, too drunk to be roused. He had several red-faced companions who were pretending to do the business of clerks. I turned over the papers to some one, not caring to whom. I felt very bad. I had induced others to enlist, to serve under what now proved to be an unprincipled drunkard. I could no longer request others to join.

The captain's face as he lay in his stupor was very red. One of his associates, who also had a red face, told me that "the captain is overcome with heat and exhausted with hard work and he has chosen to lie down and refresh himself."

I went home from Oregon that night a sadder and wiser man. I never asked another boy to enlist.

JANUARY 1863, DANVILLE, KENTUCKY

The company was called together for the purpose of electing a captain and first and second lieutenant. There was but one man in the company with enough strength of character to offer himself as candidate for captain in opposition to Dennis. The result was that Dennis was elected with the one or two blank votes cast. William Crowell,[11] a school teacher of good standing among his friends, was elected first lieutenant by acclamation and bid fair to make a good officer.

For second lieutenant, there was quite a scramble, but two men, who canvassed the position thoroughly, seemed to have the lead, E. F. Border and Hall.[12] It looked to me as if neither would go to war unless he carried an officer's commission. On the first ballot Border and Hall had the bulk of the votes, Border ahead. There were, however, scattered votes for nearly half a dozen good men—sober, upright men but their modesty had kept them from electioneering. A motion was made by a friend of the leading candidate to drop all except the two highest. The boys, of course, said aye and E. F. Border was elected at the next ballot. I have not seen Hall since. Dennis and Border were apparently sober till four o'clock, then the company broke up to go home.

A great barrack called Camp Fuller was established in Rockford for all the recruits in northwestern Illinois. We were ordered to report there. It was named in honor of Adjutant General Fuller of Illinois, a successful organizer of the troops throughout the state.

In Rockford, long barracks were erected to receive the companies as they came in. These barracks were erected of rough board; floor, sides, and roof all the same material. They were about sixteen feet wide and were run in long continuous rows from a quarter to a half mile in length, the rows partitioned so that each section would hold a company of a hundred men. Each barrack had bunks from floor to ceiling and two men would occupy a bunk. In this way five men could be literally corded up to sleep. The builders of these barracks had no practical knowledge of ventilation and knew nothing of the philosophy of the atmosphere. Every crack and crevice was nailed up and not a bit of fresh air was provided. When any of the boys were out on guard two hours in the night, he would declare when he returned that the barracks stank bad enough to knock him down. Although Rockford is in a healthy climate and Camp Fuller was in a healthy location on Rock River, yet this barrack was one of the greatest breeders of disease I have ever inhabited. The air was impure and unfit for breathing five minutes after the doors were closed for the night and the men fell sick by dozens and scores. I was one of those men and was taken to a ventilated hospital for several days to recover.

The fourth of September 1863 was a great day in Rockford. Teams from the country poured in from all directions for the day had been appointed to formally organize the companies into regiments. It was unusually bright and sunny that day and old Camp Fuller was a perfect jam with some companies arriving in cars.

General Fuller and his staff came on the round in carriages. The companies had grouped themselves together to form regiments and had agreed who should be colonels, lieutenant colonels, and majors. The ten companies to form our regiment were ordered out for inspection. We had previously all been taken separately and alone into a tent before a surgeon, stripped, examined, and all who were found wanting were rejected. But now came another examination in a different form. We stood in what is called open ranks, each surgeon examining the soldiers as he passed. One

examined the eyes, another the limbs, and still another strong, robust surgeon examined the physical abilities of every soldier. The examination by
the latter was laughable and decidedly interesting. Every man was ordered
to hold both hands in such a position that the surgeon could lock hands
with him, he would take a firm quick hold, eye the soldier in the face, and
give a sudden strong jerk forward. If the soldier was weak it would jerk him
nearly out of his boots, but if he was solid and well made he would stand the
shock with ease. About every tenth man was jerked out of the ranks and
sent to a little knot by themselves. After the examinations were finished the
little knot of men was again reexamined, sorted, and selected. The best were
sent back to the ranks and puny ones were sent home to their mothers.

After the men had all been examined at Rockford the second time,
those remaining went through the procedure of electing captains and lieutenants in the presence of General Fuller. He in turn appointed those the
soldiers had elected. Company letters were selected by throwing ten slips of
paper into a hat each with a letter from A to K. (J was eliminated because
it looked like I). Dennis, my captain, drew B.

In all there were nearly a thousand men of us all; strong, robust, and
hearty looking. The general commanded us, saying "Hold up your right
hand every man of men." The latter part of the command was given with
such a peculiar determined tone that it shot through me to the very finger
tips. While nearly a thousand men stood in this attitude, an ironclad oath
was read to us, the substance of which was that we would maintain the
constitution of the United States and obey the commands of the officer
appointed over us and that we would serve three years or the duration of
the war. After the oath was taken and some preliminaries disposed of, the
general made a three-minute speech. The first sentence was met with a
tremendous cheer. He said, "Men of the Ninety-Second Illinois Volunteer
Infantry." From that moment we were known as the 92d Illinois Volunteers.

S. D. Atkins[13] of Freeport was chosen colonel; B. F. Sheets[14] of Oregon,
lieutenant colonel; and John H. Bohn[15] of Mt. Carroll, major. As they were
public men holding a public position, every man in the regiment had his
private opinion of them and publicly expressed it, especially when none of
them was present. Not one of them was so good that you could not find
something faulty, neither were they so bad that you could not find something to commend.

Colonel Atkins, in my opinion, was a peculiar man; a talented lawyer
by profession and like many men of that profession had used his talents to

save wrong doers from getting justice done them. I never saw him drink but the boys played pranks with his bottles and more than one man has been dead drunk on whiskey stolen from the colonel's demijohn. He had a slick tongue and was fond of speech making and had a high appreciation of what he said and did. A sensitive private soldier would feel in his presence that it was a sort of humiliating disgrace to be a private soldier—that to be a colonel or general was something grand and patriotic. But to be a common soldier was a position nothing but unfortunates ever held. Still Colonel Atkins had many warm friends and admirers.

Colonel Sheets was nothing like Colonel Atkins. It is true he has many enemies but I believe he got these enemies more by doing right than by doing wrong. He does his business straight and never bothers the demijohn. I regard him as an upright man, always ready to do the right as he sees it, even if it makes him enemies.

Major Bohn is a jolly good fellow and the boys like him. He is always fond of a good joke and alive to fun. To get a "Kentucky nig"[16] on a barn door laid on the ground for a platform seemed to be the highest type of fun for the major. His face would brighten up with sunshine and smiles as he watched the darkie's feet rattle and clatter on the old barn door.[17] The major never seemed to me to be cut out for a military man destined to lead armies to mortal combat, but he is a real good fellow.

⯈⭈⬩⭇⬩O⬩⭊⬩⭇⬩⯇

While we remained in camp at Rockford we were drilling and practicing the use of arms. When I first entered camp with throngs of soldiers and thousands of family visitors I rather liked the excitement, but after a few days my mind began to want a retreat, a place of solitude, but there was no such place. During the drills, which occurred twice a day, I was in the ranks, which of course were packed with men. At meal times we stood on opposite sides of long board tables. When off drill the grounds were covered with men going in all directions and at night we were corded into our bunks. A few would have whiskey and in spite of all efforts the barracks were in a sort of pandemonium. Before I had been in camp two weeks I was repeating over and over again to myself a phrase that I had seen or heard somewhere: "Solitude, oh solitude, where are thy charms?" I had been in school and my mind was active but now the mind had nothing to do but to obey. I thought of reading and studying but there were no books and if I purchased books I could not carry them.

One day while crossing the camp, Lieutenant Crowell came up to me, locked arms and wanted to know if I had been introduced to Colonel Atkins. On being informed that I had not, he turned in the direction of the colonel's tent, clinging tight to my arm. I remonstrated and told him that the colonel was too busy to be bothered with private soldiers of his regiment but he urged and I yielded. When we arrived at the tent we found the colonel very busy. I was introduced in the usual way to his "highness." He barely glanced and bade us take seats. I felt like an intruder and wanted to skip, but a look from the lieutenant caused me to sit. In a few moments the colonel was at leisure and turning towards me said in a harsh cutting tone, "Have you any business here?" I replied in a voice that must have resembled that of a sneak, "No, Sir," and I walked out. I certainly felt worse than a sneak. I was sorry that I ever had that introduction for it left a sting on my sensitiveness that I could not easily get over and made me rather an unfair judge of the colonel. I congratulated myself, however, on the thought that there was no need of more than one introduction and never had occasion to visit his tent since.

We could not leave camp and go home at pleasure. If we went home at all we must have a furlough and a great long document written up and signed by two or three officers, each of whom must let it lie in a pigeon hole in his desk a day or two before signing. All this had to be accomplished by a soldier who wanted to go fifteen or twenty miles to spend a day with his family or friends. But if a reckless fellow would bolt out of camp, go home, and stay there until the regiment was ready to go south, it was no different for him when he returned than it was for the one tortured with a furlough for forty-eight hours.

Well I begged and begged and got a forty-eight hour furlough, as did five others. It was six o'clock in the evening, time was precious, and if we wanted to be free again and breath the pure air at home we must go at once. It was raining and the roads were muddy. We clubbed together and hired a team. It was an all-night ride even with lively driving. One of the boys bought a quart of whiskey. He told the boys not to drink much but of course when the bottle went around the driver was included and urged to "take a good pull." The boys bragged on his team, saying what fast travelers they were and the driver cracked and applied the whip vigorously so that the wheels spun around and mud flew in every direction. Wild songs were sung as we glided along the dark road and the driver got merrier after every pull at the bottle. We reached home a little after midnight with the driver so drunk he could hardly sit erect.

There was no enjoyment at home, that is, that real solid enjoyment that one feels after performing a difficult task, all was different, the hours were numbered and that took some pleasure of home away.

Shortly after returning to camp we drew Enfield rifles with bayonets and accoutrements, knapsacks, haversacks, and canteens.

The boys of Co. B clubbed together, chipped in, and bought Captain Dennis a sword, revolver, sash, and belt. The enterprise was headed by an Irishman named Tobin.[18] Tobin had taken a great liking to Dennis and they both frequently drank from one bottle.

On the morning of the ninth of October, 1862 we got orders to march, or rather, to take a train for Chicago and go south. The orders were received the night before and the news had spread into the country for twenty or thirty miles in all directions by midnight. My younger brother Richard got up in the night at twelve o'clock and came to Rockford before six the next morning determined to enlist. I tried hard to persuade him not to because of our captain, for I was satisfied there was fun ahead, a kind that would be anything but pleasant; otherwise I would have been glad of his company. But nothing I could say would alter his determination. In less time than it takes to write this he was sworn in and had a full outfit of accoutrements.

Mothers, fathers, sisters, brothers, and sweethearts jammed Camp Fuller to bid the boys good-bye. We all realized that it would be a last good-bye for many of us; we could not tell who would fall or who would return. The rebels in the South had shown more courage and strength than was expected and had won some very important victories.

The knapsacks were all packed, the regiment marched through the crowded streets of Rockford to the depot where a special train stood waiting to receive us. We all climbed aboard and turned to look back to give another longing farewell, seeing the depot and adjoining grounds literally covered with people waving handkerchiefs, parasols, canes, hats and everything which a sign of love and affection could offer. We were soon out of sight steaming towards Chicago.

Tears were gradually dried as we sped along towards Chicago. Earnest thoughts stole into the mind of every thinking soldier. What was going to be our future? We were going out for the express purpose of shooting men and other men were coming out on the other side of the line for the express purpose of shooting us. Where will I be at the end of three years of such carnage, were my thoughts at the time. But the constant hustle and bustle of the cars and men, with constant new sight-seeing along the road and the prospect of there being more as we journeyed on, all conspired to drive away melancholy and we soon forgot about home.

We arrived in Chicago about three o'clock in the afternoon. We fell into line, each man loaded with a full knapsack, gun, cartridge box, forty pounds of ammunition, haversack, and canteen. In this condition we went marching up one street and down another through the city of Chicago, not in search of rebels, not in search of anybody to shoot, and I was going to say not trying to scare anybody, but for the purpose of showing the people of Chicago what large knapsacks we could carry and taking a look at the goods for sale in the city.

We were marched into a great depot on the lake shore,[19] the largest I had ever seen. We had about one hour to wait. All the officers whose bottles and demijohns had been complaining of the drought were now taken to the proper place and soaked. Our march through the streets had shown every man where he could go to get just such goods as he wanted. But let it be said in honor of the regiment that there were but a few men who did not show a good bearing and were not an honor to their associates.

But there are, however, a few black in every fold and so it was in our case. Captain Dennis had got a good "supply" and when we got into the great depot we stacked arms on one of the lone platforms and rested at ease while Captain Dennis's face began to redden. He became very excitable, mirthful, and changeable. He ordered the company into line and walked up and down it in an excited manner, then commanded to rest at ease, then to "stand erect!" stand at a "shoulder arms," and then at an "order arms;" first one order and then another. A few of the boys who had been drinking from the same bottle laughed at him and he laughed too. He gave an order to "rest at ease" while he slipped to one side for another drink; when he returned the boys were sitting down, as the order permits. He was fuller of whiskey and still more excited. He seized the sword the boys had bought and presented him, and without unsheathing it began an indiscriminate whacking at the boys, especially all those who were sitting. I was determined to keep out of trouble myself if possible. I was standing erect where I was when he went for the drink so he did not strike at me and I was glad of it. My blood was at a boiling point. I did not say anything and the boys did not seem to mind it nor care about it. It did not hurt much and the boys acted more like children who had been switched with a very fine willow. But I did not like it and felt as ugly as "Cain." I smothered all my own feelings and kept up as cheerful a look as possible.

At six o'clock the train ran into the depot and we were ordered on board; I was glad of the change. I determined now to get a seat as far from the captain and his few drinking associates as possible. We were soon all aboard but the train did not start. Captain Dennis, instead of taking a seat and keeping it, passed up and down the aisle of our car like a caged lion. His disposition while intoxicated was treacherous, smiling at one man, looking daggers at another, bursting out into a quick hearty laugh for a short moment, and then being in a mood to thrust his best friend with a bayonet if he should utter a disapproving word. I believed that the captain should be arrested, disarmed, and put under guard; then when sober he ought to be court-martialed or hanged.

In spite of all this, nearly a dozen of the youngest boys were tagging him around, trying to turn everything into a joke and laughing heartily at everything he did and said. Among the older members of the company were several Irishmen, good sturdy fellows. Finally the captain said something disrespectful about the Irish. One man jumped up and declared that an Irishman was as good as any American. This exploded the magazine. The captain sprang to the wall of the car and grabbed a bayonet from a belt that was dangling from a hook. He was one seat ahead of me and the Irishman one seat back. I tried to keep out of the difficulty but now I was in the midst of it for every seat in the car was full and there was no other car to go to. More than a dozen men grabbed the captain and then began a general scrimmage. The men who took hold of the captain were his friends; they pulled and hauled, tumbled over seats, got the car in an uproar of excitement while the Irish boys began to get together for a sort of self defence. The boys begged and pleaded and coaxed and entreated the captain to let go of the bayonet. When Captain Dennis saw that there were several Irishmen of the same opinion, he yielded. I kept out of the melee as best I could. I did not want to see him hurt the Irishman but I was satisfied that if the captain undertook to bayonet that one, before his job was half done every Irishman in the car would assist in slaughtering the captain, the very thing I wanted to see done. I know I was very radical but I only record how I felt under those circumstances. It seemed to me to be bad enough and hard enough to fight a common enemy without such action by a drunken, crazy captain. The scrimmage had a very cooling effect upon those boys who were toadying to the captain. It was very seldom that Captain Dennis ever got staggery drunk. He could drink and drink of the poorest whiskey and still walk erect. The train started on and the jostle of the cars brought men to their seats, but the rattle of the cars seemed like an awful stillness compared with the drunken wrangles gotten up by the captain.

The steady running of the train from Chicago without stopping at any stations quieted everything in our car. About midnight the train halted and I ventured out upon the platform. To my astonishment the ground was covered with what appeared like snow. What could it mean? It was a little chilly but not enough to prevent snow from melting before it could possibly reach the ground. I got down to scrape up a snowball and to my surprise scraped up a handful of white sand. We were in Michigan City, Indiana, seventy miles east of Chicago, a city on Lake Michigan with a population of about twenty-five hundred. The soil is simply white sand.

We all slept sitting erect in our seats that night. [Fellow volunteer] "Big" Lockwood[20] was taken sick during the night with cholera morbus; Dr. Helm[21] took him to the baggage car and treated him. I went in to see him for a few moments and witnessed a man in the greatest distress I have ever seen. He lay on his back in the middle of the car, on the hard plank floor without a blanket. As he lay there, his arms swung violently up and down while he kicked with all his apparent strength with both feet, his head rolling from side to side. Dr. Helm stood over him and gave him medicine every few minutes. I thought that he would die before morning when I left the car. But the next morning he was alive, the severe pain had abated and he was in fair way to recovery.

All night long as we tried to sleep sitting, the everlasting "woo woo woo" of the cars continued to ring in our ears. There was none of that stopping and starting, whistling and ringing of bells of an ordinary passenger train. It was a long steady fast run. We might sleep if we could but there were no down beds of ease for us, for it was supposed that there were no "feather-bed soldiers" aboard, although a feather bed would have been very acceptable in my case.

Next morning, when we opened our eyes we looked out over parts of Indiana; flat and wet for there had been a great amount of rain during the past two months.

At the Wabash River we were detained a couple of hours for repairs on the railroad bridge. Our train halted on the old battle ground of Tippecanoe. We got out, strolled about and visited apple orchards and filled our pockets and shirts. Dick McCann[22] of Co. D was furiously attacked by a tame deer; and the animal helped Dick along at a lively pace with his antlers. When Dick reached the train he found holes where there ought to be patches and his apples were scattered along the race course. We crossed the bridge about noon and reached La Fayette, a city of ten thousand inhabitants on the Wabash. Here we took a grand halt, the train for fuel and we for dinner. It was not dinner at a hotel, nor at mother's table; neither was dinner set at long tables fourth of July fashion, but a peculiar one. We drew rations from a sort of government store house there that had a quantity of bacon. From this store house we were given a number of large pieces of bacon, which were cut up and subdivided in smaller pieces, each man receiving a piece of it raw. How we were to cook it or eat it did not appear on the programme. This was to be our dinner. The appearance of this meat without cutting was what might be expected of a piece of meat lying under the side walk of any city. In other words it looked and smelled as if it were perfectly rotten; but when it was cut into, the inner portion had a sound appearance. The boys all remarked "this is nothing, we have got to eat worse than this before we get through with this war." I put my meat in my haversack, chewed some hard tack and drank cold water for dinner. "All aboard" brought every man to his place and the train continued in the direction of Indianapolis.

I had a strong desire to see this rapidly growing capital city of eighteen thousand and the capitol building. We did not reach it till dark, passing through its great central depot, catching a few glimpses of the long rows of lamp lights in its streets. The train halted only for a moment and kept up its woo woo in the direction of Cincinnati, Ohio. We were all tired and very sleepy and planned for a night's rest. We turned the backs of our seats in opposite directions so that two seats faced each other, then with our knapsacks filled the space between. In this way we stretched out and went to sleep. My pillowed bed fellow was another man's feet. There were four of us to each bed or pair of seats. However much one might dislike having another man's feet serenely resting on his pillow within an inch of his nose, he had the exquisite pleasure of compelling his neighbor to gasp for breath as he whiled away the midnight hours. What happened during the night or what cities we passed I know not for I slept soundly.

At break of day the train halted and Cincinnati was announced. We got out, fell into line, and marched down through the streets of the city, to the river, and crossed the Ohio on a floating bridge made of coal barges anchored out at proper distances apart, with great beams laid from boat to boat and planks laid across the beams. The bridge would seem to rise up before you as you crossed with a team, for it would settle under the team and appear to rise higher both behind and before. We crossed the river and walked upon the "sacred soil of Kentucky," marching through Covington to a camping ground south of the city on the bank of Licking River.

Covington, Kentucky, looks like a little thinly settled town on the opposite side of the Ohio River from Cincinnati, a sort of reflected shadow of the great city of Cincinnati or Pork-a-polis. But when examined in its true light, it is quite a city, having about fifteen thousand inhabitants, larger than Rockford, Illinois. It has over twenty-five miles of paved streets and is situated on two rivers.

We went into camp south of Covington. Unbuckling our knapsacks, we laid them on the ground and either laid down, stood up, or fried meat, boiled coffee, or fried hard tack. While we were in Rockford four or five men were detailed for the express purpose of cooking and placing the food upon the long table and telling us when dinner was ready or rather, when to scramble. But now we had no tables and no one knew just where our cooking utensils were. How we were to cook, get our food, and what it would be were quite questions [sic] to me.

Well, we "drew rations," which consisted of hard tack or hard crackers packed in boxes about the size of boot boxes. A certain number of boxes came to the regiment and these were divided among the ten companies, each company breaking them open and dividing the crackers among the men. These crackers were very hard and intended to be eaten as a substitute for bread. If we could keep them dry they would keep a long time without injury, but if once dampened they soon spoiled. In addition to the hard tack we drew what we called sow belly, which is pork salted, such as the Board of Trade in Chicago speculates in so extensively. It was divided in the same way as the crackers. Then we each got a little sugar, unground coffee ready browned, a small amount of beans, and a similar amount of rice. We never drew from the government either butter, cheese, potatoes, or anything of that kind. Instead for us it is usually hard tack and sow belly for breakfast, sow belly and hard tack for dinner, and by way of change we had hard tack with sow belly for tea.

How to get dinner on this new camp ground was the theme in our minds. Some of the boys skipped out of the ranks while in Cincinnati and bought sheet-iron frying pans and coffee pots, so these men had no trouble frying meat and making coffee. Their utensils were lent and re-lent until all had had dinner. The men grouped themselves together in groups of twos and fours, sharing in their rations and taking turns at doing up the domestic work.

As during our long train voyage, there again appeared in the countenance of nearly every man that quiet thoughtfulness that is felt upon facing a radical change in life. Very many men were really homesick but were too proud to acknowledge it. I felt a little homesick myself, couldn't help it, but would not have acknowledged it at that time for anything. My brother Richard, who had so unceremoniously enlisted against my advice, now said from a look which I thought I read in his face "I wish I had taken advice." Of course he never told me so, but I was strongly of the opinion that "actions speak louder than words." I was aware of the fact that he was not legally enlisted and had he known it, I thought perhaps he might take the first northern-bound train to Chicago. I thought that he had the ice broken now and he might as well help paddle the canoe along with the rest of us. All thoughts of this kind were smothered and never allowed to be seen or heard, and we drank in all that we could of the newspaper flattery about patriotism, bravery, chivalry, etc.

The building in which we camped the first night was under the same roof that tens of thousands of our troops had slept under before us. The south wall was the high bluff rising from the south valley of the Ohio River. The west was timber, the east was the Licking River, the north was the Ohio River and the roof was the broad canopy of heaven. In contrast to the barracks of Camp Fuller, here the ventilation was delightful and we laid down tired and weary and rose up really and truly refreshed.

On our second day at Covington every man was writing letters. The regiment looked more like an army of clerks than men going to battle. Every man had a "portfolio" as we call them. Each folio is about the size of an ordinary school geography and consists of pockets for writing material. When opened out it makes a very good desk to hold in your hand and write upon. With one of these you could sit on the ground on a log, stump, stone, or lean against the fence and write. Everybody was writing letters for somebody. Every little thing that had been seen, done, said, thought of, dreamed of, or heard of had to be written about; even the smallest things received considerable attention, things as small as "grey-backs" sometimes called "Tennessee Travelers," occupied considerable space in letters.[23] Some of the boys had seen these pests, a few had felt their nibble, and a great many had scratched at the very thought of them. While the good folks at home were looking anxiously for letters portraying fearful carnage, bloody scenes, and great victories, the letters contained accounts of heavy knapsacks, meat frying, coffee boiling, and car-ride snoozing.

On the first Monday at Covington, Kentucky, the regiment drew bell tents, wagons, and mules. The tents, resembling cow bells, were held erect by two upright poles and a cross bar or reach pole. The lower edge is staked to the ground and an opening at one end can be closed with buttons. The usual mode of sleeping, after littering the ground with straw or hay if it could be had, was to lie with feet towards the center since men are broadest at the shoulders and narrowest at the feet (although we have seen this to be the exception rather than the rule). The feet were corded up in the center and our heads were out. We used knapsacks for pillows. In this way twenty men could be crowded into one tent, provided the boys would all "spoon up" just right. Twenty men could occupy one tent on the spoon principle, lying on their sides, but fifteen left it free and easy.

When these tents were staked down tight and the doorway and fly curtains all buttoned down, they made very unhealthy places in which to sleep. The material from which the tents were made is water tight and nearly air tight. The result was, after all is shut up for the night, so many men in so small a compass without ventilation vitiated the air in five minutes.

Every infantry regiment is entitled to eleven mule teams, one for each of the ten companies and one for headquarters. A mule team consists of six mules on one covered wagon equipped with two chain locks, one for each hind wheel, so that they can be made to slide or drag all the way down hill. The smallest mules were placed in front and the largest in the rear and the driver controlled the whole six with one line. He performed a very necessary duty, a work that was tiresome and laborious, and he was exposed to a great deal of danger and hardship.

I have no desire to reflect dishonor upon a mule driver but I never did like the business. My idea of a mule "whacker" is a long, lank-looking man with stubble whiskers on his chin, a man that could crack a whip so loud and swear so hard that even a dog would not bark at him. Crossing a marshy valley on a still night the oaths can be heard from sunset to sunrise as the men and mules flounder in the mud. Some swore backward, some forward, some swore at the mules, some at the wagons, some at the mud, some at the whip because it was too short and some swore that their position was enough to make a minister swear; some swore at the size of their loads, some swore because they had no supper.

After our regiment drew unbroken three-year-old mules in Covington, the swearing began at the first kick. The mule seems to be in his element when he can act stubborn and get thrashed. Two men were taken from each company to "break" the mules. To choose a mule for the wheeler was the first job. It frequently happened that when the driver got into the saddle he suddenly discovered that he had chosen the wrong mule for he would not even have a chance to grab the mule's ears as he passed over the animal's head. When these mules were once trained to mule driver talk they seemed to understand language that no white man could interpret. A driver would sit on the near hind mule and give a number of short quick jerks on the line, and at every jerk he would call out "yea, yea" and the lead mules would gee off. Again the driver would jerk the single line, call out the same "yea, yea" and the leaders would haw off.

On the fifteenth of October the regiments that had garrisoned Cumberland Gap reached Covington, ragged and footsore. I went among them and talked with them for hours about their experience at the Gap,[24] for they told many interesting stories of their hardships and battles. There was one Union Kentucky regiment in the lot. Kentucky furnished troops for both armies in pretty near equal proportion. The Kentucky boys told me a story where a young man of their regiment captured a rebel, took him prisoner of war, and discovered that he had captured his own father. Families are divided in Kentucky; brothers are fighting against brothers, fathers against sons, and sons against fathers. This was the first real, earnest-looking track of real war that I had seen.

When a regiment was exposed to an enemy, when they were so close that an hour's march or a half-hour's march by either could bring forces face to face, it was very difficult for men to keep themselves clean. They seldom took their clothes off at night when they slept for they might be called at a moment's notice. The result was that before anyone was aware of it the Tennessee Travelers get among the troops and it becomes almost impossible to get entirely clear of them while the regiment remained together.

While talking with these men I noticed they scratched considerably and my eyes began to search for small things and they beheld for the first time a regular Tennessee Traveler through a hole in a boy's shirt. He was firmly fixed with his proboscis driven into the soldier's flesh sucking up a square meal of warm blood. It made me shudder. I imagined that a thousand were crawling on me. I could not relish any more stories so I walked off, went into a thicket of brush, took off my clothes, shook, brushed, and hunted. I came out master of the situation. No such thing had as yet got into our regiment.

On the eighteenth of October the regiment got orders to march at four P.M. The tents, tent poles, camp kettles, captain's desk, etc., all the baggage of the captain and that of two lieutenants and all the extra provisions of the company were loaded into the wagon of each company, which made a very full load. The baggage of a private soldier had to be carried upon his own back so each soldier had cut his baggage to what he believed to be the lowest possible limit. Besides the suit on his back he carried an overcoat, two woolen blankets, a dress coat, a rubber blanket, an extra pair of pants, one extra shirt, portfolio, stationary [sic], and a bottle of ink. All this was placed in the knapsack. In addition he had a haversack to carry rations, cartridge box with belts, forty rounds of cartridge, bayonet scabbard, bayonet, and musket. The total outfit that we have to carry will weigh all the way from fifty to one hundred pounds or more. When we get all these things up on our backs we resemble an army of pack mules. I felt decidedly ridiculous when I first got packed and underway. I kept repeating to myself, sometimes aloud, the fragments of two to three verses I had imperfectly learned at Sunday School, such as "Take up thy bed and walk," and "Come unto me all ye that are weary and heavy laden and I will carry your knapsack." I certainly wanted some one to carry mine.

Our start was splendid. Of course we went south, or nearly so, traveling on the pike in the direction of Independence. A pike was a new thing to me, as well as to the rest of the Illinois men. Built by the state or a corporation, they are to Kentucky what railroads are to Illinois. The routes have been surveyed with care and the road bed has been graded down to nearly the same level as a railroad bed. The road bed is covered nearly a foot deep with limestone pounded into pieces about the size of hen's eggs or smaller. The surface is ground down to a sand-smooth surface, making it nearly as hard and solid as rock in a quarry. Weary travelers pay tolls at toll gates as they pass over the road.

The men marched gaily on the pike for a time, for every man wanted to be ahead and it was with difficulty that the colonel could keep the regiment from resembling a mob. As time rolled on the knapsacks became heavier and the men began to hunt for places in the rear instead of the front. Before we got into camp that night, very many had sunk by the road side. We marched thirteen miles before we went into camp, long after dark, on the fair grounds of Independence, the county seat of Kenton County. We went supperless to sleep for there was no fuel with which to build fires and cook, except the high-board fences, and they were guarded. It rained during the night in perfect torrents. I managed to keep my bed sheltered some way and slept well, but many of the boys suffered with wet and cold.

Reveille sounded at the first gray of morning and "fall in for roll call," was cried by the sergeants of all the companies. Roll call, under some circumstances, may be of some benefit. When an army is in camp drilling and preparing for war it may be advisable to call every man up at a certain hour in the morning to stimulate regularity and uniformity in rising and getting breakfast. But when an army has marched way into the night and lain without shelter in rain, it seems to be to call the men into line to shiver until every name has been called only to cuddle back into their sleeping places or stand around and shiver when it is done is more red-tape rules with as much utility as a fifth wheel on a carriage.

><>·<>·O·<>·<><

Long marches with a heavy weight upon a soldier's back slowly destroys all ability to observe, read, and think. The soldier's main thoughts are rest, food, and sleep. All the vitality that is derived from food goes through the blood to the muscles and there is very little left for brain work. I saw many objects of interest as we passed on our long marches through Kentucky, but as they were not recorded until now, they have been forgotten.

On November 1, 1862, the regiment reached Mt. Sterling, Kentucky, and went into camp. The country through which we passed was the finest in the state. We had, by this time, traveled about five hundred and fifty miles.

One night when I was on picket a negro came to our picket line. The negroes were always our friends and while I could not allow him to pass I bade him sit down and give me his history. He was a slave who had been twice married. His first wife and he belonged to the same man. His master, in need of money, offered the wife of this negro for sale. A man from a state farther south came and bought the wife and took her away although the negro begged and pleaded for her. His master tried to console him by telling him that he could marry another wench and that would do just as well. For a long time he refused, but finally he married again and was living with his second wife. I asked him in case he was free which wife he would live with? "Bless you soul, massa, I would go to the first one. She am the one I always loved the best," he said. "I could die for her. Massa, he tell me it is just as well to marry another wife. I tried it and it ain't no such thing. You white folk may think it is nothing for to stop liking your first wife, but I tell you that you don't know nothing 'bout it. I go out in the woods all alone on Sunday and cry all day. Marrying another wife don't stop it. I'll have that first wife yet if I ever get free." And so the fellow went on, warming up as he told me of his love for his first wife.

All the stories I had heard about slavery were far fetched. But now I was listening to a genuine story as it fell from the lips of a negro slave. Tired and sleepy as I was, that poor simple slave made a deep impression upon my sympathies that I shall not soon forget.

The negroes gathered around our camp fires every night when we went into camp and danced, patted "juba,"[25] and sang their melodies. These melodies usually consist of about one verse which they would repeat over again as they patted for some other "nig" to dance. A short one ran like this:

> Ole massa call me
> Fore day, fore day,
> Too soon for me.
> Too soon for me.

Another one ran like this:

> Wake up snakes, pelican, and seshners;
> Don't you hear 'um comin'
> Comin' on the run?
> Wake up I tell yu, Sit up Jefferson!
> Bobolishion's comin'
> Bobo-lish-i-on.

On our marches we passed through the beautiful city of Lexington on a branch of the Elkhorn River. This city of ten thousand is the home of John Morgan, the notorious rebel "bushwhacker" who sacked the city a few days before our arrival.

On our march from Lexington to Mt. Sterling, Co. B was brought face to face with another drunken, disgusting row with Dennis.

On the first of October we were marching through a rolling country where there were at intervals small distilleries erected for the manufacture of whiskey. The captain kept himself well supplied. As the weather was dry he drank freely of his whiskey and he got fuller than usual. Many of the boys were guarded as to what they said or did in his hearing but James Tobin, who was instrumental in raising subscriptions to buy the captain the sword, belt sash, and revolver at Rockford, supposed himself perfectly safe at all times, drunk or sober, in the presence of the captain. Dennis made some outlandish remark at which Tobin dissented and stated the matter as he saw it. The captain called him a damned lying Irish son of a bitch. This roused Tobin so that he made a retort, though it was a great deal milder than the statement the captain had offered.

The captain flew into a rage, struck Tobin with his sword, and then drew his revolver to shoot him, and it took the strong efforts of a dozen or more men to prevent it. This scared Tobin, and well it might, for he came very near being shot before the captain could be prevented. Tobin ran for his life, and Captain Dennis swore by all that was good and great that he would shoot him before morning.

I expected to see the captain arrested, disarmed, and put under guard as soon as we got into camp, but it was not done. Tobin skulked around as best he could until dark. We went into camp as usual and from the time that darkness fell, Tobin has not been seen by any member of the regiment. He deserted and I could not help but saying in my heart, "God speed him on his way."[26] Why Dennis was not arrested, court-martialed, and sent home in disgrace was never clear in my mind, for the army regulations are very clear on what to do with a drunken officer. The man who had power to act was Colonel Atkins. Tobin applied to him for protection and yet Dennis was allowed his freedom to carry arms and carry out his threat if he desired.

Mt. Sterling is a pleasant village in a fertile part of the state. We went into camp about a mile south of the village near what they call a spring. This would be called a sink-hole in Ogle County, Illinois. The water that we have had to use for drinking purposes has been mostly either sink-hole water or river water. The soil is mostly clay and will hold water the year round. When a regiment camps by one of these sink-holes or ponds it becomes necessary for an officer to designate which side shall be used for "clear" water and which side shall be used for the mules to drink from. A guard is placed on duty to watch that the one side is kept clean. I have seen a pond so small that I could take a cat by the tail and throw her across. I have seen mules drinking and men washing their feet on the one side, while on the other side we were dipping out water to drink and make coffee.

While here, the negroes came to our camp in great numbers and many of them wanted to stay and go with us. This brought a great deal of trouble, not only to the officers and men, but to the general government. My point is this:

1. Eleven of the Southern states had seceded and confederated for the purpose of destroying the Union and the Constitution.
2. The rest of the states had remained united and were trying to preserve the Union and the Constitution.
3. The Constitution supported slavery.
4. Kentucky was a slave state and supports the Union and the Constitution.
5. Kentucky sent her troops to the war to fight with us to maintain the Union.
6. The officers and men of the Kentucky regiments owned property at home, but their property in many instances consisted of negro slaves.
7. The Kentuckians believed in the institution of slavery and the Constitution was on their side.
8. The men of our regiment were bitterly opposed to slavery in all its forms but the Constitution which we were maintaining was against us.
9. Loyalty with us was to maintain the Union and the Constitution.
10. Kentucky lay nearer the seceded states than Illinois; consequently more men left Kentucky on their own individual responsibility and joined the rebel army than did from Illinois, but of course, neither state sent troops to the rebel army by state authority.

Col. J. C. Cockran[27] commanded the brigade to which our regiment belonged. Cockran was of the 14th Kentucky Infantry and outranked Atkins; consequently he had command of the brigade. Many members of the Kentucky regiment owned slaves.

Another point of difficulty arose from the fact that every man here held the opinion that he had a right to his own private opinion on all national questions without being called a traitor and no one had the right to molest him for opinion's sake. This state of affairs brought much trouble to us as well as to the officials of Washington.

When a lot of negroes came into camp wanting to stay, we all swore that we were not slave hunters who captured men and returned them to their aristocratic masters. On the other hand, very many of the slaves that came in belonged to officers and soldiers who were in our army. Union men had a right, according to this Constitution, to come and claim their slaves. To cover some of the difficulties growing out of this Congress added a new regulation to the code that governs officers and soldiers. All officers or persons in the military or naval service of the United States are prohibited from employing any of the forces under their respected commands for the purpose of returning fugitives from service or labor who may have escaped from any person to whom such service or labor is claimed to be due. . . .

While the Kentuckians had the advantage of us from a Constitutional point of view, this new regulation left us a pretty independent set of fellows. We believed slavery to be a wrong from a moral point of view and that it ought not to exist, but were sworn to uphold the Constitution that permitted slavery. The new army regulations covered a multitude of sins and yet the number of men who came to our regiment for slaves was very great.

Colonel Atkins was a lawyer and he had a splendid chance to tell what he knew about Constitutional law. The difficulties he got into were many. In fact he was hedged so closely that on several occasions he put his line guard around the regiment and gave orders to let no man, officer or private, pass in or out of the line without a written order from him; thus they could not get to him to arrest him.

About midnight at Mt. Sterling two shots were fired on the picket line; the first thing I heard was a Boo-O-O-O-OOOF and the regular roll. Needham, the drum major, was called to beat the long roll in haste. He went through three drum heads before he could steady his hand down to calf-skin strength, then he did make the old drum roll in earnest.

Awakened from deep slumber in the dead of night by the long roll, the soldiers' warning of imminent danger, made my hair stand straight up. Captain Dennis, who never seemed to sleep, jumped out at the first beat of the drum and spun round like an old hen with a flock of chickens. He cried out over and over again, "Fall in Co. B, fall in I say or I will tear the tents down over your heads!" and as he hallooed he ran from one tent to another and grabbing the stay poles shook them till the tents were nearly ready to topple over. Inside the tents it was a scramble. Every man was after his pants, shoes, hat, coat, gun, and cartridge box. It was very dark inside and no one had time to strike a light, but with all the scrambling the regiment was in line of battle in three minutes.

It was all a scare. Some negroes out coon hunting had run up to our picket line, were supposed to be rebels and were shot at. Co. B was then sent out to reinforce the picket line.

The night was still, frosty, and clear. Every picket was more or less agitated over the scare. Just before we reached the post where Barrick and Crowley[28] stood, Crowley is a short, thick set, uneducated Irishman, Barrick imagined that he heard or saw something. He fired, then turned to Crowley and cried, "Shoot, shoot, shoot!"

"And what shall I shoot at?" said Mike.

"Great God! Shoot for your life, shoot, shoot!" Mike squared himself and fired into the air at an angle of 45 degrees. The man who had first fired started to run to camp. The second man thought he would follow and started after him. The first thought the second was a rebel chasing them, a third thought he had better run in too and followed the first two. Number two thought number three was a rebel and ran for dear life. In this way five soldiers were running for dear life. One fell over a log and decided to surrender, but before he could do so his pursuers had run by him, the distance between them widening with every bound. It was an awful scene but no blood was shed.

Here the boys believed they had a good joke on our Captain Woodcock, our Sabbath school captain of Co. K. Every body liked him. All his training had made him very precise in language and pleasant in speech. Notwithstanding that he was much excited at the long roll of the drums, he could not change his manner of speech. All his commands were heard on the still night air by every man in all ten companies. "Fall in Co. K, the enemy is upon you." The boys often mocked his command in his presence, but he took it all good-naturedly and remained the same precise-spoken, good-hearted man that he always was, and the boys liked him all the better for it.

CHAPTER 2

In the Hands of a Brainless Commander

January – March 1863

JANUARY 1863, DANVILLE, KENTUCKY

On the 19th of November, 1862, the regiment reached Nicholasville, Kentucky after trudging along all day in the rain. General Baird[1] was in command and ordered Colonel Atkins to make out full reports of all the troubles arising out of the negro question. I had command of the second section of Co. E in marching from Mt. Sterling, Kentucky to Nicholasville. We passed through Winchester by sections. As I gave the command "right wheel," three men came in on the right and one of them, who said he was a lieutenant in the 14th Kentucky, came into my section and said to a negro marching near me, "Come out of here, you thick-lipped son of a bitch."

I brought my gun to the position of "charge bayonet" and told him that I had command of that section and would not be interrupted by any man. He asked me if I intended to defend the "damned nigger." I told him I did.

"I have come for him," he said, "and I will have him or die. The 92d is good for nothing but to steal niggers. I am an officer in the Union army. That nigger belongs to a Union man and he will have him if we follow the regiment to hell."

"Get out of this section," I said, "or I will run you through with my bayonet."

He stepped out to the right of the section and drew his revolver. Each of the others also drew revolvers, and he said, "I will shoot the damned cuss."

I do not know whether he meant me or the negro. I told him that if they leveled or cocked their revolvers they would be dead men, and they had better put them up, and if they did not I would order my section to charge. They then put up their pistols and the lieutenant of the 14th Kentucky said, "If you don't give up that boy, I will go to my regiment and bring it up and clean your damned regiment out."

I told him that we were ready at any moment. He said, "Are you going to give him up or not."

I said, "Never!"

"Do you claim him?" he said.

"No, the second lieutenant has hired him, and if you want to ask any more questions, go to the colonel."

I had disobeyed my orders for the first time by answering him a question. He said, "It will do no good to go to him, for he is as big a thief as the rest of you and he will give me no satisfaction; but I will go and see the damned cuss," and off he went. When he came back, he said, "The colonel says I can take him."

I said, "You can if you have force enough."

He started back to town after following us about a mile, and said as he left, "You may look for a warm time."

I told him, "That is just what we came for." This is an exact statement of the conversation I had with the lieutenant of the 14th Kentucky. And I'm willing to testify to it at any time.[2]

At Nicholasville we had a siege of rainy, cloudy, snowy, fickle weather. Mud, snow, slush, dress parade, inspection, hard tack, and sow belly were the chief sources of amusement and home comfort for the boys.

On the 26th of November the regiment took up its line of march in a snow storm for Danville. After a two-day march, sweeping along the pike, passing around the base of a cone-shaped mountain, where it is said Daniel Boone tossed an Indian heels-over-head from the cliff into the great abyss below, crossing the Kentucky River with its rocky bed and high perpendicular banks and overhanging evergreens, we reached Camp Dick Robinson.[3] This was a deserted camp of the rebels and was the first havoc of the war we had seen. Houses were deserted, fences burned, and crops eaten up or destroyed. The rebels in their flight had left fifteen hundred barrels of pork, fifteen hundred stand of damaged fire arms, and a dismounted battery. The regiment took charge of this stuff, my company was detached to guard it, and the regiment pushed on to Danville.

We had been at Camp Dick Robinson but a short time when squads of East Tennesseans began to come in making their way to Louisville, there to be organized into Union regiments. These squads would average all the way from two men to three hundred. When they reached our camp we would give them the captured mess pork, hard tack, and coffee.

I conversed with many of those Tennesseeans, and I never realized before what a tame thing it was to be a Union man in Illinois. To be a Union man in East Tennessee, and let it be known, was simply to give up the ghost and be shot or hung. Nearly every man had a sad story to relate of the loss of a brother, father, or son at the hands of those rebel fiends.

This state of anarchy led to the organization of a society that probably never had its equal for profound secrecy. The people continued to live together in communities and neighborhoods, as elsewhere, but they were about equally divided between Union and rebel inhabitants. Union men would find each other out, but a mistake would cost a man his life. To protect each other and sort the sheep from the goats, the Union men organized themselves into what they called the Union League. These Union men would meet in a house at night and so thoroughly would they blind the windows and guard from without, that no band of rebels could ever discover their whereabouts or who their members were. Their oaths and obligations to each other were ironclad. If one man should turn traitor it might be the means of taking the life of the whole league but the traitor's life would be taken by the first man who over took him.

In this organization men got together in groups and bands and actually organized themselves into companies and regiments, elected their lieutenants, captains, and colonels and appointed a day to start north. In small squads they started on foot in the night across the fields and through the woods, traveling as best they could until they reached our lines and were transported to Louisville where they all met in due time. There they were provided with implements of war and clothing. Then they would return as "boys in blue" to literally fight for their homes, wives, and children. After talking with these men it seemed to me I had never met men from any northern state that had such deep-set loyalty as that which lay in the breasts of these Tennesseeans.

While in Camp Dick Robinson we learned the art of cooking and how to make ourselves comfortable. While on marches hard tack was our bread and butter. Hard tack, made from flour and vegetables, is hard and very tough unless it gets wet at which time it soon becomes moldy and wormy. When I eat it dry I have to gnaw it, if I soak it in cold water it becomes very soft. On the march we always gnawed it but in camp we had the luxury of soaking it in water and frying it in fat.

While lying in camp we became tired of hard tack and so since we had some flour left in the store house, the boys all began to bake pancakes. They were heavy and not very palatable, but still an improvement on hard tack.

There was an old tumble-down brick chimney near camp and I got an idea that a small brick oven could be erected in which biscuits, pies, and cakes could be baked like they do at home. Accordingly I enlisted several boys in the enterprise and we went to work. Bricks were brought, the ground leveled, a hole dug for mortar, and clay and water used for cement. The floor was soon laid and walls erected.

Rubin Edgar,[4] a boy of positive opinions and a very good-hearted fellow, had enlisted in the enterprise but could not see how the brick roof was to be supported. We erected a wooden arch on the inside of the brick walls and soon had a brick arch laid on top of the wood. As the arch was nearly together on top, Rubin brought his last load of bricks, threw them down and as he did so said, "Now see here boys, this is all damned foolishness. I am willing to carry as many bricks as any fellow on this job, I'll carry a ton yet if you say so, but the moment you put fire into that thing to heat it those wooden supports and arch will take fire and burn out and down comes your she-bang."

Some of the boys pretended to think that the fire would pass under the wooden arch and leave it stand. But Rubin knew it would burn out and he got the whole company out to substantiate his opinion. The oven was completed and the fire applied and of course the wooden arch all burned out but the brick arch stood. Rubin stood by prophesying how many minutes it would take to tumble. When the fire had heated the brick walls sufficiently the coals were raked out and a dozen tins of biscuits and pies laid in where the fire had been. In the course of a few minutes we pulled out what appeared to me the nicest biscuits and pies I ever saw. The boys turned the joke on Rubin. They asked him all manner of questions . . . "why don't the she-bang tumble in?" "Where did you learn the mason trade? Did you learn of a white man or a nigger?" Rube got tired of their questions and told the boys if they would hush up he would buy the soda to make biscuits and pie crust. For a time we had warm biscuits and pie on the table three times a day.

On the 14th and 15th of December we began to get news from Fredericksburg, Virginia, of the terrible battle at that place between General Burnside and the rebel General [Robert E.] Lee. Our forces were repulsed with a loss of fifteen hundred killed and six thousand wounded. We then began to learn that the rebels were terrible in earnest and that the fighting part of the war had only just begun. We began to realize that the war was a terrible reality and that hundreds of battles were yet to be fought and thousands and tens of thousands of men must yet perish in war from the effects of bullet, bayonet, and shell. Our pilgrimage here was but a school to fit us for more ardent duties of campaign life.

The army trains were taking away almost daily the great store house of pork and when it was gone we could rejoin our regiment at Danville. It was believed that the pork would all be gone by January 1, 1863, but several days before that date we got orders to rejoin our regiment at Danville.

This brings me to the time where my diary fully begins, where I and my regiment camped in this beautiful city of two thousand inhabitants.

Captain Woodcock was acting as provost marshall of the regiments, which were encamped in almost a perfect circle embracing the whole city and some of the surrounding country. Although it took a great many men to do it, this guard line was kept up night and day. No man was allowed to pass in or out of the city without a written pass from the provost marshall.

As Danville is a city of learning, with many good schools, churches, and asylums, the captain's accuracy of speech and impressiveness of manner made him more fitted for the position than any other man in the regiment. He dealt with every citizen of the city from the highest to the lowest. Whatever opinion they formed of him was the opinion of the regiment and the regiment has not suffered from his representative position. On one occasion an old gray-haired negro applied for a pass of Captain Woodcock. The captain informed the negro that it would be necessary to establish his loyalty before giving him a pass. He was a free negro. Taking off his hat, he pulled out a copy of the *New York Tribune* and said, "For twelve years I have been a scriber to dis here paper. Do ye spose dat anything but a loyal man would take de *New York Tribune?*"

The captain was convinced, and the *Tribune* subscriber obtained the desired pass.

Since the company was re-established in camp in its proper place in the regiment, Lieutenant Beander[5] has spent much of his time in the city, for what we never knew.

>–·◆·–O–·◆·–◄

In a point of sickness the camp at Danville was a sort of Valley Forge of the 92d. Although my own health was good in all appearances, yet there was a sort of melancholy gloom that seemed to cloud our stay since we had arrived in Danville. Every morning the bugle blew its sound for sick call, at which a sergeant from each company reported to the doctor's tent the names of all those in the company who had been taken sick during the last twenty-four hours.

The sick were first taken to a large hospital tent, cared for, and assorted. Those whose symptoms were bad were sent to some building or established army hospital where greater facilities could be had for caring for the sick. Those with lesser ills were retained in the tent.

At these morning sick calls, large numbers flocked to the doctor's tent for treatment. I believe the doctors here were among the best—these were no quacks and the men had the utmost confidence in their ability while the doctors in turn worked honestly to maintain it.

At risk of repeating my earlier grievances, I found the poor ventilation to be one of the greatest causes of sickness. Here in Danville we dug into the earth about eighteen inches before placing our bell tents on top. This makes a sort of cellar, which we use for a bedroom as well as kitchen. At one end we dug out a place for a fireplace and erected a chimney. These made warm, comfortable places for winter quarters and had possible room for two or three persons. To be warm, however, they were made air tight, and with fifteen to twenty men packed into the tent the air became unfit to breathe in fifteen minutes. There was a hole on top of the tents for ventilation with a flap to cover it, but because there was so much rain it was constantly kept closed in most of the tents. Many a night I slipped out and opened the ventilator flap after all were asleep in my tent since some of the other men, knowing nothing of the nature of the atmosphere of the breath, objected to the opening of the hole on a cloudy night. Our little group was unusually healthy during the sickly times.

Another cause of sickness was the peculiarity to us of the winter. The weather was neither very cold nor very warm; some days it rained, others it snowed and then the snow melted. These causes seemed to work with terrible effect upon the regiment. Many had died and others contracted diseases so that it was necessary to discharge many from the service and send them home.

General Gordon Granger has been appointed as chief commander of all the troops through central Kentucky; all other generals are subject to his order. Granger is one of those illustrious men who were educated at West Point where it sometimes occurs that they try to cram information into a head where there are not enough brains to retain it. I fear it fell to the lot of the 92d to be in the hands of a brainless commander.

An example of my fears occurred on the morning of December 26, 1862. Rebel General John Morgan was one of the greatest rebel cavalry raiders that ever belonged to the rebel army. He reportedly had the finest and best-trained cavalry in the whole Confederate army. They were a quick, bold, dashy set, and Morgan could hurl them against a weak point of ours, capture the place, sack the town, and be gone before a dispatch could be sent anywhere for aid. He worked almost constantly in the rear of our main armies, always taking to the woods and mountains where we had pushed. It seemed his men were always in the saddle.

On that morning General Granger started with nearly all the infantry in the direction of Lebanon, Morgan, and his rovers. How Granger expected to catch Morgan's band with footmen, when Morgan's men were on horseback we never knew but away we went in a torrent of winter rain. We marched all day in the rain without dinner till dark when we turned into a plowed field to camp for the night. Here the mud was ankle deep. General Gordon Granger made his headquarters in a fine brick resistance. We were sticking arms when word came from these "headquarters" not to burn rails to make fires to warm ourselves and cook our foods, but to wait until the teams came and then unload, go to a distant forest, cut green wood, load it, haul it, make fires of it to cook our suppers. It was then dark, the teams not up, and it would take till nearly morning to get our supper. Colonel Atkins was indignant, as well as every man, and he, in the presence of the messenger, ordered us to take the rails and cook our suppers.

At twelve o'clock midnight we were called with orders to start on the chase at three o'clock. General Granger took another nap, a little more wine, and did not order the start until seven o'clock. By this time his chasing order had run dry and he ordered the whole division back to Danville. When we arrived on our old camp ground, everything had been destroyed: the cellar kitchen we had dug was filled with water and everything was mud and desolation. It was a winter night, we were cold, wet, and weary and we must sleep on the ground saturated with cold water. The next morning nearly the whole regiment answered to sick call. It has been estimated that this little march cost the regiment over fifty lives.[6]

The first of January 1863 came with warmth and sunshine. For the officers of high ranks, there was big pay, plenty of the best to eat and drink, no night picketing to do, a good tent or headquarters in which to sleep. To

them it was a pleasant New Year. They were invited out to dinner and
wine, serenaded by the regimental band, and had far more distinction
paid them than many of them would have received at home. But for a
private soldier, who must march at command, stop when told, make his
bed in a mud hole on a freezing night, see the regiment sinking into sickness and many into death, thoughts have been gloomy reflections for the
New Year.

JANUARY 12, 1863, DANVILLE, KENTUCKY
Honorable Joshua White and Captain Weld of Marion, Illinois, came to the
regiment to visit friends. While they were visiting with us a little drunken
incident occurred that roused the indignation of Colonel Atkins. Dress
parade was called.

Dress parade is one of those red-tape affairs in the army that has no
genuine utility in it. It is all show. The men put on their best clothes, the
officers their best clothes and wrap their bodies around their waists and over
their shoulders with flashy colored belts, red-tape, or red sashes. Each takes
a flimsy sword in his hand and stands up very straight and stiff. The regiment is put into line of battle with the captains and lieutenants all in their
proper places in their respective companies. The colonel takes his place
directly in front of the regiment, facing the men. The adjutant is a sort of a
clerk, waiter, or lackey, a fellow that does lots of everything and not much
of anything. When the adjutant gets the regiment into line with all the officers standing correctly, he then makes a sign to the leader of the band and
they begin to toot their horns and march down the whole length of the
regiment, passing between the colonel and adjutant on the one side and the
line of officers and men on the other. The adjutant then orders the men to
"shoulder arms, present arms!" and when the men are all holding the guns
in that position he waves his sword about his head and tells the colonel that
the regiment is ready. The colonel then in a tone that might be expected
from the statuary of the Tennessee state house, commands, "shoulder arms,
order arms," and we put our guns with butts on the ground, standing by
our side. The line officers of the ten companies, captains and lieutenants,
thirty in number, are all brought to the front and forward to the colonel.
When they get there the colonel gives them orders. The adjutant steps out
and dismisses the men. This dress parade always takes place just before sunset. Well, we were on dress parade one evening when White and Weld were
taken there from the north. Colonel Atkins, Lieutenant Colonel Sheets, and

Major Bohn were all downtown and the ranking captain had to stand in front as colonel. Captain Dennis was now the ranking captain and had to take the colonel's place. It so happened that he was beautifully drunk that evening but as usual could walk tolerably straight. Quite a number of ladies and distinguished gentlemen from the city were present to hear the music and see the show. Captain Dennis could not stand straight. He seemed to be standing on the hub of a horizontal mill wheel, the ground spinning round rapidly. The adjutant got everything [ready] and the band tested their horns. The officers were all standing straight. When the adjutant saluted the drunken captain and told him that the regiment was ready, he walked down around behind him and up by his side. Captain Dennis looked at the regiment and tried to give some command, but it was no use, his tongue was too thick and his lips too stiff. He turned, looked the adjutant in the face, and grinned like a driveling idiot. The adjutant stepped forward, gave the proper commands, and dismissed the regiment. Captain Dennis staggered off to his tent.

Retribution came at last. Captain Dennis's crime could not be overlooked. Although he had insulted every respectable man in the company, tried to shoot Tobin and frightened him until he deserted, got drunk on every favorable occasion, yet no notice was taken of it until he had insulted red-tape. He was given the choice of resigning or court-martial. He took the former, resigned, and was on his way home.

Just previous to the captain's resignation, Lieutenant Bander of Co. B had put in his resignation also and the acceptance of both resignations reached the regiment about the same time. Bander, whose strange conduct had utterly severed all respect of the intelligent part of the company, nevertheless had one or two fast friends of his own stripe in the company. When the returns of Captain Dennis's resignation came, Bander made an effort to get himself appointed captain to fill Dennis's place, notwithstanding his own resignation had been accepted and he was no longer a soldier or a member of the company. He caused a petition to be drawn up recommending the colonel to apply to the governor of Illinois for a captain's commission. He found a man to circulate his petition. The plan was secretly laid and the petition cunningly circulated. There was a large number of the boys in the company who knew nothing of political trickery. The youngest boys were approached and requested to sign their names below those of Bander's associates. When they asked "what for?" all kinds of joking answers were given. The boys thought it was all right anyhow, and added their names to the petition. The man circulating the petition took pains not to let the older men know what was going on.

Suddenly there came an uproar in the company. The matter leaked out after nearly three-fourths of the men had signed it. The petition was quickly withdrawn and before a remonstrance could be thought of the petition was laid before Colonel Sheets. There in the colonel's hands in black and white was a genuine petition with nearly three fourths of the company's signatures, praying for the appointment as captain of Co. B., a man that was a known whoremonger. Colonel Sheets knew him even better than the company. It was a disgrace to the company. What would Colonel Sheets do? Would he dare to refuse the expressed wish of three-fourths of the company or would he grant their request? I was ashamed to approach the colonel's tent so I decided to take what would come. It was a very trying experience for Colonel Sheets; he knew the character of the man but if he refused the whole regiment would raise the cry that Colonel Sheets would not allow Co. B to select its own officers, as is the practice in all companies. Colonel Sheets pleasantly but firmly refused to recommend the appointment. This was a noble act of his in my opinion that may have cost him a great many friends and earned him many enemies. Soldiers in all the companies were writing home to their friends denouncing the colonel for his action.

Captain Dennis and E. F. Bander, two misguided wretches, one by whiskey and the other by whiskey and lust, were soon wending their way homewards and a great deal of shame and disgrace began to roll off the reputation of the company.

>·+◇·-O·-◇·+·<

On January 8 the paymaster paid off the regiment. Long payrolls were made out and every man signed his name or made his mark if he was not able to write. The paymaster took his seat in the middle of a large tent open at both ends. He had two clerks; one read off the name of the soldier who was to be paid, the other clerk counted the money from the great stacks of greenbacks and handed it to the paymaster who in turn counted it a second time and handed it to the soldier. A guard stood at the door of each end of the tent and let the soldiers in one at a time as the names were called. I was guard at one door. This gave me an excellent opportunity to see the large piles of new greenbacks with which we were paid. The amount of my pay on this occasion was $22.50. Soldiers receive $13 per month.

On the 13th of January we moved our camp about a mile from the low land to a higher position. While making the change it turned cold and began to snow. It is not very pleasant living and sleeping under a cloth tent on the ground in cold rigorous weather. The morning of January 15 the ground was covered with snow.

We had no stove in our tent and we lay and shivered all night. It looked like hard work serving one's country that morning. My brother and I traveled all around the neighborhood in search of a stove. We got an old cook stove and the next night things had a more comfortable appearance. I wrote in my diary by a bayonet candlestick: an ordinary candle stuck into the hollow end of the bayonet while the sharp end was driven into the ground.

The following day it fell to my lot to go out on picket. The picket line had to be kept up through snow and sunshine, heat or cold, night and day. It was severe on feet to stand in the snow and during the coldest weather we were prohibited from building fires on the picket line. We scraped the snow away with our feet at night and built large fires of rails, then sat by them. The whole campground was surrounded in this way by a circle of picket fires.

SUNDAY, JANUARY 24, 1863

Orders came this day to march to Louisville and there we were to take transports and go down the Ohio River and up the Cumberland River to Nashville, Tennessee. This was one of General Gordon Granger's movements. Everybody in the camp was cheerful over the idea that we were to march on, since none of us really liked staying in camp. We would rather move on, even if we endure more hardships.

We started out for Louisville at six o'clock on the morning of January 26, joyful and happy. It would take at least five days to reach the city. Nearly every day while on the route it rained or snowed. At night we had to erect tents to protect ourselves from the rain and snow. When the tent was up a bed had to be made on the ground that was saturated with melted snow or water. To make a bed on cold mud was a thing we had to do whether the idea was pleasant or otherwise. On some occasions straw could be had, but on most of those nights there was no such luxury. A soldier, however, soon learns to make the most of a bad job. Every man had a rubber blanket. If the mud was very soft the rubber blanket would be laid on the mud and a piece of rail or a pole slipped under all around the outer edges to prevent the mud and water from coming over the edges. On top of these rubbers the woolen blankets were laid and we could get in between them and with knapsacks of pillows sleep quite soundly and comfortably. The mud was soft and acted like a featherbed.

While on this muddy march some one at headquarters got the idea that a quantity of whiskey issued to each man in the evening would be beneficial to the general health of the men. Consequently whiskey was given to every man. In my opinion this was nonsense but of course it was my duty to obey and not command or offer advice. A soldier can look on, observe, remember, and keep still. I watched its effects. There was not enough given each man to make him drunk, even if he should drink it all at once, but there was just enough to make the men boisterous, excitable, talkative, and foolish. After the drinks there was a sort of pandemonium in nearly every tent. The men would not go to sleep until nearly twelve o'clock at night so they were robbed of sleep and rest they should have had. The next morning, after issuing the first rations of whiskey, two men in Co. H got into a desperate fight; one of the men thrust his thumb into the other man's mouth and got it bitten nearly half off. It created quite a sensation among all the men and it took considerable work to restore quiet and good order.

We arrived in Louisville at the end of five days' journey on January 20, 1863. On the morning of the 31st we marched through the city of Louisville in platoons. There were many Kentuckians who preceded us there still wishing to secure their negro boys that were acting as cooks and waiters to the officers. In the city many wealthy people who sympathized with the South laid a plot to injure our armies all they could. They had contributed funds to purchase citizens' clothing and kept them in a dry goods store. A soldier who would desert could go there, trade his uniform, and even up for a suit of citizens' clothing.

In their employ was a cripple whose leg had been amputated and who went about on crutches. He was a red-hot rebel sympathizer and a very earnest and glib talker. The regiment halted in the middle of the street and this fellow was soon hobbling all around among us, talking secession boldly and above board. Hot words frequently passed, whereby any of the men could have clubbed his brains out had he not been a cripple. It seemed to give him a passport to go all through among the men and talk his rebel doctrine, a thing that would have cost a well man his life. His work there took two men out of my company. They deserted that night.

These seemed to be the darkest times of the war. The rebels had been successful in different parts of the country and evil designers are scattered all through our country.

JANUARY 31, 1863, LOUISVILLE, KENTUCKY

At the wharf in Louisville, a large number of steamers, transports, and gun boats lay to receive the troops. To get all on board was no easy task. Wagons had to be taken apart, lugged on board, and packed in the hold and between decks.

A large portion of the 92d, including my Co. B, got on board the *Tempest* and the rest got on board the *Arizona*. The *Tempest* was a very fine-looking double-decked side-wheel steamer. The upper deck, the cabin deck, was nearly all used up in finely finished cabins with snug little berths on the sides. These cabins were long and nicely carpeted with an open deck all around the outside. They had windows at proper intervals where one could look in from the outside and out from within. Of course a cabin like that could not be occupied by either soldiers or mules unless the soldier had a handle to his name as lieutenant, captain, major, colonel, general, etc.

The boiler deck was next below. This large, mostly open deck with the boiler in the middle was also the working deck. As a place of shelter it might be compared to a mammoth cattle shed with all the weather boards knocked off. On this deck the private soldiers and mules were stowed and packed, and the officers took the cabin above.

When we first entered the boat I felt a thrill of joy pass over me. We were to have a long boat ride down the Ohio and up the Cumberland Rivers, where we could ride by day and night, view all the beautiful scenery and catch a glimpse of four or five states, one of which would be our own dear old state of Illinois. We could watch the sunbeams, stars and moonlight sparkle, glitter, and dance on the waves of those beautiful rivers. But little did I dream of what would follow.

Co. B was about the first on board and of course, there was lots of room. Our company was moved from place to place as the column continued to pour over the plank on to the deck. The officers were around among us spacing off the deck to the different companies, wedging us in together, compelling each company to occupy the least possible space, leaving just enough room so that all could lie down on the deck. We were wedged in like a stock farmer wedges hogs or cattle into a car to ship to market. Co. B changed positions several times and, when all was settled, we found ourselves on the side and left front of the boiler. Our position would have been a desirable one in hot weather, but if it should turn cold and windy there would be a good chance of freezing to death. Co. K on the other side was similarly situated. All the other companies were more or less protected by the boiler and wheel-houses on the two sides.

We had just begun to make the most of our limited space when a rope was stretched close to the water edge of the deck and the mules were led on and tied to this rope. Their heads were out and heels in and they occupied one-half or two-thirds of our limited space. We felt confident now that Co. B and K would surely get some new place, but there was no room any-where except on the narrow cabin deck or in the cabin and none was offered. Lieutenant Crowell, who was in command of the company, was not a military man and had no influence with the officers or men. He was a scholar and his ability was other than military.

The officers all went into the cabin, a guard was put on the cabin door and no soldier was allowed to pass in or out unless he was sick. A guard was put on the foot plank and no soldier allowed to go off the boat.

It was hard to find an officer outside the cabin before whom we could lay our cause. When we found one, we discovered we were unfortunate. Colonel Atkins, who was in command of the brigade, had several regiments under his command. He commanded a body of troops that army regula-tions require a general to command, while he used the boat as headquar-ters. No one could now approach his royal highness without a commission in his pocket and a strap on his shoulder.

There was no place for us on the boat except the cabin, and that could not be occupied under any circumstances, so we were compelled to accept the situation and made the best of it. We found that by lying with our heads close up to the boiler fence and feet toward the mules, well curled and drawn up, that we could all lie down, provided of course, the mules did not back up. We lay down to sleep, well knowing that if we were not stepped upon, our feet and blankets would be buried in the offal from the mules. By nine o'clock that evening my first impression of joy was reversed and I was mad—downright angry and indignant.

If there are personal reflections cast from impressions derived at that time, I have forgiven all and try to hold now no hatred or dislike to the parties.

The weather turned colder. We had no cooked dinner or supper but had gnawed and munched hard tack and we could sleep in the open air with a mule if we could curl our feet enough. The boat did not leave that night. I lay down behind a big, ugly mule and politely told him that in case I got good natured enough to drop to sleep, that whatever he did by all means not to step on my feet.

I had dozed a while when I heard strange voices on the shore and at the guard on the plank, so I got up and picked my way out over the sleepers as best I could. I went up on the cabin deck in front of the cabin door where one of the engineers was boiling with rage. The whole crew to the backbone was rebel in sympathy.

The Kentuckians who had lost their slaves at Mt. Sterling and other points had followed us and had laid a plan to get all the negroes away from us, by theft or any other means. The guards at the foot plank had instructions to let the boat crew off and on at pleasure, but no soldiers were allowed to go ashore. The boys on guard that night were not well versed in the ways of the cunning. One of the engineers was very daring. He walked up to a negro who lay sleeping, wedged in among the soldiers, took him by the collar, shook and waked him up and told him that the colonel had ordered him off the boat. He led him to the foot plank, told the guards the same story and they like geese accepted the lie for the truth, and allowed the negro to be led off. As soon as he touched the shore, his master stepped up and collared him and led him away.

One negro cook after another was led off that way. When the engineer came to the big, stout, sharp negro of Co. B (the same man they attempted to capture in Lexington) he showed fight and muscle too, so that the engineer did not dare risk a tussle but it made him frothing mad.

The noise brought Colonel Atkins out, who did some good swearing. He hushed up the engineer and gave him to understand that if he made any more such moves he would be arrested, bucked, and gagged. The guards were blessed in a similar way and new orders were given.

I picked my way back as best I could, offered a prayer to the mule and went to sleep.

> Here I curl me down to sleep
> If I should stretch before I peep,
> I pray the mule keep off my feet.

FEBRUARY 2, 1863, ON BOARD THE *TEMPEST*

In the morning I woke up from under the heels of "his majesty," the big ugly mule, shook the offal from the blanket, rolled it up and laid it in the same place where I had shivered all night. It had turned cold during the night and the snow which had been melting began to freeze. The wind was rough, boisterous, and high. As there was no protection for those of us who were at the front end of the boat, we were left as a sort of wind target for the cold blasts. Even the mules were entitled to some pity, but neither the men nor mules received any. The wind shrieked, howled, and whistled across the deck, screeching at every corner and flapping every loose blanket. It splashed water against the side of the boat where it froze. It also played pranks with the manes and tails of the mules who flapped their long ears and brayed. I thought a breakfast would strengthen me but where could it be had? There was no stove over which we could cook, and camp fires could not be built on board ship. As no warm meal could be had I thought I would go and look on and see other men eat in a warm comfortable room, as most of us had done when at home. I went up on the cabin deck and walked rapidly to and fro to keep warm and at the same time surveyed through the window into the cabin.

There was a big blazing fire, pictures on the walls, carpets on the floor, a great dining table in the center around which sat Colonel Atkins, all his staff officers and waiters, and all or nearly all the officers of the regiment that were on the *Tempest*. The table was loaded with hot meats, tea and coffee, and all the dainties and luxuries of a first-class hotel. At the door stood a guard so that a man like myself who would condescend to sleep with a mule as my companions and myself had done that night, could not even enter to warm, to say nothing about a breakfast. I looked on for a time as I passed backward and forward, stamping my feet to keep them warm. I tried to feel meek and calm but I could not. I had never seen men eat under such peculiar circumstances before. My blood boiled in spite of the cold blasts.

I picked my way back to my position behind the mules, too mad and indignant for words. I took some cold tack from my haversack and sat down on my knapsack to breakfast. As I munched hard tack I could not help thinking, thinking how the men who would endure the most hardship, would be respected least when we returned home; how the men who appropriated all the comforts here would appropriate all the honors when we arrived home.

After our breakfast of hard tack and river water, my brother decided to write a letter home and tell Father all about our condition. I advised him not to do so until the trip was ended and the hardships over, that if he wrote now his letter would leave us in the midst of our trip and would only tend to awaken the deepest sympathy in those who could give us no assistance. Although the ink froze to his pen while he wrote, he persisted in writing the letter. (This letter had even more effect than he desired. It created more sympathy than he wanted Father to spare, and although he had written nothing but the truth, yet he regreted later that he had written it.)

We boarded the *Tempest* Saturday about noon and lay at the wharf over Sunday. All day Sunday as it grew colder and colder there was a general talk of entering the cabin by force, and if the colonel undertook to resist, to throw him into the river. It could probably have been done, had not two things prevented it. In the first place the men were all loyal and no one wanted to do anything of that kind. Another reason was that all the companies had positions except B and K. While they were very poor and cold, their positions were bearable. These two companies—B and K—had no rash men in them that wanted to do anything of the kind unless it was the last resort as a means to preserve their own existence. All appeared to agree, however, that it would serve the colonel right if it should be done. We realized what abject slaves men become when soldiers if those in command see fit to put them under the heels of mules. If we made an effort to force the guards and go ashore for shelter, or force an entry into the cabin, we would be booked as deserters and our names would be published as such connected with all the disgrace ever attached to any deserter or mutineers, but if we stayed with the mules and contracted diseases that would carry many of us to our graves, we would have a little cheap glory pronounced at our funerals and those who lived through it could go home at the close of the war and shout when those men who drank from demijohns and ate and smoked in the comfortable cabin came around making political speeches. We decided to cuddle down under the mules and preserve all the glory for our funerals.

At two o'clock on Monday morning, February 2, the fleet was loosed from the shore and we went steaming down the Ohio River, the wind whistling, the blankets flapping, the mules braying, the boats whistling, and the men shivering.

FEBRUARY 3, 1863, ON BOARD THE *TEMPEST*, CUMBERLAND RIVER

When we first got aboard the boats a great many men had their rations of whiskey and others had their appetites so whittled up that they stole out of their ranks while coming through the city and got their canteens filled with bourbon. Many of the men got beastly drunk in a few hours after getting aboard. There was one man in Co. B who claimed to have lately come from the South. He had arrived at Byron just as recruiting was going on, enlisted, and went with us. He among others was drunk. Scarcely a word passed before the Co. B Southerner took a pen knife from his pocket and stabbed another man. The wound looked insignificant but it had set something internally and the stabbed has died a few days later. My brother saw the wound and gave me the names of both men—but I will not record them.[7] There has been but little notice taken of the affair.

I awoke this morning shivering with cold. A landing on an island was effected where we all went ashore with orders to cook three days' rations. The island was soon ablaze with the light of the many camp fires. The chance to stand and warm ourselves by the camp fires was a treat. The mules flapped their big ears and brayed for equal rights but it was of no use for we were their superiors for nearly a brief hour and a half. After finishing the cooking we steamed down stream. Following warming by the camp fires and eating a warm meal, we felt better and were now prepared to stand the cutting winds with more fortitude. Some of the men, however, had begun to fail in health under the constant exposure. Colonel Atkins had been prevailed upon to allow those who were taken sick, who could get a written permit from their captains, to sit inside the cabin. My brother was put on guard at the cabin door and his orders were to let in sick men with written permits and a few soldiers at a time to warm themselves. Since the guard could stand on the inside of the cabin door, it was a warm treat to be put on guard. My brother interpreted the warming part of the order quite liberally and allowed nearly every fellow in to warm himself. The colonel occupied a stateroom where he could not see how many entered the cabin.

The captain of the boat and his crew were proving themselves more and more to be rebel in sympathy. Seeing the men warming themselves in the cabin he wanted to drive them out and let no more in. He therefore selected one of his boat's crew who went pompously up to my brother and told him that he was relieved and that now he would guard the door himself.

My brother brought his musket down and gave the captain to understand that he had been placed on guard here with orders from another source and that he proposed to hold his position until relieved by the authority that put him there. The captain then changed his tactics and was very pleasant and affable. He told my brother that at Louisville he had offered to Colonel Atkins to take all the furniture out of the cabin and let the men have it but the colonel would not have it so. He also told that after it had turned cold he had offered to land his furniture at any town along the river but Colonel Atkins forbade it and told him that the soldiers should not enter the cabin. Since that was the colonel's plan he wanted my brother to refuse to allow any of the soldiers in. The captain then tried to buy him up with whiskey. He told him to go to the bar, call for whatever he wanted, as he had instructed the bar tender to let him have whiskey. My brother hated the entire rebel crew as well as the men who appropriated the cabin to themselves while compelling him to sleep in the open cutting air under the feet of the mules. He held his position, drank no whiskey, and allowed as many men to enter the cabin as orders would permit. The captain was boiling mad but thought it best to say nothing to the guard.

During the day my curiosity led me to stroll about on the cabin deck and look in the windows viewing the comforts. The table was spread for dinner, the officers gathered around, drinking, joking, and laughing while the strollers like myself slapped our hands, kicked our feet to keep warm and saw comforts on the other side of the wall. I could not help thinking how we had enlisted to fight for equality and were practicing the utmost inequality. The only equality I see now is that existing between the mules and the men.

One of the coldest nights was clear and the moon shone out brightly. About midnight, I happened on the stern of the boat and looking back it seemed as if a prairie fire was rushing on to overtake the boat. The water which boiled in the vessels' track glistened in the moonlight and it resembled fire so much that it was hard to believe it was not. About the middle of the afternoon the pilot told us that the right bank of the river was the south end of Illinois. We all got up on the hurricane deck and gave three rousing cheers for old Illinois.

On the evening of the third of February we reached Smithland, a town of about five hundred inhabitants at the mouth of the Cumberland River. Here sailors and loafers congregated to lounge and loaf, tell vulgar stories, chew, smoke, drink, and talk politics. The boat hauled up at Smithland and

Co. B and K were ordered to get out of the way; they wanted the place occupied by these two companies to put the coal. We questioned—where will we sleep now? The colonel did not allow us to enter the cabin. Great heaps of coal three or four feet deep were piled where B and K had been sleeping. We couldn't get into the cabin even now and our cup of bitterness seemed full to overflowing. The boat pushed off up stream, up the Cumberland River in the direction of Nashville, Tennessee, past Fort Donaldson [Donelson]. We supposed the coal in our sleeping place was a curse but it soon proved a blessing. Some of the boys commenced crushing and smashing the large chunks of coal into powder and leveling it down so that the whole surface was soon leveled. The hay bales for the mules were broken open and spread on the top of the coal. This gave us a slant height so that we could lay out straight at night.

Our attention now was attracted elsewhere. A telegram had reached Smithland that a second battle was in progress at Fort Donaldson. Added to this there were constantly roving bands of rebels roaming up and down the Cumberland River trying to check the navigation of the river. These bands would aim first to kill the pilot, let the vessel run aground, then after pillaging it, they would burn it.

We were now steaming up a dangerous river with fighting ahead and our presence was needed. In the fleet were several gunboats clad with iron who took the lead. We loaded our guns and prepared for any emergency. The pilot houses on these steamers were small rooms on the top near the middle whose sides were made of glass windows. In order to protect the pilot our boat had a boiler iron shield placed on each side of him. These shields were about the size of half a hogshead but longer and so thick that a musket ball could not penetrate them. As we entered the Cumberland River we could faintly hear the cannonading away up the river at a great distance. We spread out our blankets under such circumstances, not knowing what moment we might be called up with the crack of the rifle and the whiz of bullets.

FEBRUARY 5, 1863, ON BOARD THE *TEMPEST*, CUMBERLAND RIVER

On February 4 we awoke to find we hadn't been fired on during the night by any roving band. The firing at Fort Donaldson had ceased [but] how the battle had terminated none of us knew. The officers were uneasy.

The pilot was watching every object that he could see on either shore, and the boats steamed slowly and carefully up the river. If the rebels had won the battle and captured the fort, it would be foolish nonsense to run the transports filled with soldiers up to the landing and let the rebels tear through our wooden boats with their shells. Consequently, we effected a landing and the 92d deployed into a line of battle and marched out to see what we could find. A little way from the bank stood a house and from the inmates we learned that Wheeler and Van Dorn[8] with their two forces of rebel cavalry had, the afternoon before, made a furious attack upon our forces stationed at Donaldson,[9] or Dover; that our forces still held their positions and the rebels had withdrawn. We marched back to the boats and steamed up stream.

The weather was cold for this country; it snowed nearly all night until quite late in the morning. We arrived at the landing of Fort Donaldson about noon. The men on shore hailed our arrival with shouts of joy, as they had been sorely pressed with a force of not less than five to one and they did not know whether the rebels might return to the fight with redoubled energy.

I had read long accounts nearly a year before of the great battle at Fort Donaldson and thought I should be delighted to visit that place and see all the old battle scars and landmarks made famous in history. Now the opportunity was before me but one thing discouraged me. It was nearly a year since the great victory of Fort Donaldson was won, and only yesterday another battle was fought to hold it. It seemed to me that the fighting ought to be farther south after a year's campaign and fighting.

I found myself on shore as soon as the boat landed and steered straight for the battlefield where the men were at work burying the dead. I had never seen a man intentionally slain in my life. Although I had gone on to the field all fortified to see the bloody war, yet I cannot describe the feeling at the first sight of the slain. There were two parties of our men burying the dead; one was burying rebels and the other Union men. There were only eleven or twelve Union men but one hundred and forty rebels killed. The Union men had all been picked up and carefully boxed in as good boxes as could be had and each soldier was buried good and deep, and after each box was lowered and dirt thrown in, a squad of men fired three volleys in honor of each as a sort of sermon or funeral service. At each grave our men tuck two pieces of board at head and feet with name, number, and date on each headboard.

But the other squad, oh my! What a burial! A great big army wagon with six mules attached drove up to the squad just as I got there. On the ground lay two dead rebels, and in the wagon were fifteen more. The great bulk of the dead had been buried but this load had been picked up around the ragged edges of the battleground from under logs, trees, fences, in gutters and every place where a man could crawl or walk to get a place to die in peace. These poor fellows (I cannot help pitying them) had all been mortally wounded, and crawled or walked off to some place of concealment to die. Their life-blood had ebbed away while they lay unsheltered in a snow storm and were picked up cold and stiff the next day, thrown into a wagon in great heaps, and then dumped into a shallow grave. The wagon came up and the men began to unload. They were pitched out at the end gate of the wagon in about the same style that a farmer would throw off cordwood when he did not wish to cord it. The appearance of these men was simply horrible in the extreme to me. Nearly every one of the rebels had died lying on his back, face up and arms extended out to the right and left. The snow had sifted all down among their hair and stuck to their clothes. The eyes of some were open and there was a deadly stare at me from the promiscuous heap of dead bodies, no matter what position I would take. As the men unloaded the bodies they would keep talking in an animated tone of voice, telling us where they found each one as they tumbled him out.

"This one was shot through the lungs and had been dead all night; this one was shot through the bowels and died hard, he kicked a great hole in the dirt and snow; this one has not been dead long, he was warm when we found him," and so the conversation ran on. They dug a hole to start with about two feet deep and wide enough to lay two men side by side, heels to head, that is, the heels of one by the head of the other. When the two were in they commenced digging by their sides to make room for two more and threw the dirt as fast as they dug it on the last two buried. No coffins or boxes were used. The men were buried as they fell—clothes and all on.

By close inquiry I found that the 83d Illinois Infantry and Co. C of 2d Illinois Artillery was all the force we had there, about seven hundred or eight hundred strong, that Van Dorn and Wheeler had assaulted them with a force estimated at eight thousand. Colonel A. C. Harding of the 83d Illinois was in command. How they had held out against such odds was a wonder. The battle was fought not in the old earth works called Fort

Donaldson, but in the outskirts of the little village called Dover, a town of about five hundred inhabitants in times of peace. Dover was badly dilapidated and almost deserted. I took a hasty visit to the hospital where the rebel wounded were cared for. There were a large number of them, about a hundred in all. Each one was badly wounded. Every rebel that had been slightly wounded and was able to stick to his horse had gone away with his command, but every rebel that was so badly wounded that he could neither walk nor ride had been left behind for the 83d to care for. These men were all in great agony, as the wounds were bad. They were stored away in an old dilapidated two-story building and were lying on straw, old blankets, and the bare floor. Their groans were painful to hear. I took a hasty look over the building and gladly departed. The truth was the 83d had its hands more than full. They fought hard for their own existence and had killed and wounded more than they could care for. The whole regiment was at work picking up the dead, burying the rebel wounded and their own; fifty of them caring for the latter, and at the same time keeping a strong picket line. They were doing the best they could and had not an idle man to spare.

I went aboard the boat at night and in the morning took a stroll over the fighting ground of Fort Donaldson, but I had not been there long before I longed to be away. There was a dead, desolate silence pervading there that I had never witnessed before. My idea of Fort Donaldson was that it was a large square fort with walls very thick and roof to correspond, that it had cannon pointing down the river on the river side and on the other were cannon pointing the other way or land side, but there was nothing of the kind. Fort Donaldson, so called, was nothing more than a long pile of dirt one-half or three-quarters of a mile long, running parallel with the river, resembling a sod fence, only thicker. There were several piles of dirt to get behind down the river. In viewing these grounds everything seemed dead and gone and I resolved never to advise any tourist to visit a battle ground. There was not a pig to squeal, a cow to bellow, a dog to bark, a cat to mew, nor bird to sing in all the country around. It seemed like the deadest spot on earth I was ever on. I went back, got aboard the boat, sick of sight-seeing around Fort Donaldson and Dover.

The balance of the fleet has caught up with us, some seventy or eighty steamers in all. They were lashed together two and two and we all are now steaming slowly up stream, not knowing what moment we might be fired upon from the shore.

FEBRUARY 9, 1863, NASHVILLE, TENNESSEE

On February 6 we steamed up the Cumberland River, all the boats lashed together two and two, and it was a beautiful sight to see the great columns of smoke rising from nearly eighty vessels. It was pretty generally believed by all that we would be fired upon from a land force before we should arrive at Nashville. The boats had been lashed together so that in case we were fired at and one boat should be disabled, both boats would probably not be injured at the same time, and the uninjured boat could preserve the injured one. There were several gunboats in the fleet as a sort of protection. These boats both took the lead and brought up the rear. They were much smaller than the transports, and very securely built. The boiler was placed as low in the boat as possible so that the water should be a wall of protection. The wheel that propelled each was at the stern all under water and out of sight. It was called a screw steamer, that is, the propelling wheel lay in the water like a screw on a carpenter's bench and turned very rapidly, and the water acted as a block for the screw to turn in, and pushed the boats forward or backwards as the engineers desired. These screws lay so deep in the water that a cannon ball could hardly ever get them. The sides of these gunboats sloped from the waters edge, up, and these sides were plaited with heavy boiler iron. If a musket ball should be fired at it, it would strike and glance off and up and pass over. A small cannon ball would do the same. There were small port holes where muskets could be fired through from the inside; also there were several larger ones to shoot through. Each boat had four or five cannon on board, all ready to shoot at a moment's notice.

Before reaching Clarksville where the iron railroad bridge had been destroyed, leaving portions of the iron work hanging to the piers and into the river, somewhat obstructing passage, Lieutenant A. M. York[10] of Co. I, heard the captain of the steamer *Tempest* in conversation with one of his pilots predicting a disaster at the bridge. The lieutenant believed that it was the intention of the captain and pilot, who were rebel in sympathy, deliberately to wreck the steamer *Tempest* and the steamer *Arizona* lashed to its side on which the 92d was being transported. Colonel Atkins, who was in command of the brigade, ordered the lieutenant with a file of soldiers to take the same pilot and captain to the pilot house, and there inform them that if any accident happened at the Clarksville bridge to shoot them both. Lieutenant York did as directed, and we passed the Clarksville bridge without an accident.

Clarksville is quite a pretty town situated on the south bank of the Cumberland River, nearly fifty miles northwest of Nashville. Its citizens, besides being rebels, have done what they could to make the world nastier and filthier by raising and shipping large quantities of that weed called tobacco, fifteen thousand hogsheads is no unusual crop for them to ship to the outside world, where boys love to eat, chew, and smoke it, and they learn to swear and become lazy, filthy loafers.

On the morning of the seventh it was very clear and somewhat warmer, and it was a beautiful sight to see such a small river as the Cumberland having a depth of water to float such a long fleet of vessels. The river, as a whole, is a very narrow one and would almost seem as though there would scarce be room for another boat to pass down, especially while our boats were lashed two and two.

We arrived at Nashville about four o'clock on the seventh of February. We did not unload that night but waited until the next morning. The city of Nashville was brim full of wounded and sick soldiers from Rosecrans' army, after his great battle of Stone River.[11] These sick and wounded were being loaded on to boats in large quantities preparatory to going down the river under escort of the gunboats that came with us. On the morning of the eighth of February we unloaded our boats, and about noon we marched in order through the city. It looked so different from a Northern city that it was the notice of all how different in appeared. Its main streets though beautiful do not appear to be more than half the width of our Northern cities.

The regiment had marched on this whole journey, eighty miles by land and four hundred twenty miles by steamer. It was only one hundred seventy miles straight across by land, and could have been made easily in several days less time and much less exposure and a great many thousand dollars [less] expense to the government. It has been estimated that the trip cost the government fifty lives by exposure that led to sickness and death.

The sick when we landed were all taken to hospitals. Nashville was full of hospitals and they were numbered as hospital No. 1, No. 2, and so on up to twenty and thirty, and each one was well filled and getting fuller. Many of the boys were carried from the boats to the hospitals, and when they came out they came in a box, feet foremost. We camped south of the city on a rise of ground in a field. The ground was all mud from the melting of snow. We got our tents erected so that by February 9 we were at rest once more.

FEBRUARY 10, 1863, NASHVILLE, TENNESSEE

Nashville is a beautiful Southern city and the capital of the state of Tennessee. It is situated on the south bank of the Cumberland River, two hundred miles above its mouth. The river was spanned by a suspension wagon bridge, but when the rebels found, after the battle of Fort Donaldson, that they must evacuate the city, some rebel citizens with coal chisels and hammers went to the great cables that held it to the shore and chiseled and cut wire after wire, or strand after strand, until the weight broke the balance and the whole structure tumbled into the river. The Cumberland River, though narrow, is navigable for considerable portions of the year several hundred miles further up to Carthage. The streets of Nashville are narrow and yet beautiful. Being situated as it is, Nashville is easily approached from the north by land and water, railroad and steamer, and it was made the great military center to accommodate military supplies and munitions of war. The citizens were all rebel in sympathy and to guard those magazines and store houses was no easy task. Rebel spies and bushwhackers were going in and coming out dressed as farmers, women, negroes, and the like, crawling through the guard line under cover of darkness, getting ammunition and supplies to shoot our men with from behind a tree or under a bush. A head guard line night and day completely encircled the city, and no man, woman, or negro could pass in or out unless he prove his loyalty, and yet a heavy patrol was kept constantly scouring the streets night and day. A great many bushwhackers and villains were shot down in the streets from time to time and a few innocent men. Thousands of women and men were arrested and put under guard for a time.

On one back street of Nashville, filthy with dirt and filthier in morals, commonly known as "Smoky Row," nearly the whole street was inhabited by women—women without shame and without character. These women had collected there from the North and South and others were native born. Their ways were dark and they covered themselves with infamy and shame. They became a great source of annoyance to the authorities; accordingly a plan was laid, a trap set to catch and dispose of the whole batch at one scoop. A very large detachment of soldiers were ordered to go on to that street at a certain hour of the night and arrest every woman. The plan thus far worked and they were all taken down to the Cumberland River, some two or three hundred in all, put on board of government transports and the boat steamed down the river and up the Ohio to Louisville, Kentucky.

But word had preceded them by telegraph and the citizens of Louisville were indignant in the extreme. They felt they had all the bad characters they needed and to receive a fresh cargo was more than they would bear. The consequence was that the citizens of Louisville rose up en masse and armed themselves with revolvers, shotguns, clubs, spikes, and hammers and went down to the wharf to receive the cargo. When the boat arrived the mad populace gave the captain to understand that if he allowed that boat to land on Kentucky soil they would shoot him and his whole crew, burn his boat to the water's edge, and drown the women in the Ohio River. The captain of the boat was confused and did not know what to do. He anchored in the middle of the river, not daring to lash the boat to shore. The female cargo was devouring provisions at a rapid rate and he could get no fresh supply. If he landed the women on a barren, uninhabited shore they would perish of starvation and cold. Something had to be done. Finally the captain weighed anchor, steamed down the Ohio and up the Cumberland and landed his female cargo in the city of Nashville from whence he had taken them and the women all returned to their former dens of shame and infamy.

In addition to the guard line that surrounded the city and the patrol that scoured the streets of Nashville, there was also a detective force constantly at work. These men discovered that the horses and mules belonging to private families in the city were dying off at a rapid rate and they all died very suddenly. A southern lady would go to the provost marshall's office and with tears in her eyes relate the sad story of the death of their family horse and ask for a permit to drag his dead body out of the city limits and beyond the guard line for burial. Of course the permit was granted. But after the death rate began to run up the detectives investigated. It was found that these horses and mules had been intentionally killed or smothered with fumes. The entrails were all carefully removed and disposed of and the inside filled and packed with bottles and packages of quinine.[12]

Nashville is a great city for theaters. There are three or four at full blast every night and they are all well attended. The audiences are of a mixed character—soldiers, Southerners, and negroes. There is a bitter dislike among soldiers of the North towards Southerners and they have no respect for the rules and necessary regulations of a theater. Northern men have gone south to put down the rebellion, but it seems as though nearly every man has lost more or less respect for all law and order once he crossed

Mason Dixon's line. The result is that to run a theater it is necessary to put guards of soldiers all through the audience, both above and below, in the gallery and in the pit. A sergeant takes about twenty men with guns all scoured until they shine and glisten, the soldiers in full uniform and white gloves. The sergeant stands in the gallery where he can overlook the whole house. He then divides up his men and sends one to every part of the house. If anyone makes the slightest disturbance the sergeant orders the soldiers in that part of the house to arrest the disturber. While attending such a theater I heard someone in the audience burst suddenly with one of the most piercing whistles I ever heard. I could not tell how he made it. The sergeant ordered the soldier in that part of the house to "take him out," and the soldier was on his feet in an instant looking for his man, but for the life of him he could not tell which one whistled.

Everything was again quiet and the play went on; but when we again got our attention all fixed upon the play, the piercing whistle came again, throwing everything into confusion. The sergeant repeated his order with double emphasis but the soldier was compelled to reply that he could not tell the man. The sergeant then told the guard that the next time that whistle blew to "bring out that man." The play went on. We had all got intensely interested in the play and forgotten all about the whistle, when all of a sudden the wax seemed to fairly jump from our ears. But the guard had his eyes on the suspected locality and he had detected his man. He was a Union soldier in company with a squad of his friends and had been drinking just enough to be devilish and bold. The guard ordered him out but he refused to go.

"By God," said the guard, "my sergeant said 'come out' and you are coming." The guard took him by the collar, jerked him into the aisle, put his bayonet behind him and told him to go and he went. He was taken down and out to the guard house and here my knowledge of the matter ends. Order was quickly restored and the play concluded.

From the seventh of February, the day of our landing, for a whole month, the regiment lay in a muddy camp near the city of Nashville. While thus lying inactive in camp we were all dissatisfied and uneasy. The men preferred anything to inactivity. Hardships were a pleasure compared to it. We came out to fight and we would rather now go right at it and have it done with. To lie in camp with nothing to do is one of the most disagreeable things in the world.

On the 15th of February Lieutenant Crowell handed in his resignation which was quickly accepted and Co. B was without a commissioned officer. On the 16th, Horace J. Smith,[13] first lieutenant of Co. K came into the company and took command, as he said, until someone was elected or appointed. By degrees we learned that he had really been appointed as our captain before we left Danville, Kentucky.

CHAPTER 3

We Were All Anxious for the Fray

March – June 1863

MARCH 1, 1863

In an army the private soldier loses all individuality. He is sworn at the start with a solemn oath to obey the officers appointed (not elected) over him. He is no longer a man in the light of the Republic. He has no opinions that will ever be heard, much less heeded. It is his duty to obey and never be heard. He is supposed not to know anything about the business he is engaged in—the war. It is his duty to come when called, and go when sent—and no questions as to the whys and wherefores. He is at liberty to eat what is given him and sleep until "roll call." The doctor decides when he is sick, the captain tells him when he is mean, and decides whether he shall be put in the guard house or tied up by the thumbs, and if he is very mean the captain decides that also—and orders him "bucked and gagged." This latter punishment however was of very rare occurrence in the 92d. It is a barbarous affair to look at. The soldier is taken, his wrists snugly bound together with a rope or strap, and he is then seated on the ground and his feet drawn close to the body in such a way that the knees project up in front of his face. His arms are drawn down around the outside of his legs, and then a hoe handle or something of the kind is slipped through under the knees and over the arms. Whatever position a man is put in, he cannot move. He can be rolled over and over and wherever he stops rolling there he will stay until relieved by some one—he cannot help himself. The gag was simply to take an ordinary bayonet and tie it into his mouth like a bridle bit on a horse—it held his mouth open and prevented him from talking. This punishment was never resorted to unless some negro or soldier got crazy mad and utterly refused to obey all orders and abused officers with the foulest of foul language and threats. I have seen several negroes and only one man of the 92d so punished.

In army life the officers decide whether a soldier goes on picket or stays off, whether he can have a fire on picket or go without it, whether he can go home or stay. If he goes home without permission, officers call it desertion, and decide whether he is to be shot dead or allowed to live. Officers decide how sick he is, whether he can stay in his tent, the hospital tent, or go home to his mother to die, or get well. Every particle of individuality is locked up and must be smothered in his own bosom until his time of enlistment has expired, and he once more becomes a free man. The private soldier is a volunteer slave during his term of enlistment. But as far as I know it is a necessity. War is a dreadful calamity at best, and in order to get men to be hurled up to the very cannon's mouth at the command of one man— each man must volunteer to become a willing slave.

The organization of armies commenced way back in the days of barbarism and has since been improved and reflected by all the great military minds from that time to the present, and every change and improvement has been to make the minds of the soldiers the willing tools of their master or commander.

New officers make very many blunders of necessity. Some of these blunders seem mean and unpardonable in the light of after knowledge. We hope no reader of these "notes" will ever hold any officers to account for any blunders herein described. These blunders were as much on account of the peculiar division made among men in the army regulations, as it was an evil design on the part of the officers.

The colonel is mounted on a horse while the men go on foot. His pay is about $250 per month while the privates get $13. He is dressed with the richest broadcloths, gold cords, red sash, fancy belts, revolver, and silver-mounted sword. While the soldier wears coarse woolen clothes with a few brass buttons, and when on the march carries a greasy haversack filled with rations, a canteen of water, cartridge box, belts, bayonet, musket, and on top of all is a huge knapsack filled with extra pants, shirt, tent, overcoat, woolen blanket, rubber blanket, love letters from his girl, portfolio with paper, pen, ink, and pencil to reply to letters, a needle book, needles, pins, threads, and buttons.

At night the colonel sleeps in a large tent guarded all night by soldiers, while the soldier sleeps in a small pup tent, unguarded. The colonel has waiters take care of his horse for him, cook for him, write for him, and wait on him. An officer or colonel, lifted into office under such circumstances has every reason to believe himself a wise man, and the military laws all acknowledge him to be a superior man, and the dress, rank, and position all point to his superiority, and he is as willing to believe it as the men are compelled to concede it. It stimulates into action all the pride and conceit that the colonel ever had. He imagines himself what the law makes him—a man of superior ability. The ladies all admire the colonel and look at the men. A citizen feels it a great honor to speak to the colonel. The officers of lower rank will laugh and wink with an air of great appreciation at even a stale joke from the colonel. The silly-minded soldier will cower, creep, and fawn to the colonel for an approving look. The conceit and arrogance of the colonel is strained to the highest tension that law, dress, show, favoritism, and flattery is capable of raising it. His judgment, for a time, is smothered with self importance and conceit. While in this frame of mind, nearly every new colonel leaves a record of blunders behind him. But after an active service in the presence of an enemy, that conceit is beaten out of these colonels and other officers by hard experience. After one or two years of blunders and experiences these officers frequently become valuable commanders.

Nearly every other day while the regiment lay in camp at Nashville, we would get orders to be ready to march the next day, but for some reason we did not march. A force of rebel cavalry got north of us while here and cut the railroad once or twice, which affected our supplies of rations. To the squad and tent to which I belonged there were seventeen men when "all were at home." We used to take turns about cooking. One man would cook one day, another the next, and so on, so that about every seventeenth day I had to cook. It came my turn to cook one day when rations were short. In fact there was scarcely anything in the whole regiment to eat, but rations were expected daily and almost hourly. I managed to get a scanty breakfast, but for dinner I did not know what to get. I searched in every pail, bucket, haversack, and kettle, and the only thing that I could find to cook was about a teacup-full of beans. How to get dinner for seventeen men with a teacup-full of beans was a stunner, but dinner of some kind must be had. I decided however to make bean soup. I got a kettle that held about two pails of water, filled it up, and set it on the camp fire, poured in the teacup-full of beans, and took a stick and began to stir to prevent them from burning. Although there was not much to burn, still I thought I would stir. I boiled and stirred the pot till plum noon, and by that time the beans had all boiled to pieces and dissolved, turning the water to a milky white color. There was not a particle of bean left the size of a pin-head in the soup, so thoroughly had they dissolved. I had just set the kettle off the fire when Charley Ames[1] came along and saw my big kettle of bean soup. Charley's squad, like ours, was short of rations. He saw the soup and very meekly asked me if I would not give him a dish of soup, as that looked so delicious. Wishing to be generous I said certainly, and told him to bring around his soup dish. Charley got his soup dish and I filled it and he thanked me very gentlemanly. He walked off to one side and began to stir and cool it. He examined it and tasted it. It tasted like water, but he stirred again and again tasted it. He then turned around, brought his dish back, held it out and said, "For God's sake just give me one bean, so that I can say that I have had bean soup for dinner."

MARCH 5, 1863, NEAR FRANKLIN, TENNESSEE

On the 26th of February, news reached camp that a bill had passed Congress to raise more troops. This was joyful news to the regiment.

The papers at home were all ablaze with denunciations of Copperheads[2] at the North. Everybody felt bitter in the extreme towards those who were opposing the war and lending their sympathies towards the rebels. On receipt of this news the officers of the regiment appointed themselves as a committee of the whole to express the indignation of the regiment. No private had a voice in the matter. In fact no private even knew that an indignation meeting was to be held, or even thought of, unless it were the colonel's clerk or guard at his tent. Not a private had voted for a delegate to the meeting, and not a private was recognized as a member of the meeting, and yet every private could have the privilege of saying, "aye" to their resolutions when all were in line. To say "aye" to each resolution would do no harm nor good, and to say "no" would leave an unpleasant sting.

The meeting turned out two whereases and seven resolutions. These resolutions breathed the true spirit of loyalty in the extreme, and a few extravagant ideas, and others a little inconsistent. Resolution four read:

"Resolved, that we oppose all secret organizations organized for any political purpose, believing it to be an unmanly way of gaining political power."

At the time when the above was penned, the Union League, a secret organization, had been organized and running for months in East Tennessee, and it was snatching innocent Union men from the jaws of rebellion and death, and assisting them to skulk from home to a place of safety in the North, where they could be organized into regiments to fight for the Union. The League was then spreading all over the Union as a secret

organization to preserve it. Those company officers were brim full of ambition—to get a higher rank—and patriotism. In their drafting resolutions it
must not be expected that they were statesmen. The Knights of the Golden
Circle was a secret organization to plot and overthrow the government. The
resolutions were fixed up for the Knights of the Circle, but they could not
see that it tore the secret institution all to pieces, of which nearly every
Union citizen was a member. The resolutions were read to each company,
and they were all permitted to say "aye" to them, and then on the third of
March Colonel Sheets presented them to the regiment, while on dress
parade, for an expression there, and of course every man, except three,
voted for them with mechanical precision, and those three voted against
apparently out of pure deviltry. The tone of the resolutions were [*sic*] very
loyal and expressed in radical inconsistent language. To put such questions
or resolutions before a regiment of men, read them aloud, and call for a
vote without further consideration or debate, when nearly every private
soldier did not feel at liberty to vote against it if he wanted to, was simply a
farce. The standing in line listening to the mumbling of such documents by
embarrassed clerks, and the subsequent "aye," is the most complete system
of machine voting known to men familiar with a Republic.

On March 5 the whole regiment was out on what is called battalion
drill, a drill practiced in sham battles and other movements preparatory to
warfare. While on battalion drill, word came to get ready in five minutes to
take the cars for Franklin, a town on the railroad some fifteen or twenty
miles south. The order was to leave all luggage behind and to go in light
fighting order. All was hustle-bustle, hurly-burly, get ready quick, take a
day's rations, lots of ammunition, and be ready to fight. Cannonading could
be distinctly heard in the direction of Franklin. Franklin was the right wing
and front of General Rosecrans' army, and Gordon Granger commanded
the right wing. We were soon at the depot, but had to wait until six o'clock
in the evening, listening to the continuous roar of artillery, before cars came
for us. The cars consisted of old rickety cattle cars. The 92d, and in fact the
whole brigade boarded the train, that is squeezed in, pushed in, climbed on
top, and hung on to anything and everything that would ensure a man a
place to ride in safety. The weather had been clear and cool all day, and
towards evening it moderated a little and the sky was overcast with a deepening haze, and as night came on it intensified the darkness until everything
seemed absolutely dark. The engine puffed and tugged with its heavy load,
and seemed almost swamped. In these cars there were no seats. At first the

men were full of jokes, but as we neared a point where the cars dared not go farther a silence began to prevail, and the darkness of the night lent a peculiar air to the silence. The engine did not run with that head-long speed that is so pleasantly indulged in our northern roads in times of peace, but it ran cautiously as though it were afraid, checking up and starting again, and frequently stopping and standing still. We could not tell whether we had passed stations, crossed rivers, or run over dangerous tressel [sic] works, everything was so dark. At eleven o'clock at night the train halted and we were ordered to get out. Everybody wondered what station we were at. Everything was so pitch dark, and we had no lanterns and there were no conductors, brakemen, or newsboys to ask. We got out and the train backed up. We found ourselves in a muddy cornfield, and concluded that this must be Cornfield Station, inhabited with old corn stalks. The wealth of the station, the corn, had all gone into the rebel army. The clouds were deepening and everything was as still as death. None of the regiment had ever been there before, and where we were none seemed to know. Our beds that night were all made on soft mud between the rows of corn.

Many of the men slept soundly. Two men agree to sleep together; each has a rubber blanket and a woolen one. They locate the spot where they will sleep, and one stands there while the other, knife in hand, gropes in the darkness and cuts and gathers old corn stalks and weeds. When he is loaded he calls to his companion and guides his way back by voice. These stalks and weeds are laid on the ground until the mud is completely covered. On the top of the stalks a rubber blanket is laid, then two woolen ones, and on the top of all is another rubber. The soldiers crawl in between the woolen ones, clothes on, guns by their sides, ready to jump and fight at the first alarm. We had hardly got our beds made when the rain began to fall in torrents. In order to prevent the water leaking in, the soldiers lie spoon fashion so as not to permit a hollow or sag in the blankets between them. During the heavy dashing of rain he curls up his feet and cuddles down his head under the rubber to keep the rain from his feet and face, but during the drizzling mists he stretches out and sleeps with face to the open air and holds his position until the torrents drive him back to his hole again.

MARCH 8, 1863, FRANKLIN, TENNESSEE

On the morning of March 6 we woke up from our muddy, wet beds looking more like drowned rats than men. It is impossible to make a bed in the open air and sleep through a drenching rain without getting wet. Water will work through somewhere, even if you have rubber blankets. Daylight found us on the north side of Harpeth River overlooking Franklin. The town was situated on the south side and we were encamped on the north. The rain continued to fall in torrents all day and there could be no fighting under the circumstances. We remained in the cornfield all day and the constant tramp of the men and the constant fall of rain thinned the mud and left the ground in a horrible condition.

The day before, Colonel Coburn's brigade, consisting of the 22d Wisconsin, 23d Indiana and 49th Michigan regiments, about twenty-five hundred strong, all that were fit for duty, were sent out towards Spring Hill and left unsupported, fighting about eighteen thousand rebels under Van Dorn, Forrest, and Wheeler. Coburn's brigade made a gallant fight, but surrounded and left alone with such terrible odds were at last compelled to surrender, only a few making their escape and returning to Franklin. There was a blunder somewhere, and it was believed by every soldier and officer that General Gordon Granger, the general who had command of all the troops in and around Franklin was the blundering party.[3] He is believed to be an incompetent man by every one from colonels to privates. Coburn's brigade had fought nearly half a day within a few miles of Franklin. General Granger had two or three other brigades at Franklin, but never sent a man to assist Coburn, although word had been sent for help several times. The rebel cavalry had worked their way in behind Coburn's brigade of infantry. Only when he had fired all his ammunition into the rebel ranks and could do no more did he surrender. The troops stood at their guns around Franklin and listened to the rattle of musketry and the roar of artillery and longed to be sent out to assist Coburn's brigade, but Granger would not give the order and that is how a brigade of troops was lost.

In the United States there is a military school located at West Point where young men are sent at government expense and taught the known arts and sciences of civilized warfare. They are thoroughly trained in military tactics. In times of peace these graduates hold commissions as lieutenants, captains, and colonels, but in time of war many are lifted to generals. In a general way this is a good plan, but it has its drawbacks. It frequently occurs that a student is sent there who is considerably destitute of brains and education does not give men brains, only improves what they have. It sometimes occurs that some soft-handed fop, with a softer brain and curly mustache, through the agency of some political friend, will get appointed to the military school. He readily learns to keep his boots black, his collar white, his hair slick, his coat well brushed, and to stand erect in the ranks. He manages to commit his lessons to memory and mumbles them over to his teacher. After four years of training of this sort he graduates, becomes a lieutenant or captain of the regular army, and in the case of war, if he has strong political friends, he becomes a major general of volunteers. Such a man is General Granger, stylish, haughty, and indignant. Granger is a cipher at the wrong end of the number where there ought to have been a digit that would count. It was almost the universal, half-smothered expression among all men of the different regiments and brigades of his command that "Granger is a damned fool." Such half-smothered expressions can be heard almost daily on picket or in camp. They were deeper and far more frequent after the loss of Coburn's brigade.

All weak-minded men are fond of dress and show. The rule applies to Granger and to get the troops out on parade was his greatest delight. On almost every possible occasion he sent orders all through his command to prepare for a grand review. He selected some field, meadow, or prairie, mounted upon his finest horse dressed in his finest coat, red sash, sword, belts, gauntlet, gloves, and top boots, and then with his bodyguard of about forty men sitting on their horses in the background, compelled his whole command to march by him on review. It could take from half to three-quarters of a day sometimes to complete the review, but long as it was the general would hold his position and occasionally salute the colonels as they rode by. Every regiment seemed to feel it is a misfortune to belong to his corps.

Franklin is a rebel town and it was reported that the citizens had sent word to Van Dorn, Wheeler, and Forrest[4] to come take supper in town on the evening of the sixth, but the rebel generals did not like the company that had forced itself upon the town, so they modestly declined and stayed away. It rained all day on the sixth, but by night our tents came and we were once more under cover, but not out of the mud. On the seventh, the bridge across Harpeth River was completed and on the eighth many troops of cavalry and infantry came to Franklin, under the command of General Sheridan,[5] and reported to Granger. It was evident now that a move would be made and we were all anxious for the fray. Everything was in readiness for a battle.

MARCH 14, 1863, FRANKLIN, TENNESSEE

On the eighth of March troops began to arrive, train load after train load until Sheridan's whole division of infantry came up and some others. Sheridan's troops had mostly enlisted and had been in the service six months earlier than the 92d and other regiments stationed about Franklin. Each of the six hundred thousand troops that enlisted when the 92d did got $100 bounty over and above his monthly pay. Sheridan's troops had enlisted earlier and at that time had received no bounty, nor promise of any. His men felt a little sore at the inequality of the distribution of bounties.

When Sheridan's troops came marching from the cars to places from camp, the joking commenced, of course, and the 92d rather got the worst of it. The main feature of the joking with Sheridan's men was calling us "hundred-dollar men." We sent back pretty good bumpers and told them that they would like to have had the hundred dollars, but that they were not sharp enough to get it. They in turn told us that our patriotism had to be bought at a hundred dollars a head and we retorted with the idea that they were not worth a hundred dollars nor a hundred cents and so the joking went on, every man that felt so disposed putting in his lip.

On the ninth all the troops about Franklin started on the march south to wake up the Johnnies. About five miles out, crack, crack, crack went the guns of our cavalry advance. The rebels were driven back, but they fired on our advance from every favored spot, and reluctantly retreated. The first wounded man the 92d got to see was a cavalryman who came riding back in search of a surgeon. He had a ballshot through the left hand and the blood was dripping from the end of his fingers. It was bleeding freely and he held it out from the body and guided his horse with the right hand.

We reached a little town called Spring Hill and camped a mile and half south of it. Two of our cavalrymen were killed and four wounded during the day. The rebels left one dead man behind, but how many of them were killed and wounded we had no means of knowing. We had no tents and about midnight it commenced to rain and continued twenty-four hours without ceasing. It rained so hard that we had to stand up a considerable part of the time to let the water run off. It was very disagreeable standing in a cold rain.

On the morning of the tenth we did not expect to march on account of the rain, and the men began tearing down some old buildings near at hand and made temporary sheds of lumber. We had scarcely got up a place to dodge rain drops when orders came to move on. We resumed our march about ten o'clock since we could not wait for the rain to cease. The cavalry was soon skirmishing and our progress was slow. At every convenient knoll the artillery was unlimbered and the timber in advance shelled. We did not get far when the cavalry came dashing back to the rear. Rumor was afloat that the rebels were trying a flank movement and the cavalry was sent to prevent it. As they passed back the joking commenced between the cavalry and infantry.

The privates had no responsibility and, notwithstanding the nearness to the rebels and constant skirmishing, it was a pleasant pastime for the infantry to joke the cavalry and vice versa. We told them they were making a bold charge on the rear to draw their sabers and "go in," there was no danger of getting hurt. We told them in case they should find anything in the rear that we would come and settle their hash as soon as we whipped those fellows that scared them back. They called us a blasted set of web-footed mudwaders; rain was good for ducks and the harder it rained the louder we squawked.

Every fellow would strain his thinking cap and sometimes some fellow would get off the sharpest of sharp hits that would bring a roar of laughter as far up and down the line as he could be heard, on one side only. These jokes were rough, keen, and sharp but there was no real bitterness; it was done for fun and excitement and to enjoy an occasional hearty laugh.

We formed into a line of battle on the north side of a creek, while on the other about a mile back the rebels formed into line of battle. I got the privilege of looking through an officer's field glass and their lines could be distinctly seen with officers riding up and down giving orders and preparing for battle. Just over back of the rebel line was Duck River, at flood tide from the heavy rains and all the bridges gone. Now was the time for a decisive battle. We had from two to three times their number, and an attack on our part was anxiously waited for, or rather, we waited for orders to advance to the attack, but no orders came. Granger was in command. The artillery was brought up, and the rebels were shelled at long range from right to left. The rebels feebly responded, but their shells burst high in the air, doing us no harm. The day was spent in this way until night came on. It was evident that the opportunity of capturing or drowning those rebels was lost, for they could erect a temporary bridge during the night and skip.

We were called up at three o'clock in the morning of the 12th, and stood in line of battle until after sunrise. And sure enough Duck River was between us and the rebel cavalry. Everybody felt disappointed, and we were ordered back to Franklin. Sheridan's troops took the lead. They started off like quarter horses to show the newer soldiers what older ones could do. The 92d kept up and nineteen miles were made in six hours. Just before reaching Franklin, a squad of rebel scouts fired on our rear guard, and the 92d was thrown into line to ascertain what was after us. We reached camp tired, wet, footsore, and hungry. We had been on a wild goose chase. Had Sheridan been in command we would have got some geese. The next day we got orders to keep three days' cooked rations on hand and on the 14th General Granger got all the troops out on one of his stylish grand reviews.

MARCH 21, 1863, FRANKLIN, TENNESSEE

While in Franklin, all the troops have undergone the effects of all General Granger's red-tape foolishness.

The usual method of standing picket is this: a place where it is deemed necessary to keep three men constantly on guard, twelve men are detailed or selected for that purpose, two noncommissioned officers and ten privates. One of the privates is selected as supernumerary and the other nine privates are divided into three groups with three men in each group. These groups are numbered one, two, and three but are called relief, first relief, second relief, and third relief. The first relief of three men takes a position where the road or country is to be watched. They load their guns and are ready to shoot at the slightest evidence of an approaching enemy. While these three are standing the other nine men rest in a free and easy manner a little way back, where they build a fire, cook, eat, and sleep. But every man must keep his cartridge box, belt, and ammunition constantly buckled to his person, his gun in his hand or lying by his side. When the first group of three men or first relief has stood two hours then the second relief goes and takes its place and sends the first relief back to the fire. At the end of two more hours the third relief takes the place of the second and thus they go round and round. At night, those who are by the fire lie down and sleep. No man is allowed to take off his boots, coat, or any part of his clothing while he sleeps. Every man must have his gun by his side loaded and capped, ready to jump and shoot in the shortest time possible. The two noncommissioned officers and supernumerary divide themselves into three watches the same as the men. One stands by the fire all the time with a watch in his pocket to keep the time. During the night he wakes up the reliefs and places them on picket and relieves those who have been standing two hours. In addition to this the man at the fire wakes up every man at the slightest alarm or unusual noise that cannot be accounted for. It matters not what the condition of the weather may be; these men must stay there twenty-four hours.

Sometimes the storm clouds come sweeping over the country and the night becomes black with darkness, and the winds blow and the rain pelts and drenches every man until he is wet to the skin. At other times it sleets and snows and sometimes it freezes, but the soldier just stays at his post. After the rain, or the snow, or the sleet, the soldier can warm and dry by the fire at the reserve post, after standing two hours in the storm.

Some commanders, who are more timid than wise, will sometimes forbid the fire after night at the reserve post. General Granger, like the old granny he is, seemed to think the best way to make good soldiers was to find as many ways to make them uncomfortable as his weak mind could invent. He forbade all fires on the picket post either night or day. Of course the order was easily defended on the ground of safety, but for every life saved in that way from distinction by the bullet (if any had been saved) there were a hundred lives lost for want of fire during the long, chilly, rainy, sleety, freezing, variable nights. Twelve hours of such exposure with three warm meals and eight hours in a warm bed a man could stand with ease, but with twenty-four hours of cold rains, without a fire to warm and dry by and cold, poorly cooked poor food and no place to sleep except on the cold, wet ground, under such treatment men fell victims to the exposure and the sick list was very large. It seemed but a matter of little time, if Granger held command of the troops, until the whole command was wasted with sickness. Granger has enlarged his order now so that men were compelled to stay twenty-four hours without a wink of sleep, a fire to warm by, or anything warm to eat or drink. Added to this, Granger issued another order that compelled every regiment to get up at four o'clock and stand in line of battle until after sunrise. To stand in those damp, chilly fogs that rose from the Harpeth River three hours in the morning was more destructive to life and probably was the means of more deaths than all the men killed by bullets in all the battles Granger ever fought. Nearly one-half the regiment with which we left Rockford was either on the sick list or troubled with some sort of complaint that such exposure produced.

Plans were laid by the engineers and other officers to fortify a hill on the north side of the Harpeth River that overlooked Franklin and a plain level tract of country lying to the south, west, and east. The fort was laid off in about the same way a farmer lays out a pig pen or cow pasture, only the engineer wears fine clothes and has a soft hand, and measures the ground with a tape line, while the farmer measures off his pig pen with a pole and wears coarser clothes and has a hard hand. The soldiers were then detailed to dig a trench and use the dirt for a thick dirt wall. When the trench was dug and made into a dirt wall, the patch fence in the fort was completed, just the same as the farmer's pig pens. The trench was on the outside and the dirt wall was on the inside and about as high as a man's head. This dirt wall was about ten feet thick, so that a cannon ball could not go through. There were a few breaks in the walls, but more in the ditches for cannon to shoot out of.

On the 15th of March, 1863, I was detailed to work for the first time on a fort. There was no particular skill needed in building it. Any one that could strike with a pick or throw dirt with a shovel could work on it.

I was sent out on picket during the day and night of the 17th and 18th, on the main line running south. During the night twelve negroes came in bringing four mules and reported rebels in Spring Hill, the next little town south.

On the 19th I worked in company with large details from the regiment on the fort.

The next day the whole regiment went on picket, guarding the whole front on the south of Franklin, across the main road running to Spring Hill. Granger's orders were strictly obeyed and no fires were built and no one was allowed to sleep. The night was cold and chilly and if a vote could have been taken probably every man would have voted for fires on the reserve; for one I felt as though I would prefer cooling off after I was shot, than cool off first while waiting to be shot. If I had got to die on Southern soil I wanted to be warm enough to let the blood run.

Granger never stood on picket as a soldier in his life. He issued his orders in a room by a blazing fire with plenty to eat and drink and his wine gave him a good appetite for sleep. Nor was he disturbed about getting up and standing in line of battle at four o'clock in the morning. His orders were for the soldiers, but did not apply to officers of his rank.

APRIL 8, 1863, FRANKLIN, TENNESSEE

While at Franklin the rebels were hovering around our picket lines and shots were frequently exchanged but no attacks were made by them of any note until the morning of March 25, when firing was heard at daylight in the rear or in the direction of home on the line of railroad on which we came to Franklin. The firing was at Brentwood, a little station on the railroad about eight miles back towards Nashville.

The 92d was in line of battle in accordance with Granger's orders, before daylight. The regiment stood in a peach orchard for hours till long after daylight when it was ordered out. It was jestingly remarked that there was no danger, as Granger would keep us in line of battle in the peach orchard until the rebels would have time to complete all their mischief at Brentwood and go away before he would let any assistance go there. We got on the road for a considerable distance and then returned, as the rebels had completed their work and gone.

At Brentwood were stationed all the teamsters, convalescents, and debris of what were left of Colonel Coburn's brigade captured at Spring Hill. These men had been stationed at Brentwood, a place exposed to the enemy and were there to fortify and guard the railroad against roving bands of rebels. Colonel Bloodgood of the 22d Wisconsin had command. They had been in their new position but a few days while the rebel General Van Dorn took a night ride in a circuitous route, got to Brentwood in the morning, and Colonel Bloodgood surrendered without firing scarcely a gun. A few of the men, however, got into a stockade, refused to surrender, and did some fighting, but when Van Dorn got his artillery trimmed on the stockade and sent a few shells tearing through, they surrendered also. Our boys all declared that Van Dorn had found the Ulster roll of Coburn's brigade and had come back after the balance of the command, for they got them all, toted them all down to Dixie, and threw them into Andersonville prison.

About this time sickness among the men was very great and the men were being poured into the Nashville hospitals at a rapid rate. I had a good constitution and had little or no fear of sickness but carelessness overcame me.

On the morning of the 24th I was sent out on the picket line. It rained nearly all day and all night. Under Granger's orders there could be no fires either night or day. Although we wore rubber blankets, our lower extremities were soon drabbled and wet to the skin. We remained standing on our feet nearly all day and night. Towards morning I became tired and drowsy while at the reserve post. I took my rubber off and laid it on some rails, so as to make a little shelter, and carelessly lay down on the wet ground with my head and shoulders under cover and the balance of my body exposed to the continuous cold rain. I thought I would lie only a few moments, but I fell fast asleep and slept soundly for four hours until I was called at daylight to stand as vidette. I woke up numb, wet, and cold. My clothes were saturated with the cold rain, except a little about my shoulders. I took my position as vidette and walked rapidly backward and forward until the blood was again in circulation. On our way to camp after the relief came I felt a sore on one ankle. By the time we got to camp there were sores on both ankles and in an hour after reaching camp my limbs were nearly covered with a perfect system of bunches resembling boils. I was not sick but badly scared. I went directly to the hospital tent and applied for treatment and Doctors Helm and Winston took charge of me.

On the 27th Colonel Sheets got orders to be ready to march in fifteen minutes. The regiment was soon in line and on the march. We reached Brentwood about midnight in what appeared to me the heaviest rainfall I ever experienced. Although I was on the sick list with my limbs literally covered with a mass of strange-looking blisters, yet I was in the rain, drenched to the skin and helped to erect our tent, staking it down by the light of the occasional flashes of lightning. When the tent was up the mud and water inside of it was ankle deep. We made our beds on that mud and we lay down and slept soundly, wet clothes and all. Every other man who was on the sick list was in no better condition than I was. If a man is sick and chooses to go with his regiment he must stand the hardships of the regiment. When men were very sick they were taken to the cars in ambulances and shipped to Nashville, sometimes by the car load. I had a dread of the hospitals at Nashville and preferred staying with the regiment.

The next day the regiment moved two miles to a good camping ground and the regimental hospital tent was erected. The doctors took charge of me and kept me inside the hospital tent. In every regiment there was one large tent kept on purpose for the sick, inside of which were a lot of small bunks for soldiers to lie on. There were two or three men kept for the express purpose of cooking and nursing sick men. Whenever the tent was filled with the sick and there was no longer room for more, all those who were bedridden were sent away to some general hospital.

The town of Brentwood was fortified and on the eighth of April the regiment was ordered back to Franklin as other troops had come to take our places. All the sick who were not able to walk were ordered sent to Nashville to the hospitals and I came within the range of the order as I was now unable to walk, although I suffered no pain. To go to Nashville to a hospital where soldiers were being carried to their graves by the dozens and scores daily was no pleasant thought to me. About two o'clock we were taken to the cars and put on board, how many I have no means of knowing as my diary was very deficient in many things during my illness, but I had a great dread of the hospital.

I had never been really sick in my life and had never seen the inside of a genuine hospital, and it seemed to me like going to the hospital was the first downward step to the grave. We were hustled aboard when the train arrived, the bell rung, and away we sped for Nashville. There were plenty of well men sent along to assist and we were well cared for, each man taking such a position on the cars as was best suited for his sickness. There was a melancholy gloom spread over the midst of the sick soldiers. Scarcely a word was spoken or groan uttered although some of the men were very sick with but little prospect of ever recovering. We arrived at Nashville about two hours before dark and army ambulances came and took us all up to Hospital No. 3. Waiters came out and a physician with them and his practiced eye could easily tell those who were the sickest. All those who, in his judgment, ought not to be allowed to walk were laid on stretchers and carried into the hospital and up the stairway to the wards where they were to remain. When we were all unloaded and in the wards, those who could sit were given chairs and all who could not were laid at once upon beds. The nurses then came round and stripped us piece meal of everything we had on, from the crowns of our heads to the soles of our feet, and a clean hospital suit was put on in its stead. Our clothing was all packed in our dirty-looking knapsacks, each one properly marked and packed away in the store room, a room kept for that purpose. As soon as this stripping and redressing was over, all who would eat were given supper and put to bed. I, for one, was exhausted and all my dread and fears were soon drowned in sleep.

>-+-<>-O-<>-+-<

Hospital No. 3 was a large building with six floors, counting the basement. It was built of brick with a brick wall running through the middle, lengthwise of the building, dividing it into two sets of rooms. Each room above the basement was a ward, except one which was used for an office in part and in part for a store room. The basement on one side was for cooking and the other for a dining room. There were nine wards in the building filled with patients, averaging about forty to each ward, or 360 in the whole building. All patients whose stomachs were supposed to be sound, who were able to go up and down stairs, were compelled to dine at the general dining room table. There were no potatoes nor butter used on this table. The chief article of food was bakers bread, boiled beef, and mixed vegetables. There were two tables running the whole length of the building. Although the cooking was done on a large scale and there was plenty for all and waiters to get it, yet if you called for beef steak you got boiled beef. If you called for pie you got bakers bread. Calling for oyster soup would bring vegetable soup. It was a regular round of diet. Vegetable soup, beef, and bread for dinner; bread, beef and vegetable soup for supper; and for breakfast it was beef with vegetable soup and bread.

There were nearly thirty hospitals in the single city of Nashville running on this grand scale. Nearly all were full to overflowing with sick and wounded soldiers. When the hospitals became full and more came, a steamboat load or several steamboat loads would be sent down the Cumberland and up the Ohio to Louisville which city also had a lot of hospitals.

My case, Dr. Winston told me, was a rare one. Nothing like it had occurred or been reported in the army. It would be treated the same as erysipelas; hence he had booked me as with that complaint when I was sent, but he informed me that it was a real case of scorpute.[6] My new-made friend declared that I had the black leg, as they were badly swelled and the skin turned black. Dr. Winston very kindly gave me private instructions before leaving camp. He told me not to take much medicine and to live upon vegetable food to the fullest possible extent. I never felt a genuine streak of severe pain during the whole of my sickness, if it could be called sickness, but I was weak and languid. I could stand on my feet and walk a little during the whole time, although on two mornings in succession I had no use whatever of my hands or arms. They were numb or paralyzed and I had to be dressed by my friend who joked glibly over the process and called me his "big infant."

The butter in the hospital ran low and we were allowed a very trifle if any. I managed to get a pass and a permit to go down and out for an hour in the middle of the day. I made my way slowly to Market Street in search of butter. I found a house at last that had a small amount of greasy looking white variety. I inquired the price and the shopkeeper told me it was only 75 cents per pound now. I told him I would take a pound before it went up again. I returned, put the butter in my little stand beside my bed and at meal time my bread was spread with butter. The butter was rather weak at first, but it grew stronger with age and in a little time it was strong enough to go alone and before it was used up the last of it could have been driven out of the hospital with a level field and plenty of drovers. The cost of Southern butter crawled up so high that I did not buy any more.

There was one old quack medical notion taught by the medical fraternity. The water in Nashville was said to be bad. It looked clear and clean but it had to be neutralized with liquor. Every patient was prescribed a wine glass of liquor three times a day to neutralize the effects of bad water. The patient could choose beer, wine, or whiskey. There were a few soldiers who would have been pleased if the doctors had prescribed all liquor and no water. In fact, they were pleased that the water had been pronounced bad.

There was a doctor who had charge of my ward when I first went there whom all the men liked very much. We all had confidence in his treatment and I began to improve nearly from the start. He belonged to an Illinois regiment which was at the front and he longed to be there with his men. He finally decided to go and the boys in the three wards where he had been operating raised by subscription $150 and purchased a gold watch and presented it to him. The presentation took place in our ward and all the sick from the other two wards who could sit in chairs or walk were brought in or walked in to witness the ceremony. The gift was a happy surprise, he made some very touching remarks, and many were brought to tears.

After the departure of the army doctor another was sent to fill his place, a citizen doctor from the North. The next doctor came, took the books, and began to prescribe. He changed the treatment of nearly every patient. I had no particle of confidence in him. He looked to me like an old fussy hen-hussy quack. He changed my treatment as well as the rest. I was doing so well I ventured to request him to let my former treatment stand as it was on the book, but he would not and prescribed a lot of pills. The doctor prescribed and the nurses gave the medicine three times a day, morning, noon, and night. I made up my mind not to stand any risk and take doubtful medicine from a doubtful-looking doctor. The nurses came around with the pills prescribed for me and I told them in plain English that I did not intend to take the pills. They asked me if I would shoulder the responsibility and I told them that I would and they passed on around.

Nearly a week passed and the doctor examined and prescribed the same pills every day. I was gaining rapidly in health and spirits and my limbs were returning to their natural condition as rapidly as could be desired. One morning on his regular rounds prescribing, the doctor examined me more closely than ever before. Finally he looked me in the face with a knowing look and confident air and said, "You have been doing a great deal better since you commenced taking my medicine. Let's see, how long have you been taking my medicine?"

I told him bluntly that I had not taken any. If a boy were to throw his hat into a brood of young chickens the old hen would not do as many foolish things nor cackle as much nonsense as did that foolish quack. He flew uncontrollably mad, blustered and blowed, jawed me with all the bitterness there was in him, threatened to have me arrested and locked up. He called up one waiter after another and scolded them fiercely and finally assailed my new friend with a storm of abuse. I told the doctor that it was my fault and that if he would let it pass this time that he would have no more trouble from that source. That statement quieted him down some and he went on his rounds, occasionally letting a jet of steam either at me or one of the waiters.

My plans of taking pills was to put the pills in the mouth and take a glass of water and not let the pills go down with it. When the nurses came around I took the pills, put them in my mouth, took a sip of water, but the pills did not go down. As soon as the nurses were gone I spit the pills into the spittoon. The spittoon got along nicely with the pills although it looked as though it needed physic and a hot injection. In course of time, after I left, word reached us at the front that this doctor afterwards got into trouble and was discharged and sent home in disgrace.

APRIL 15, 1863, NASHVILLE, TENNESSEE

Still in the hospital I was witness to a strange act. A soldier belonging to one of the regiments stationed near the city was taken out and deliberately shot to death by a volley of musketry from his own companions in presence of nearly all the troops about the city. The doctors pronounced me unfit to be out, otherwise I should have been an eyewitness to the slaughter. A large number of the soldiers went out to witness the shooting and from them I gathered these points.

There had been large demands made for fresh troops, and states all over the North were straining every nerve to raise them. Large bounties were offered to men who would enlist. Each town, city, and county had a certain number of soldiers to raise and if any town failed to raise its quota the state would make the able-bodied men of the town cast lots as to who should go. To prevent the draft the people of a town got together in meetings, raised a large sum of money, appointed an agent, and sent him out with this money to hire young men and middle-aged men to go to war and be counted as a man who enlisted for the town that hired him. Some towns and cities give $300 apiece for all who would enlist, others give $500 and others $1,000 apiece. There are rascals in the army as well as out and the man shot here was a rascal. He deserted from his regiment, went North, put on citizens' clothes, enlisted again for another regiment, got four or five hundred dollars for enlisting and as soon as he got the money he deserted again, changed his name and his clothes, and enlisted again from another township, got another bounty, and again he deserted. The government detectives on the track of this bounty jumper traced him from place to place and finally caught him. They put handcuffs on his hands and shackles on his feet and brought him back to the regiment at Nashville where he belonged. He was then taken before a court-martial and tried for his life, then condemned to be shot to death in the presence of all the troops about Nashville. The reason he was shot in presence of all was to terrify all evil-designed soldiers from committing the same offence.

All the troops were assembled in long lines overlooking the spot where he was to be shot. A number of soldiers had previously been appointed to do the shooting. The guns were loaded by one man, half were loaded with blank cartridges. The doomed man was led to the coffin blindfolded, his hands tied behind him, and he was given the privilege of standing, sitting, or kneeling. He knelt down upon the coffin and awaited the signal to fire. At the command "fire" the rifle blast sent a score or more of balls piercing his heart and body and he fell across his coffin, gave a few shrugs of the shoulders and twitchings of the limbs, and he jumped bounties no more.

The soldiers who returned from the scene and offered me this description were much moved by the sight. Those who were able to be up and about the wards had been gathering, talking the matter over, of how he must have felt while kneeling on his coffin, inquired as to where he lived and all about his history; then, in the evening, we got a copy of the *Nashville Daily Union* and read the reporter's account of the affair. By an oversight his name is not recorded in the diary and I cannot recall his name nor the number of his regiment.

MAY 5, 1863, NASHVILLE, TENNESSEE

There had been as near as I could estimate at the time, about three deaths per day in the hospital. Some days there were none and others there were five and six.

While in the hospital I had two occasions to be made glad by the presence of old neighbors from Ogle County. Joshua White, of Stillman Valley, called to see me and scrutinized things very closely. The next day along came Samuel Hamaker of Ogle County. These visits were encouraging as each person was very anxious to know all the particulars as to our comforts and conditions of health so that when they returned to Ogle County they could give a correct account of every patient in the hospital.

I began to recover rapidly and I got a pass every day to travel the streets around about until my strength was exhausted, when I returned and retired to rest at an early hour. I applied for my hospital discharge that I might again go to the front.

I stopped taking wine that "neutralized bad water" and at the skipping of the first drink I found I had a hankering after that neutralizer.

There was some red-tape in getting a hospital discharge to go to the front. Henry Middlekoff[7] of Co. K had also recovered and we went together. After we got our discharges we were given back our regular suits. We returned our hospital suit and got rid of the gown which will make any well man look sick. We were put under guard and taken to the Zollicoffer house. Every soldier leaving the hospital must pass a night there to get covered with glory and lice. The building was designed for the finest hotel in the city, built of brick and it is new and not completed. The walls, roof, and floors are up and that is about all. It belonged to the rebel General Zollicoffer[8] so the Union forces confiscated it and used it as a sort of stopover house for soldiers going to and from the armies. Only three articles of food were used on the table while I was there for supper and breakfast: bakers bread, coffee, and fried pork. We took a bedroom, swept the floors and walls, and spread our blankets on the floor for a bed. I suggested to Middlekoff the propriety of getting some tar to make a lice fence around our bed, but he thought it would be no use, as these fellows were too breachy to be fenced out in that way. He thought that if they failed to scale the tar fence that they would crawl up the walls to the ceiling and drop down upon us while asleep. We laid down upon the floor, taking pains to lie in such positions so as not to let our bones punch holes in the floor and, with boots for pillows, we enjoyed an evening chat over the idea that we were no longer feather-bed soldiers and then dropped to sleep. The next morning after a breakfast of bakers bread, sow belly, and coffee, we were escorted under guard to the train where we started south to the front.

MAY 22, 1863, FRANKLIN, TENNESSEE

On board the train on which we were transported from Nashville to the front at Franklin, were twenty-five or thirty other soldiers who had recovered their health at the Louisville hospitals. We were all in the charge of the same guards who saw to it we were transported almost precisely as a farmer transports a car load of cattle or hogs to the Chicago market. Our names with company and regiment were given to one man on a slip of paper like a freight bill. We were put in a stock car and when we arrived in Franklin we all got together in line with the man with the freight bill at the head and marched up to General Granger's headquarters to have our noses counted. When we arrived in front of his tent, out came one of his lackeys to receive his freight.

At first glance one not acquainted with army life would be led to believe the body guard of a general were the best men in an army. While there are a few fine men sometimes among these waiters and orderlies, as a rule, they are the biggest set of boobies, sycophants, fawners, and louts in the whole army. Weak, silly-minded men seem to think that it is elevating to their own individual greatness to be in the company of men of rank, even though they are compelled to black the general's boots, shave his face, or fry his meat and boil his coffee in order to be in his company. They will praise the general for everything. They will praise his foolish doings as well as his wise ones. When in the presence of other soldiers these fellows will wear an attitude of self-importance that is quite disagreeable to look at. Every act and motion is made to talk as much as possible and seems to say to the common soldier, "I have an order in my pocket from my general which leaves me at liberty to arrest you and punish you as I may in my better judgment see fit; you better look out." The poor coots really have no authority to do anything, only to wait on their master. Some of them—not all—are men that would prefer to be tied to the general's curry comb, blacking brush, slop pails, coffee pots, and frying pans than to be a soldier, stand picket, and meet the enemy in battle. They usually keep their clothes very clean and hair slick and trim their hats, coats, and pants with all the hold lace and other gew gaws possible without infringing upon the marks and signs that indicate rank. It frequently occurs that the finest dressed ones are the most illiterate blockheads. There is always a little rivalry or jealousy existing between the common soldier and the officers' lackeys, as they are frequently called.

Well, when we arrived in front of Granger's headquarters, a very finely dressed fellow came out to receive us. He wore the regular uniform, well decked with gold lace cords. Around his body was a flashy belt with saber and revolver attached. He was a private soldier in rank and a regular lackey by selection, an ignorant booby, and that made him all the more desirable for such a general as Granger. He took a position in front of our little squad and called out in very pompous military tones "Attention! Right dress! Front!" and then took the freight bill and began spelling out our names. When he got one made out so he could pronounce it he would call it out very loud and receive a reply from the soldiers in line of "Here." The wink, the nudge of the shoulder quickly passed down our line while he was spelling out our names. Whenever he pronounced a name wrong there would be no response from anyone; then he would spell the name over and again guess at another pronunciation and again there would be no response. Occasionally he would guess one correctly and get a reply. We enjoyed a half-hour's sport at his expense until finally he was compelled to call upon a soldier to help read the names and the work was quickly done. We were then turned loose and each to go to his own regiment.

On reaching the regiment and company the meeting was much like the reuniting of an absent member of the family again. As I was a sort of newcomer the captain actually offered the invitation, which I accepted, to eat dinner with him. It was a little odd, but I, a private soldier, actually ate dinner with Captain Smith, ate from the same cracker-box table with him. Captain Smith was not badly swelled up with gingerbread dignity and the less of it he had the more the men respected him.

There were many changes that took place since my departure and return, although the regiment had been shoveling dirt and chopping timber most of the time during my stay in Nashville. A great dirt fort had been built and the timber chopped away so that the artillery could have a clear sweep over a large area from the fort in case of an attack.

The regiment had given up their bell tents—tents that would accommodate from ten to twenty men each—and received dog tents in their place. These were received with many barks and growls at first and the men found all manner of fault with them but time demonstrated that they were the best thing that has been devised for a fighting, moving army. Each soldier received one and since it is so small and light he could roll it up and put it in his overcoat pocket if he wished. Two soldiers could button their tent pieces together and then with two little poles four feet long standing erect, each holding up the centre of each gable end, and with two small ropes standing out and down to the ground staked fast; the four corners of the two sheets staked down complete the tent. Two men can find just enough room to sleep. A soldier could sit on the ground under the tent and write a letter or write in his diary by the light of the camp fire, even when it was raining.

As soon as I reached camp among the boys each one had to detail the account of the rebel general Van Dorn's raid into Franklin on the tenth of May. It appeared that when General Sheridan went back to Murfresboro with his division of troops, rebel sympathizers got the idea that the bulk of all the Yankees had left and that there was nothing left but a few troops, just enough for a sort of post to do picket duty. The 40th Ohio Infantry regiment was on picket just south of the town and cavalry pickets were on all three roads running south. About ten o'clock on the evening of the 11th the cavalry pickets came dashing back to the infantry pickets on a dead run with Van Dorn's rebel cavalry at their heels, riding at top speed. The 40th Ohio emptied their muskets into the rebel ranks, but it did not halt nor check them. On they went with mad impetuosity into the town of Franklin, leaving the 40th Ohio in their rear. One rebel in his headlong recklessness ran to the pontoon bridge, ordered the guard to surrender and the guard leveled his gun, fired, and killed the rebel in his tracks. The troops were quickly in line of battle. The guns at the fort were rapidly manned and unlimbered, loaded, and sent shot and shell into the rebel hordes. As soon as the rebel saw the great lines of infantry on the north side of the Harpeth, they wheeled about and dashed out as quickly as they dashed in, and the 40th Ohio from behind rail fences, houses, and barns and other out buildings, gave them parting volleys that did good execution. The 40th Ohio lost two killed and seven wounded and the rebels lost twenty killed, the most of which were killed by the 40th Ohio. The canteens of the dead rebels were filled with gunpowder and whiskey. The next day a large number of rebels were picked up in the grove south of Franklin, badly wounded, and carried to our hospitals.

CHAPTER 4

The Rebels Seemed Determined to Fight

June – September 1863

JUNE 2, 1863, FRANKLIN, TENNESSEE

The regiment got a new chaplain—a minister of the gospel. O. D. W. White had been the chaplain of the regiment for nearly six months and probably did not preach a half dozen sermons during the time, although he was drawing about $150 per month. In other words, these sermons cost the government about $200 apiece and the boys usually swore harder, longer, and more viciously after each sermon than ever before. He was not adapted to army life and he displayed the most judgment of his whole army career when he concluded to resign. This brought us a new chaplain.

A better man for the position than Chaplain B. H. Cartwright[1] of the Methodist Rock River Conference would be hard to find. He was odd and extremely good. He was extremely active and awkward and there was not a lazy bone in his body. He could not put on a particle of military style for the more he would try the deeper he would get his foot in it. If he tried to wear his epaulets they would not get on the shoulder in the proper place. There would be a lop, lean, inclination, depression, twist, skew, rip, flap, break, or pucker. At first the colonel seemed to have hated him for his awkwardness but was compelled to love him for his goodness. In addition to his preaching he appointed himself as a general superintendent of the sick of the regiment, wrote letters for them, sent home detailed accounts to friends of those who died or were killed in battle, and assisted with stretchers in time of battle in carrying the wounded back to places of safety. Whenever he received the mail of the regiment he would get a central position in the camp, cry out in a loud clear voice, "Oh yes, oh yes, oh yes, the mail has come." He would hardly get to the end of this sentence when the last of it would be drowned by the glad shouts of the men as they all charged up to the chaplain.

On the eighth of May one Dr. Peters of Spring Hill stepped in to the rebel general's headquarters, put a revolver to Van Dorn's head and shot him, killing him instantly. Intimacy with Dr. Peters' wife was the cause of the rebel tragedy. The doctor fled to the woods and the next morning was within our lines at Franklin.[2]

General Granger was pleased to think his able opponent was dead. He drank some wine from his demijohn and felt jolly. He conceived a plan to send a flag of truce to the rebels and have some of his officers drink wine with the rebel officers. He fixed up a letter in the form of a dispatch and selected Colonel Atkins to carry it and guard the demijohn and cigars to the rebel line, and to assist in drinking the wine and smoking the cigars in style when he got there. A few officers and a hundred cavalrymen were taken along as body guard to Colonel Atkins.

When Colonel Atkins and his men reached the rebel picket lines they were halted. Atkins informed the rebels that he wanted a rebel officer of equal rank to receive his dispatches. Word was at once sent back to the rebel headquarters for a rebel colonel, while Colonel Atkins had to wait on the outside of the rebel line for the return of the officer. While they were waiting, supper had been ordered at a private house near at hand, supper for the colonels and staff officers of both rebel and union. They sat down at the same table, ate, talked, and chatted like relatives at a marriage supper. After supper they all smoked Havana cigars and drank wine sent by Granger. They talked over the prospects of the war and other topics when some of our officers spoke about the sudden take off of Van Dorn. The rebels pretended ignorance of the affair, while one man related all the particulars of the case without telling them how they came in possession of the news. They continued to drink wine and smoke cigars till a late hour. About midnight when the wine gave out they separated, each to go to his respective abode. This was one of Granger's stratagems, to drink and smoke their officers to death, but the joke of it was the rebels could stand as much of that kind of soaking and smoking as the best Yankee officer.

We were frequently called out at all hours of the night as if an attack was expected. We got up nearly every morning standing silently in line of battle.

On the morning of June first the sick were all put on board cars and sent to Nashville. The next day, June second, we started on a march for Triune.

JUNE 11, 1863, TRIUNE, TENNESSEE

On the second of June we were called up in good Granger fashion, at three o'clock in the morning with orders to get ready to march, but as usual there was no stir made to start until about nine o'clock, after Granger had leisurely drank his wine and eaten his breakfast. Triune was the place we were destined to go to. It lay east of us and was a sort of centre of the lines of encampments between the right and left flank of the army. The rebels had shown many designs of attacking that point and capturing it and thus divide our army into two parts. We started and marched hard all day and reached Triune by dark.

It was the first march for our new chaplain. The early part of the day was warm and pleasant and the weather bid fair to have pleasant weather the rest of the spring. As the day warmed up the load each man carried seemed heavier. The knapsack, blanket, tent cloth, rubber blanket, overcoat, rations, haversack, canteen, cartridge box, ammunition, and gun, all combined, tended to load each of us down in good pack-mule style. The men were determined to lighten their loads so they began throwing away blankets and overcoats. Good new blankets, overcoats, and other articles were strewn by the wayside in great numbers. The chaplain knew the nights were cold and would be for some time to come and that the men could not stand to lie out upon the ground without blankets. He got off his horse,[3] picking up blankets and strapping them upon his horse. He went on foot and led him and by sunset his horse was well loaded. When the men got into camp that night he called out in his usual loud voice for the men to come and get their blankets. A great many called for blankets who had not lost any. The chaplain, supposing the men all as honest as himself, told each man to select his own blanket from the lot and of course each man selected and the chaplain busied himself in preparing supper and lodging. When he got through supper he went to his horse to get his own blanket and to his surprise found that all the blankets had been taken away, including his own.

About three o'clock in the afternoon my strength began to give away. I got shaky in the knees. To all appearances I was knee-sprung like a horse. They would tip down when I wanted them to tip up. I was only ten days out of the hospital and not quite all the vigor necessary to march had returned. I stepped to one side, sat down by the roadside and let the column pass. At the rear of the regiment Dr. Helm rode on his horse performing regular duty, riding up to every 92d man that stopped by the wayside to ascertain if he was exhausted or unwell. He knew my condition and was surprised I had held out so long. He wrote on a slip of paper and handed it to me with instructions to present it to ambulance No. 1.

I held my position by the roadside until regiment after regiment passed by, then the artillery with its long train of horses and wagons and cannon and blacksmith wagon with its shop on wheels, with the smith hammering away as leisurely as the home blacksmith. There were six cannon to each battery and to each cannon wagon were attached six horses, one driver of the rear horse of each team. The wagons were mounted over the hind axle of each cannon wagon, while over the front axle was a huge chest for ammunition bolted fast. With each cannon wagon was an ammunition wagon which also had six horses attached. This ammunition wagon had two huge chests, one on each axletree filled with ammunition—heavy cannon balls and powder. Six cannon wagons, six ammunition wagons, one blacksmith wagon, and one wagon for feed and equipment, or fourteen wagons, six horses to each, eighty-four horses in all and about one hundred men constituted a battery of six guns.

Several regiments and the battery passed and then came the ambulance train for the sick. An ambulance wagon is rigged nearly like one of our omnibus wagons at a fair, only lighter, is covered mostly with white canvas, and will seat from twelve to sixteen men and shelter them from the rain. Four men can sleep comfortably in one of them at night. The seats are cushioned and have a drop-cushioned leaf on each side that can be quickly raised up and the whole inside is changed into a bed where three or four wounded or sick men can be laid down flat in case they cannot sit. The ambulance is mounted on springs and is drawn by two horses. I presented my slip of paper to ambulance No. 1, which led the van. There were about twenty ambulances in the string, each one having in large letters and figures on either side No. 1, No. 2, and so on to the end of the string. Dr. Winston had charge of the whole ambulance train, he received my slip of paper and wrote on another for me to hand to the driver of No. 12. I started back to find No. 12 when the doctor told me to get into No. 1 along with him.

No driver would allow a soldier to get into his ambulance without an order from Dr. Winston. The doctor was as busy as a bee giving permits to exhausted soldiers, assigning them to the different ambulances. When the doctor by mistake or otherwise would get two or three more men in one ambulance than in another, the driver of the full ambulance would whine and find fault about it like children at the supper table over a large or small piece of pie. By evening the wagons were all heavily loaded, more waiting rides than could be accommodated. The doctor went through all the ambulances and requested that all the men who felt rested enough to walk to do so, but he would not drive anyone out. Those places vacated were quickly filled with other exhausted men. When the army camped at night all went home to their respective companies and regiments.

At Triune the rebels seemed determined to fight. Our cavalry pickets were exchanging shots almost daily. On June 5 and 7 there was quite a brisk skirmishing between our cavalry pickets and the rebels, but on June 11 the cavalry pickets were all driven onto the infantry pickets and they in turn were pushed farther back, although heavy forces of skirmishers were sent out to support them. Everything was quickly in line of battle. Tents were torn up and loaded into wagons. Ambulances were all in readiness with horses hitched on and drivers in their seats ready to go anywhere. The baggage trains of six mule teams were all hitched up and moved into the road, headed back. Artillery horses were all harnessed and hitched to the wagons ready to do anything needed. Everything was ready for a general engagement.

In front of us was a clover field nearly three-quarters of a mile across. In the centre of this field was a deep wide gutter, worn by water during flood rains. No horse could cross it except in the roadways. On the opposite side of the field was timber, in the edge of which our picket line was firing. Suddenly the pickets came running back on foot for dear life, a column of Forrest's rebel cavalry[4] at their heels yelling like demons, swinging their sabers, ready to split open the heads of the first "Yanks" they overtook. It was evident that the pickets would not reach the ditch in time and many must lose their lives or be captured. At this juncture two batteries that had been placed in position pointing their guns in that direction opened upon that charging rebel column, sending their fiery explosive missiles into the charging column. In less than a holy minute things had a different appearance. The pickets were reaching the gutter and the rebels were trying to dodge our shells. They halted, became confused, and then charged back to the woods.

While this had been going on other rebel forces had also been active. A battery of rebel artillery had been placed in position and the first shot fired was at the 92d. The men were standing erect in line of battle, without any cover of barricade or earth works. The rebels had not yet been within musket range of the regiment. The first missile came screaming over the regiment not six inches above our heads. It was a shell with a fuse lit. It made an unearthly screeching noise. It knocked all the bravery out of me (if I ever had any), stood my hair on end, and laid my body flat on the ground in less time than it takes to form one letter of this entry. It seemed as though we could hear it coming when it was within twenty rods of us, and it seemed as though it would hit every one of us for the width of about two companies; indeed every man for nearly two companies' width went to the ground, lying face down in the least possible time that it took to get there. I hugged the ground as though I were frantically in love with mother earth. The whole regiment was then commanded to lie down.

The artillery duel went on with fierceness for a short time until some of the rebel guns were dismounted and they pulled off. There was a large brick house to our left front on the picket line and our skirmishers were hovering around that, shooting from every concealed corner about the house and out buildings. The family and all the plantation negroes streaked in to the woods at the opening of the fight. General Granger rode up to one of the batteries and ordered the gunners to turn the guns on the brick house and riddle it. The gunners told the general that those were our skirmishers in and around the house. The general declared that they were rebels and repeated his order to fire upon the house. The gunners refused and the general rode off. The skirmish lasted until nearly night, when the rebels withdrew.

When the wagon train was loaded and ready to move away when ordered, one little black-and-tan wooly-headed negro thought he would steal a ride. He climbed up and stood on a chain that was stretched across the rear end of the wagon box, stood straight taking hold of the wagon bows and the wagon cover hid him from the driver. He could peek over and see the head of the driver and watch his movements but the driver could not see the colored gentleman. The first cannon ball that came so close to the heads of the regiment struck the chain between the darky's feet, passed through the corner of the box, took a spoke or two out of a wheel and went on and afterwards exploded. The darky fell to the ground, supposed himself dead and shot all to pieces. He opened his eyes and saw a hole and two chains where there had been but one. He got up on his feet and found his legs would walk, and he put them to good use. The last seen of the darky that day he was pointing to the rear at the top of his speed, his coat tail floating in the wind, presenting enough horizontal surface for four nigs to play "seben up."[5]

JUNE 14, 1863, TRIUNE, TENNESSEE

After the skirmish at Triune we found that we had but two killed and nine wounded, but the 92d lost none of this number. The rebel newspaper put the rebel loss at twenty-one killed and seventy wounded. The number killed compared to the number wounded as near as we could ascertain, throughout the different battles and skirmishes, used to range from one killed to five wounded, or in other words, when six men were hit one was killed. Yet there were some battles nearly every man hit would prove fatal.

The June weather in Tennessee is delightful during the intervals between the gushing showers and pouring torrents. It was always a good night's rest to lie down upon the green carpeted earth of a pleasant night, with nothing but a blanket under and one over and breathe the pure air of heaven.

The warmer weather brought a disposition on the part of both armies to fight. Scarcely a day passed that a little skirmishing or artillery firing was not heard along the fifteen miles of front stretching from Murfresboro to Franklin. Granger kept up almost constant orders to have two or three days' cooking rations on hand. We were frequently called out into line of battle at all times of the night and day as if a fight was momentarily expected. The men were becoming tired of the cooked rations order and filled their haversacks with hard tack, called it cooked rations, and then leisurely cooked their rations from meal to meal as though no orders had been issued. To get a good square night's sleep all night was almost impossible. Either rebel scouts or General Granger's wine was the means of getting us out at three o'clock or two o'clock in the morning. Granger, of course, slept undisturbed as far as the rebels were concerned.

There were many fine apple orchards in this part of Tennessee and in June the fruit was well enough matured to make into green apple pies or apple sauce or apple jack. To bake pies in an army of men camped upon the open ground with a stove or brick oven would be a curiosity to an Illinois cook. If a cook in Illinois who had been born and raised there were to be blindfolded and transported to the kitchen of a Tennessee farm or plantation and then be unmasked and required to get a meal of victuals, although he should have the full cooking kitchen outfit, I imagine he would be at his wits' end. There was no stove in any part of the house with an oven to bake in and no brick oven for a substitute. There was a fireplace with its back logs and blazing fire, above which are iron bars with hooks. In the chimney corner was a cupboard in which could be found frying pans, spiders, iron pots, and skillets, many with iron covers. The potatoes and other vegetables were boiled in kettles hung above the blaze of the fireplace. The tea kettle was boiled in the same way. We fired meat in a skillet heated from coals raked out upon the hearth. For baking we used a larger skillet made of cast iron. The bread, "pone," corn cakes, biscuits, potatoes, meat roasts, or whatever was to be baked or roasted was put into this large iron skillet, the hot embers were raked out upon the hearth and the oven was set upon them. Then the heavy cast iron cover was put upon the top, which covered it up tight, and a shovel of burning embers were thrown on top. This kind of baking gives the food a finer flavor than can ever be produced in a stove-baking oven.

When the army was not too far from the base of supplies we could get some flour instead of hard tack. Then the soldiers could go to the negro cabins and dwelling houses and unceremoniously borrow or carry away these bake ovens. One could bake anywhere with them, in the house or out of doors, rain or sunshine, wherever hot embers could be obtained. Soldiers could get green apples, slice them into thin pieces, roll out crusts made from the flour, lay in the sliced apples and cover with another crust. Huckleberries, raspberries, and blackberries were now getting ripe and the boys had begun gathering them.

When the regiment first went into camp at Rockford each company of eighty or a hundred all ate at one table with three or four men detailed to cook for the whole company, but when we reached Kentucky it was found to be impracticable on marches to prepare meals for so many at one mess. Consequently the companies are divided up into five messes of about eighteen men each, then sometimes subdivided into smaller and smaller messes to suit their tastes and friendships. The men squadded together according to their liking into groups of twos and fours. A few hateful, quarrelsome men were left out in the cold with no one to squad or chum with.

The great study of soldiers when campaigning was to cut their luggage down to the lowest possible weight. The cooking outfit for two men consists of one very light-handled sheet from a frying pan, one tin coffee pot with handle melted off and wire bail attached through two bayonet holes at the top, two tin cups, two tin plates, two knives, and two forks. The coffee pot answers the triple purpose of boiling coffee, rice, and sweet potatoes. On the march one carried the coffee pot and the frying pan and each carried his own tin cup, plate, knife, and fork. When the army camped for the night one man of each squad went for rails or the fuel for a fire and the other went for water. A fire was quickly built, the coffee boiler with water for coffee was placed upon the camp fire, the frying pan with slices of meat was by its side, a rubber blanket was spread upon the ground near the fire, then two tin plates, two tin cups, two knives and two forks, one little rubber sack filled with sugar and one with salt were set out, haversacks filled with hard tack were opened and supper was ready. In half an hour after camping a whole army of thousands, yes, tens of thousands, was eating all divided into groups of twos, threes, or fours.

JUNE 25, 1863, SHELBYVILLE PIKE, TENNESSEE

On June 22 it was evident that a tremendous campaign had been planned and that the armies on both sides were keen for war to the hilt. During the campaign of the season before, in 1862, the Union armies had gained nothing decisive over the rebels that tended either to crush their armies or their spirits. Both sides had won important victories. The old ship of state hung in the balance, so to speak, and we were just ready to fight, slaughter, capture, and imprison each other, until one army or the other should be annihilated. There was a constant movement of troops all along the lines, skirmishing, scouting, and the like, but no general movement of the whole army had yet begun, although it was liable to move any day.

We had almost no information to tell what the other side was doing. When a general wants to know where the body of the rebel troops is he sends out a scouting party, a party large or small in proportion to the exactness of the news he wishes to obtain. The scouts proceed in the direction that the enemy is supposed to be. The first signs of rebels they see are rebel pickets. Of course the rebel pickets shoot at the advancing scouts as soon as they get in range of their guns. If the scouts press on they of course return the shots and the rebels stop and return the fire as they retreat. When these rebel pickets are found there may not be over five or six, or a dozen in number, and there are no means of telling how many rebel troops there may be in camp way back somewhere. There may be one thousand rebels in the camp, or there may be fifty thousand. Thus, finding a picket post, and getting shot at, gives no information whatever of the rebels' whereabouts, or their numerical strength. To get such information as is desired one of two things must be done, and done quickly too. A sudden dash or charge must be made upon the pickets with cavalry, spurring their horses to the top of their speed, shooting at the pickets as they run, and if some poor Johnny gets his horse shot, or his horse falls down and gets mired in the mud, or he falls off or happens to be on a show horse, he is caught.

The excitement of the men of both pursuers and pursued is necessarily very great at such times, as all appreciate the great danger their lives are in, although their numbers, perhaps on both sides are small. The officer in charge of the pursuers rushes up to the captured men, with revolver in one hand and perhaps sword in the other, and instantly demands of the prisoner the name of his regiment and brigade, the division and corps of his brigade, where camped, and how many troops in the vicinity. The captors quickly gather around perfectly frantic with excitement, as the circumstance always creates it. Every man demands that he tell the straight truth and quickly too or they will riddle his body with balls in less than a minute. They tell him further that if a single sentence proves untrue they will riddle him. Under these exciting circumstances the prisoner opens up, he is scared nearly out of his wits, and well he might be, for I have been an eye witness on one or two occasions when I really trembled for the prisoner, for fear the excitement of the skirmish and chase had carried some of our men to such a high state of excitement that they would shoot a prisoner after he had surrendered—a barbarous act that none of us really approved of. Under such circumstances a prisoner will shake and tremble as though he would fall to pieces, and I would if I were ever placed in similar circumstances. The prisoner will call upon God to witness the truth of his statements. The statement of the prisoner made under these circumstances can be relied on. He is taken immediately back to the rear of the camp in the presence of the commanding officer, and there questioned in detail in the presence of the man who led the squad who captured him, and the desired information obtained. The prisoner is turned over or put into the hands of a squad of men who take care of all the prisoners brought in. The men who did the capturing laugh and joke about the affair after they get back into camp.

But it sometimes occurs that they fail to catch a man, and then infantry forces must be sent out. They find the picket line and the firing commences. The men are deployed into a skirmish line, one man about ten or twenty feet from the other and advance forward. They are at liberty to walk erect or stooped over, or crawl on their hands and feet as danger and circumstance require. Every time a rebel gets in sight they shoot at him and keep advancing. The line goes on and on, until they meet with heavy opposition that they cannot drive. When such opposition is met of course that is the enemy's position, and they quickly retreat to avoid an engagement, which would annihilate the scouters if they should accept battle. Several wounded rebels are usually obtained in this way and taken back and questioned by the general in command. When there are several prisoners each is questioned separate from the rest, and in this way all the information which they have can be brought out.

On June 23 the rebel positions were well known, and orders came for a general forward movement of the whole army. We pulled up stakes on the 23d, knowing as we believed that the campaign had opened in dead earnest. The great long wagon trains bothered us on the first day so that we did not get under way until nearly or quite ten o'clock in the day. The army was entering on two great thoroughfares, both running south. We were moving towards and getting on to the Shelbyville Pike. We were two days getting there, and untold numbers of troops had passed down that pike ahead of us and were fighting their way steadily down, the rebels contesting every inch, but they kept falling back.

Dr. Winston of our regiment had been placed in command of the ambulance train of the whole brigade. The doctor had previously cautioned me against the propriety of entering upon the campaign so soon after leaving the hospital. He claimed that my legs were not yet sufficiently restored to stand the long and fatiguing marches of a general campaign. Two days' marching, part of the time raining, only convinced me that the doctor was the nearest right after all. The driver of the doctor's ambulance was rather refractory in conduct, and was a good able-bodied man, so the doctor sent him to his regiment to again carry his musket, and sent for me to come and take the driver's place. Under the circumstances, being nearly petered out, I gladly accepted the doctor's kind offer. This new position, although I would not be called on to undergo so many hardships, perhaps, would give me a much better position to watch the doings of the army, and study the country more that we passed through. I was given ambulance No. 1, the ambulance in which the doctor rode, and in which he transacted all his business when on the march. The old driver swore all sorts of bad oaths when I arrived to take charge of the team. His conduct showed plainly that the doctor had just cause for removing him and I had no sympathy for him in losing the position that he seemed to think so much of. The team was a medium-sized span of horses, a bay and a gray, and the bay was naturally balky. At night I could now sleep under cover off from the ground without building a tent. By raising the drop leaves inside the ambulance a nice cushioned surface was arranged for three or four to sleep on. I had hardly got possession of my team when orders came to move on.

JUNE 28, 1863, MURFRESBORO, TENNESSEE

On June 25 we were ready to move but did not make headway. The cannonading at our front showed that the rebels were trying to check our advance. Our advance troops had captured two passes in the long range of hills, gaps through which the roads led on to Shelbyville and farther south.

Beside the pike on which we were traveling stood a church known as Walnut Church. We had camped in the fields and woods all about it. While there a little incident occurred in which the awkwardness of our new chaplain came in collision with the red-tape of General Granger. Whenever we pass a church structure or edifice, our new chaplain always takes occasion to examine it and study Southern Christianity and Southern institutions from what information these means afforded. General Granger had made Walnut Church his headquarters. The chaplain, as soon as he saw the opportunity afforded, made straight for Walnut Church. He paid no attention to who were inside or outside, but bolted straight in at the door and advanced towards the pulpit, making some quaint expressions as he passed up the aisle. General Granger was sitting by the pulpit. He looked at the chaplain as he came marching up the aisle, with an air of astonishment mingled with contempt and indignation. Granger broke out with an expression about as follows:

"God damn you old man, what are you doing here? Get right out of here."

Colonel Atkins, who happened to be present on some military duty that had called him there spoke and said in substance: "Why General, that is my chaplain, or the chaplain of the 92d."

"Oh, is it? Well chaplain, you can stay if you want to," responded Granger.

The chaplain had not particular love for the general's company and was soon out of there. But with true Christian spirit he bore the insult without a murmur, as many other men did in the army, sacrificing everything for the good of our common country.

All the knapsacks and luggage was sent ahead to Murfresboro to lighten the men's trip for a fight.

On the 27th all the troops moved in the direction of Shelbyville. We were bound to take that place or get the worst of a battle. If the rebels held it longer they were going to have to fight for it. The cavalry under the command of General Mitchell had the advance. It had been raining almost night and day, sometimes in torrents, but the pikes with their thick beds are always good roads, rain or shine. It was the opening of the campaign and the men of both cavalry and infantry were really keen for a fight. Our cavalry knew that the roads were lined with troops for miles back, hastening to back them if they got more than they could handle. They felt bold and confident, formed their lines for a charge and dashed upon the rebels with headlong fury. The rebel lines broke, retreated, ran, and skedaddled. Our cavalry was excited and flushed with success and charged on after them with drawn sabers.

Duck River flows by Shelbyville with its rocky bed and steep rocky shores. The late rains had swollen the stream until it was on a regular boom. By the time the rebels struck this bridge across the stream they were completely panic-stricken. By some means the bridge was instantly blockaded with rebels and a perfect jam rushed upon it until horses and riders were crowded over the edges into the stream. Many jumped their horses into the stream, expecting to swim and ford, but never again reached either shore alive. Five hundred and five of them with all their horses, guns, and two pieces of artillery surrendered on the spot. The number that were killed or drowned, that tumbled off the bridge or were shot or drowned trying to swim across may never be known. Their bodies went down with the flood and many at different places were drawn out of the river.

The rebel prisoners now had to be cared for. The cavalry brought them immediately back to the infantry and turned them over to us before we got to Shelbyville.

On the morning of the 28th this large batch of prisoners was handed over to the 92d to be taken care of and guarded back to Murfresboro. Before starting back the prisoners were first put into a pen like a herd of cattle. The fence posts of this yard consisted of men of the 92d and the rails were guns. In other words, the men stood in a circle about ten feet apart with an opening of two or three across of ground on the inside. While the rebels were in this yard they were given hard tack and sow belly to eat, the same as we had, and great camp kettles filled with coffee. Large crowds of soldiers gathered around the enclosure and talked with the rebels. After they had eaten, they were marched out into the road. A few of the 92d went ahead; the rebels followed, taking the centre of the road and the balance of the 92d, all with their guns loaded, strung out on either side of the road so as to completely shut the rebels into a long narrow pen nearly a quarter of a mile long. Many of these rebels had received bumps and bruises and all could not stand the march all the way to Murfresboro. Accordingly Dr. Winston was ordered to follow the column with his ambulance train and carry all those who, in his judgment, were not fit to travel on foot. This was fun for me. I drove my ambulance right up among the rebels and the others followed. The doctor took all the rebel commissioned officers into our ambulance. We pulled down the side curtains and the doctor said "Now gentlemen, I want to talk with you about these war matters and I want you to speak your minds just as freely to me as though there was no war, and whatever you say to me shall be all right."

We had a splendid time. They were pretty smart men and I got lots of information. Dr. Winston is a whole-souled generous man and the prisoners felt perfectly at ease in his presence. The two most intelligent rebel officers were the captain of the battery that our cavalry had got and a rebel major. The arguments and conversation were continuous and lasted the whole day long, except as the doctor was called upon to assign some rebel prisoner a ride in some ambulance.

When we got eight miles up the pike we met the 92d Illinois Infantry and we were all turned over to that regiment. The 96th went back to the front but the ambulance train went on. Soon after starting there was a rebel sergeant, a real bright, keen-eyed fellow with black hair and a cultivated appearance, fell back for a ride. I requested that he ride in our ambulance and sit on the driver's seat with me. The request was granted and he was soon on the seat by my side. He was a Southerner of aristocratic birth and education. We debated the slavery question, the cause of the war and all its peculiar features, each claiming his side to be in the right. He was a perfect gentleman in conversation. He thanked me cordially for inviting him to my seat and for the freedom of conversation and general treatment. For dinner the troops all lunched from their haversacks and I gave my rebel companion, or divided with him from my stock, hard tack while the doctor fed the officers in the ambulance. My new acquaintance told me one story that I shall never forget. He belonged to Van Dorn's cavalry and was at the second battle of Fort Donaldson, the battle that was fought just before the fleet reached there when the 92d was aboard. He said that he was sitting on his horse's back upon a hill; that Van Dorn was forming his men into line for a charge upon our men at the fort, when a great big thirty-two-pound ball from our siege gun struck his horse square in the chest as he stood facing towards the fort. The ball went lengthwise through his horse, but at the flank on the right side it broke through the skin and covered his right boot leg with about an inch of mince meat. The horse is dead now but the rider was not hurt in the least.

JULY 1, 1863, SHELBYVILLE, TENNESSEE

While we were in the ambulance the rebel officers discussed the slavery question while I sat and listened as a private soldier. I could ask questions, but it would be undignified of me to offer a rejoinder, because aristocracy everywhere treats men in the common walks of live with silence, or silent contempt. I chose to keep silent to the officers of rank except to ask questions and draw them out on points where it was not plain enough to suit. But my seat companion's rank was not much above a private, and I debated with him to my heart's content.

The rebel officers claimed that the field work of the South, in raising cotton and cane, was done in the hottest weather, and that no white man could stand it to work in the hot sun. The hoeing of cotton and cane must all be done by hand. The cutting and topping of the cane must be done by hand. The cotton must be picked by hand. No machinery could be invented to do that work. The black man could do that work and stand the heat and the white man could not. Consequently slavery was a necessity, or else the white man would have to abandon the country and leave it all to the negro if we set him free.

This argument seemed to have weight throughout the whole South. And yet the rebel armies were marching, campaigning, bivouacking, and fighting in every state of the South in the hottest seasons of the year. These campaigns and long marches are much harder and more fatiguing work than any plantation negro ever does in the field.

The prisoners all seemed resigned to their fate, and none tried to escape. We turned our prisoners over to those in charge of Murfresboro, and the troops stationed there. These rebel prisoners were kept but a few days when they and all others that had been picked up by the whole army were put aboard cars and sent north to some great rebel prison pen and there held until they were exchanged for an equal number of Union men that they had of ours, or until the war closed.

We stayed in Murfresboro over night. The doctor went to a hotel and I slept in my ambulance to watch the team, but the next morning the doctor came and invited me to a breakfast at the hotel. It was the first regular meal for me under a shingled roof since leaving home, except what

I got at the hospital. It took us all day until after dark to catch up with the regiment.

On the morning of June 30th we were early on the road to Shelbyville. When we entered the little city we found it one of the prettiest places in all Tennessee. The stars and stripes decked nearly every house. Shelbyville was a strong Union town, and none but a Tennessean knows what it costs to be a Union man when you are living in the midst of rebel armies. Rebel General [commander of the Army of Tennessee Braxton] Bragg had his headquarters there, and had tyrannized over those Union people with cruelty that will never all be written.

There was disposition among the troops to pillage, taking everything they could find from houses, barns, sheds, or smoke houses, without ceremony. To prevent such conduct on those Union people, General Granger very properly issued very stringent orders against such pillaging, with orders to have such offenders shot unless a court-martial should see fit to make the punishment lighter. This had a good effect and pillaging was unknown there.

Shelbyville was the home of Stokes' regiment of Union cavalry,[6] and when the fight was made that Tennessee regiment led the charge into Shelbyville. When the rebels were whipped and captured, the Tennessee cavalry then rushed up into the town, each one going to his own home. Such sights as followed have probably never been witnessed in this country under similar circumstances. Great stalwart soldiers in full uniforms with gun and sabers by their sides, revolvers in their belts, clothes all scented with the smoke of battle, returned from the bloody carnage the moment the rebels surrendered, and in a few moments were in the arms of their wives, mothers, sisters, and parents, hugging and kissing those whom they loved so dearly, when but a few moments before they had been butchering their neighbors in mortal combat. The strongest hearts and bravest soldiers wept like children.

To be a Union man in the North was easy, but to be an able-bodied Union man in Tennessee was either to lay down your live or "give war to the knife and knife to the hilt." For a number of days afterwards refugees from the North returned to their homes. These refugees had fled to the North to save their own lives on account of their loyalty to the Union.

The regiment crossed that fatal bridge where so many rebels were killed, drowned, and captured, and then went into camp. The rebel army had made a long retreat, and Bragg's headquarters were now established at Chattanooga, nearly seventy-five miles farther south and east.

On our march from Triune down we found that only about one-half of the tillable land had been farmed this year. It was not certain with the rebel farmers whether Bragg could hold it or not, and if it was fought over it would ruin their crops anyway. It was the 30th of June, and the wheat fields that had been sown were ready for the sickle, or nearly so. But the troops had formed so many lines of battle in fighting their way down that the grain was trodden down completely flat to the ground. There was no harvest in store for those who had tried to raise grain along the line of our march.

Bragg's army was in full retreat towards his new base of operations. The mails came up, and it was learned that Grant and his armies were besieging Vicksburg, and that the rebels were completely hemmed in. It was evident that the rebel army must surrender unless they struck some decisive blow to Grant's army from some unseen point. Everybody was waiting and watching with breathless silence, so to speak, for the result. If Grant should need more troops, one-half of our army could now be spared with safety, sent back on cars to Nashville, down the Cumberland and Mississippi Rivers on boats to Vicksburg, to his assistance. Under all these circumstances the army went into camp for a short time to wait for developments.

While here Colonel Atkins performed an act that was popular with the regiment, and he is entitled to much praise for his efforts. All the officers and men of the regiment were tired and disgusted with General Granger, and all longed for the day when they could slip from under his command. The Army of the Cumberland (that was the name of our army under Rosecrans) was rather short or weak in cavalry forces. Rosecrans, to obviate the difficulty, had mounted on horses three or four regiments of infantry, armed them with the seven-shooter repeating Spencer rifles, and put them under the command of Colonel Wilder,[7] a brave, bold, daring, dashing officer, the commander of the mounted infantry. This brigade with their superior guns were winning laurels everywhere they went. No rebel troops could stand the racket of those repeating rifles when once brought to bear upon them. Colonel Wilder's mounted infantry could not be driven an inch from a front charge, no matter how thick the rebels came. Atkins set matters on foot to have the 92d removed from under the stale old wine-bibber's command, the reserve corps, and attach the regiment to Wilder's brigade of mounted infantry, and there armed with the new seven-shooter repeating rifles. No one hardly dare hope for success, but were willing to await the result of the effort.

JULY 12, 1863, WARTRACE, TENNESSEE

To feed a great army of fifty or a hundred thousand men, to furnish food and carry it to them is a proposition few ever think of when listening to stories about fighting and sight-seeing. To feed our army—the Army of the Cumberland as we were called—to furnish all the grain for the mule teams or wagon trains and all the cavalry horses, and bread, meat, and other provisions for the men would take, according to the best estimates that I could make, about two train loads per day, or all that two freight trains on a railroad could haul.

A great many persons sometimes wonder why it is that when the rebels retreat so rapidly, and so far, why they do not follow them closely. A large victorious army may follow for a day or two, but when they get two or three days' travel from the base of supplies, inland, away from water or rail communications, there is no method of feeding the army.

We were driving the rebels south down a railroad that ran to Chattanooga, then south through Georgia. Of course as the rebels were forced to retreat they would burn every bridge, culvert, or trestle work along the line of railroad they left behind. To follow them up and drive them down preparations had to be pre-arranged to build the railroad anew, or all that part destroyed. A construction train was put in the advance with a very large force of men, graders, pile drivers, bridge builders, and other mechanics. Way back up at Nashville and other stations carpenters were at work framing bridges and preparing the material to build new ones, perhaps to take the place of those not yet burned, still in the hands of the rebels. By this means the railroad was reconstructed about as fast as we advanced where there was no large river to cross.

Sometimes the constructing corps would push the repairs and their train clear up to the lines of battle, and blow the whistle while the engine just over and across the other end of the disputed railroad would blow its whistle also. After crossing Duck River the army was forced to wait for the bridge to be built across the river.

The recent marches and fighting, for some strange reason, had put the men in the best of health and spirits. Duck River was a clean-looking pebbly-bottom stream, and the men liked to bathe in it. On the second of July its banks were lined with men or their clothes, while the river was full of bathers.

The water in those Southern streams was as soft as the purest rain water. The men would go to the river with soap and towels and shampoo the whole body, and then swim and play like water spaniels for a time, and then leave the stream and dress up. After such a bath the soldier felt a new vigor and the skin felt like velvet. But there was a little unpleasantness in swimming in Duck River. It sometimes occurred when diving to the bottom in deep water that the diver would strike the body of a dead rebel. To unexpectedly come in contact with a dead human body has that same horrifying sensation, even in the army as it does every where else. The fact that it was the body of an enemy does not take it away. Quite a number of dead bodies were found in this way, and dragged ashore and given a decent burial.

On the third of July the regiment moved to Wartrace, a station on the Nashville & Chattanooga Railroad, a distance of about eight miles. While on this little march a flood rain came pouring down, the like of which we never saw before. Every little rivulet was filled in less time than it takes to record it. In a few moments the men were wading knee deep in the little hollows and depressions. The ground was everywhere covered with water. The men in such a rain storm simply put a rubber blanket, that has a hole in the middle for the head and neck, over their shoulders, and march on as though they cared nothing for it. The shoulders and body are pretty well protected, but the feet and legs usually get wet from top to bottom with mud and splash and wading the streams.

On July 4 we were relieved from all ordinary camp duties to perform, and allowed to enjoy ourselves if possible. But what was there to enjoy? Our country was convulsed with internal warfare and had been for two years, with the result still in the scale of doubt and uncertainty. The rebels were up in Maryland, and seemed to be rather unmanageable for the Army of the Potomac. Grant had them pretty well starved out at Vicksburg, and important news from that department was hourly looked for. We had routed Bragg and his army in our department, but yet he was preparing to renew the fight.

Blackberries were ripe and many of the men strolled in the fields and woods gathering blackberries. Blackberries in Tennessee grow so large and plentiful that it almost seemed as though the army might march on and pick blackberries for a living. Any soldier that wanted to celebrate the Fourth of July, all he had to do was to make a noise by shooting off his gun and then sit down and eat his blackberries and hard tack for a Fourth of July dinner.

On Sunday, the fifth, the chaplain gathered what men that were not out blackberrying together and preached as usual, but as soon as the sermon was over the men were hungry for blackberries and away they went into the fields and woods gathering blackberries on the Lord's day.

On the sixth of July the regiment was sent seven miles to Rouseville, on Duck River, to build a wagon bridge so that the wagon trains could cross. While at work on the bridge Colonel Wilder came along, and seeing the men at work took a fancy to the 92d, and declared his intention of having the regiment detached from the reserve corps under General Granger and attach it to his daring brigade of mounted infantry armed with the seven-shooter repeating rifles. Wilder made an application to General Rosecrans and was successful.

On the tenth the bridge was completed and the regiment returned while we were relieved of that stale old commander General Granger.

We learned the joyful news that Grant on the Fourth of July had captured Vicksburg with all its troops, guns, equipment, forts, and other munitions of war.

The construction corps pushed the railroad repairs right on south and waited for no one. Our advance lines were one or two stations farther south, and on the eighth a returning train from Tullohama, the next station south, came loaded down with rebel prisoners and deserters. The men rushed up around the train to talk with the prisoners, and while here one of our men found an old friend and acquaintance among the rebel prisoners. It seemed a little odd, but the meeting was warm and friendly.

News from the North was cut off on the tenth.

Colonel Sheets went to Nashville for equipment, and a detail of men went to Murfresboro for horses. The country was scoured for horses, as there were not enough in Murfresboro to mount all of us. To procure horses, saddles, halters, blankets, and other equipment for a regiment of men is no small task. The army was moving slowly down and we were in a hurry to get ready for our share of the fun.

JULY 28, 1863, DECORD STATION, TENNESSEE

By the 17th of July most of the regiment had been mounted, and I went up to headquarters to get an order to dispose of my team. I did not want to drive ambulance any longer. I wanted to go with the regiment. Lieutenant Lover told me to wait until all the men about headquarters were relieved and I would be relieved at the same time.

On July 18 I received two months' pay. They were paying off the army. It was a bad time to do it as there was no safe way of sending the money home. It was nearly a hundred miles back to Nashville, every rod of the railroad was exposed to bushwhackers, and then it was two hundred miles across Kentucky, which was nearly as bad, and now John Morgan[8] was on the north side of the Ohio River destroying railroads and robbing trains. There were no post offices from which we could even send a registered letter. To send money home was like giving a bottle of whiskey to a drinking man for the keeping—he would keep it safe and never return it. Nearly every man had from $25 to $50 in his pocket and no place to invest it.

On the 20th of July I received orders to go to my regiment. I had received a horse, but could not leave the ambulance until another man was sent to take my place. The regiment was now at Rousville, a little station by name only, without length, breadth, beginning or end.

On the 21st I mounted my horse and rode down to the regiment. Atkins and all the headquarters officers, teamsters, and orderlies went along. The weather was fair and the roads in fine order. The whole of Wilder's brigade were camped about in the timber. They were active, rough-and-ready men and always wanted something to do. There were no rebels in reach of us. The men had their pockets full of money and it was burning holes in their pockets. It seems to be perfectly natural for men to spend their money some way; even bankers cannot carry money in their pockets, they prefer to lend it to someone else. As soon as I got into camp I fed my horse and got some dinner, and took a stroll out to take in the situation of the timbered camp. I had not gone far when I ran on to a group of men belonging to some regiment of our new brigade, seated upon the ground trying to spend their money. They were playing chuck-luck. The games were running at a rate of about one bet a minute, the bets ranging from $1 to $50.

Upon further examination I found that there was a perfect chuck-luck mania passing through the army. Nearly every regiment and company had men, sometimes more or sometimes less, who were daily playing chuck-luck and the only reason I could give for it was that the men all had their pay and there was nowhere the money could be spent. Boys who were not yet out of their teens, were now studying the mathematics of the chuck-luck board as eagerly as they had studied the testament at home and at church. They would slap down a dollar on the number as freely as they had dropped pennies into the boxes at Sabbath schools. Cards had been used to some extent to gamble with in five- and ten-cent ante poker but that was too slow. Men would go out on a green plot to graze horses, drive a stake in the ground, tie the horse to a long cord, take their rubber blanket and dice, and go right into the "banking" business. If there came a shower of rain they would put their money and dice in their pockets, the rubber over their shoulders, and as soon as the shower was over, down went the rubber and the bank was resumed.

On the 22d a part of the regiment went on a scout down Diver River after horses, mules, rebels, and negroes. There were about six hundred, all told, on the scout and they were gone about a week. When they returned they had about fifty rebel prisoners, picked up from rebels at home on a furlough, between sixteen and seventeen hundred head of horses and mules, and about eight hundred able-bodied negroes to muster into a colored regiment.

On the 25th three hundred and eighty horses came down to us from Nashville. The next day the regiment started on farther south and came in full view of the mountains in the distance. To me the sight of those mountains with a smoky haze hanging over their summits was the grandest site I had yet seen. We pushed on, passed through Tullahoma and camped five miles south of that station.

On the 27th we marched all day in full view of the mountains and right towards them, but did not reach them. We camped at Decord Station, and went into regular camp to drill and wait for the railroad to be brought up or repaired up.

AUGUST 19, 1863, SEQUATCHIE VALLEY, TENNESSEE

By the 16th of August the plans for the campaign had all been laid and a general forward movement ordered. The infantry were to keep on the railroad in a southeast direction, striking the Tennessee River below Chattanooga at Bridgeport, while all the mounted infantry and cavalry would cross the valley, scale the mountains, and strike the Tennessee River above Chattanooga and pretend we were going to force our way across the river above at all hazards. This, of course, was to be all sham to deceive the rebels so that the main army could really put up a bridge and cross the river at the lower place: Bridgeport.

On the morning of the 16th it was all motion and hurly-burly in the camps. Everybody was busy over-hauling his rolls among cavalrymen and knapsacks among infantrymen, cutting their luggage down to the lowest possible extent, throwing away trinkets and every garment that was not an absolute necessity. Everybody was girding to see how little he could get along with.

We got started at twelve o'clock, noon, crossed the valley and began to climb the mountain height. A thunder storm set in, and the rain poured and the thunder roared, echoed, and reechoed along those mountain caverns. The water came rushing down the mountain sides, leaping, tumbling, gushing, roaring, bubbling in pools, falling over precipices, washing out rocks, gullying out roads, carrying in solution the rich elements of the mountain side to be deposited and fertilize the valley below. Amid it all the regiment moved on and up, up the mountain height in the zig-zag road, a road that was nearly everywhere on a curve running at every point of the compass, and scarcely anywhere in a straight line. Every man was dressed in black, the rubber on every soldier's back presenting a glossy black as the falling rain dashed over the smooth surface. This uniform black dress reminded me of the mourners of a great funeral procession. The thought stole through my mind that this was a great funeral procession in advance of some great calamity that might befall us before we ever returned this way again. But, again, the thought came that war is but a continued procession of mourners following friends and companions to the grave.

A mountain road was one that the prairie boys from Illinois had never seen. We had all seen pictures of mountain roads with their systematic zig-zag, but that was no true representation of the road up these mountains. Sometimes it was zig-zag, then perhaps winding around a knoll like attempted streets to the skies in the ancient Tower of Babel then darting off for half a mile or more following the dip of the rocks on a great projecting rocky shelf, passing within a few feet of perpendiculars, where, if a weary night traveler should step out of the beaten track he would tumble headlong thousands of feet into eternity. Every step is up, up, wind, twist, curve, climb, push, pull, step higher, and lean up. Every man walks and leads his horse and both man and beast must literally climb the mountain.

I saw so many grand sights, so many perpendicular masses of rock, caverns, ledges, and lofty peaks that I cared nothing for the dashing of the rain, but really enjoyed the ascent and looked eagerly for the new sights that each turn of the road brought to view. Finally we reached the top and here too I learned a new feature of the mountain. I had always supposed that when once on top that within a few feet or few rods beyond, the mountain would again descend, but here I was deceived. After we had passed on for a short distance the surface of the ground had that same general appearance that it does elsewhere. As we journeyed on the land would be level, then up hill, then down hill, here a little brook, there a little farm and farther on a town, village, or city and when we lay down to sleep at night and arose in the morning it was hard to realize that we were on a mountain, a part of the time perhaps, above the clouds.

We marched ten miles in all and camped on the mountain top at a little town known as University Place. The army trains did not keep up with us, so we had but little or no feed for our horses. We took them out to graze as there was plenty of grass in places. I led my horse as close to the mountain's edge as I could, tied him to a little bush around which he could graze, went to the very edge of the precipice, and sat down upon a rock to take in the situation. The valley below was not the identical one we had just crossed. My first impression was that what afterwards proved to be valley was a large river or lake. I put my hand into my side pocket to get a map which I carried to find if I could what body of water that was before me, but while thus searching for the map I discovered a hole in the lake or river and a green spot at the bottom. It was a very nice, clear day, but the fact was, I was looking down upon clouds and mistook them for a body of water. I gazed for a long time upon the beauty of the scene and then seated myself upon a rock.

Such a beautiful sight of the marvelous works of nature I never before looked upon. It looked to me like the prettiest land in the world and as though the happiest people in the world might reside there. But, when we marched through the valley how different the scene! Deserted log cabins, a few only, occupied by negroes, who lived as best they could. War had laid its destructive hand upon the valley. Even the birds refused to sing and nothing was heard but the neighing of horses, the braying of mules, and the rumbling of cannon wheels and wagon trains.

On the 17th we traveled twenty miles towards the east slope of the mountains and camped there, near a town called Tracy City, a coal mining town where a railroad [had been] constructed up the mountain by a system of curves on the mountain side.

We marched all day on the 18th, still in the direction of the eastern slope, and again camped at night on the mountain. My company was sent out on picket on the main road leading to the southeast.

All passed off quietly during the night but at daylight two rebels made their appearance in the road, coming towards us, unarmed and barefooted, carrying their shoes in their hands. They came forward and gave themselves up as they were deserters from the rebel army. They were tired and sick of war and were trying to skulk their way back to their homes in Tennessee. Our boys struck a spirit of inquiry and asked them how they came to enlist and become rebels. They said that when the Southern armies were being enlisted that Southern leaders in their stump speeches had appealed to their patriotism and excited their prejudices against Northern people. They had misrepresented the questions at issue and they really believed at the time, that it was their duty to enlist. But now they believed that the South was wrong and the attempt at secession a failure. They were worn out with hardships and if they were only allowed to live, they cared nothing what became of them until the war should be over.

AUGUST 22, 1863, SEQUATCHIE VALLEY, TENNESSEE

On the 19th we reached the mountain crest about noon, and began to descend into the valley. The 92d had the advance. On reaching the foot of the mountain, we encountered rebels and had a brisk little skirmish, but we put them to flight. At night, Co. A was on picket on a road leading to Jasper, a little town in the valley, when they were fired upon by the enemy. Colonel Wilder sent our four companies of his old regiment, the 17th Indiana. This regiment was conceded to be the "boss" regiment, armed with the Spencer rifle, which they handled and knew the effectiveness and value of. This squad was gone for a short time, found the rebels, killed one, wounded one, captured eight, and returned to camp without receiving a scratch. Another party was sent out on another road, surprising a party of rebel conscript officers in a church, killing two, wounding four, and capturing twenty prisoners. Among the number captured, were eight Union men, three of whom had been sentenced to be shot the next day, but their lives were saved by the entire party being captured by the Yankees. We were now in the Sequatchie Valley. This valley is a mere defile in the mountains, when viewed from the top of the Cumberland Ridge, but when once in the valley, it appeared to be about a quarter of a mile in width, and in reality, ranged from a mile to a mile and a half in width. The valley lies between two ranges of mountains, which wear the local names of Cumberland Mountains to the west, and Walden's Ridge, to the east, but in most school books they are put together and all called Cumberland Mountains. The mountains rise two thousand five hundred feet, almost perpendicularly on either side, which gave the valley the appearance of a walled-in road way.

The Sequatchie River courses its way from side to side down the valley. The river is small and is easily forded; only when the water is high from flood rains. The soil up and down this valley is the richest of the rich. It is thickly settled and many small inland towns dot the valley. Sometimes the clouds gathered in the valley, about half or two-thirds as high as the mountains, and the rain poured, and lightning streaked across from side to side, and the thunder rolled and echoed along the mountain caverns, while all is simply sunshine and pleasant on top. One could sit on a pinnacle of rocks and bask in the sunshine and throw stones at his neighbor below who was being drenched with rain and frightened with thunder and lightning. Such are some of the peculiarities of mountainous countries.

Our wagon trains could not climb those high mountains and draw up loads of provisions. If Wilder's brigade pushed over and across Walden's Ridge, how could he supply his forces with provisions, was the question. Wilder was equal to the emergency. He had planned ahead. The wagon trains had come with us, but with very light loads, and a part of those loads were pack saddles for pack mules.

While it was all for the best, I did not like the pack saddle. These baskets were filled until the poor animal would fairly stagger under the great weight, and there it would stay from early morning till late at night without a single moment's rest. If the column stopped for one, two, or three hours, it was too much work to get one off while loaded, so the animal had to stand and hold it from morning till night. There were not humane societies in Sequatchie Valley, so there was no use in a mule protest. They were heavily laden and no one to give them rest.

On the morning of the 20th, the next morning after getting into the valley, the provisions were all packed on the backs of the pack mules, and Wilder and the whole brigade started up the mountains to the east across Walden's Ridge, and companies A and B and all the wagon trains were sent back up the Cumberland Mountains to Tracy City, after more rations. Companies A and B were simply guards to prevent bushwhackers and scouting parties from capturing and burning our train. We wanted to go with the command, but that did no good, we had to go where sent. We started and traveled hard all day, reaching Tracy City about ten o'clock at night, after traveling thirty miles, and sank to rest without anything to feed our tired horses.

The cars had not yet made their appearance in this city since it fell into our hands. We waited all day on the 21st without any arrivals. I strolled around the town to learn what I could of it. Coal mining was the principal occupation of its inhabitants. A coal mining company owned the mines and the railroad. The company had succeeded in erecting a railroad up the mountain by a system of curves, twists, winds, and steep roads, like a vine up a tree. Then, with one engine to pull and another to push they could get up with a half-dozen cars. This mountain road tapped the Nashville & Chattanooga Railroad, and made a splendid outlet for their coal. This road was now to be the means of supplying Wilder's brigade in his exploits up the Tennessee River country. Tracy City had one church and one saw mill, and in times of peace supported a newspaper.

About eleven o'clock at night of our second night's stay, the much-looked-for train came in at a very slow speed. Men were detailed and went at once to work preparatory to an early start. Long before morning the goods were all aboard wagons. We started early with the determination of making the valley again that night, and we reached our destination, the old camp in the valley, at eight o'clock at night. We stayed in the valley, arching up and down, guarding trains, etc., and for the first eight days we received no mail of any kind, either letter, telegram, or paper, and it did seem as though we were shut out from the world.

A rebel picket was found on the north side of the river who rapidly fell back and crossed on a flat boat. The rebels had all the boats on their side of the river. The rebels had rifle pits, back of which were cannon bearing upon the river. Our colonel was examining the position with his field glass, when a puff of smoke on the other side indicated danger. The leaden messenger passed over the colonel's head, through the arm of W. C. Patterson[9] of Co. D, the first man of the regiment to be wounded with rebel lead.

To walk down to the river's edge for water in open daylight was like walking into a grave. The regiment would frequently conceal themselves behind trees and underbrush, and every time a rebel's head appeared above the bare earth works they would shoot at it across the river. This was more like squirrel hunting than real warfare.

SEPTEMBER 5, 1863, JASPER, TENNESSEE

The 92d continued to scout and skirmish up and down the Tennessee River at the different fords for several days, and all the skirmishing, marching, fighting, and camping was more like an animated excursion party on a general hunt than deadly warfare. The Tennessee River was a division between the contending forces, and a skirmish at long range across the river with no opportunity for a charge either way made it less hazardous and the destruction of life could not be great—yet, there was a good opportunity to take a good square look at a rebel running at large, armed and equipped, ready to fight at the drop of the hat or crack of the gun. And another thing that made the scouting interesting was the fact that when a soldier felt that he was spoiling to shoot a rebel all he had to do was to crawl up to a tree on the river bank and blaze away at a rebel's head behind the earth works, and then he could try his hand at dodging when the rebels returned the fire.

Some very interesting scenes and incidents occurred. The first time the regiment struck the Tennessee River they deployed into skirmish line up and down the river, every man concealing himself behind some object, such as a tree, stump, stone, hummock, or tuft of grass or brush, and each man tried his hand at rebel heads at long range, and kept it up until the novelty wore off, when they withdrew, went into camp, got supper and went to sleep.

A scouting party was sent high up the river, and they discovered a small rebel steamer concealed at the mouth of a little creek, and the boys captured it and burned it to the water's edge.

On Sunday, August 23, Wilder, Minty, and Wagoner spent their time shelling Chattanooga across the river at long range.[10]

The 92d had a section of the battery—two guns to shell the rebels with occasionally across the river.

On the 24th the regiment returned again to Harrison's Landing. The rebels had covered their rifle pits next to the river with brush so as to conceal their heads. Upon a hill farther back were earth works and a battery bearing upon the ferry. The colonel concluded to have an artillery skirmish this time. Rebel gunners could be seen scouting and sitting around on the parapet. The lieutenant of artillery would not fire for some time. He held a little brass instrument in his hand and was waiting for a rebel to stand up straight so that he could sight him with the instrument. By and by a rebel accommodated him and stood erect, and the lieutenant sighted him, then figured on a slip of paper, then cut two shells, loaded both cannon, pointed them apparently skyward and fired both of them at once. As soon as the smoke cleared away there was not a rebel to be seen anywhere; neither did they return the fire as was expected from their artillery. Our gunners continued to drop shells around where the rebels were supposed to be for an hour, and then left them to enjoy life for a while longer. We had no means of knowing whether our guns had done them any harm or not, but a day or two later one of our scouting parties succeeded in getting a copy of the *Daily Chattanooga Rebel,* that was printed the next day, which contained an account of how the first two shots of the Yankee guns at Harrison's Landing had killed four rebel soldiers and dismounted one of the rebel guns.

Nearly every morning, early, the rebels would send a squad of cavalrymen across the river on the ferry boat, who would prowl around until they found our pickets, fire a few shots at them, retreat hastily and cross the river in their ferry boat.

One morning, or one night around one o'clock in the morning, a detail of men were sent to the landing with orders to conceal themselves in the woods and underbrush by the side of the road in two different places, one close to the landing and the other farther up the road. The concealed men left their horses behind in order that their concealment might be more complete. About sunrise the rebels commenced hallooing across the river. The woman at the house of the landing soon answered to their call by waving her handkerchief, a signal that no Yankees were there. Six horsemen and a few dismounted men soon entered the flat ferry boat and paddled and poled it slowly across the river. The six horsemen mounted their horses, rode up to the house, conversed with the woman for a short time, and then proceeded cautiously up the road. As soon as they passed the party nearest the house they stepped into the road behind them, and the men in front stepped in at the same time. The rebels saw that it was a trap and that they were fairly in it, and they surrendered without a gun being fired. The men next rushed down to the river to capture the boat and the men left to guard it. The rebels shoved it quickly from shore, jumped in, and lay flat down to prevent the balls from hitting them. The boys demanded their surrender and tried to riddle their old boat with balls, but the sides were so thick that musket balls couldn't go all the way through the sides of their boat. The rebels lay flat on the bottom close to the side, and each paddled with one hand. The current and the paddling soon carried them out of reach, and they managed at last to reach the other shore. The woman's house at the landing caught fire in less than half an hour afterwards and was burned to the ground with all its contents. We never knew of her being in the "signal service" afterwards.

On the third of September several companies and details were on picket at the different fords, ferrys, and landings. Co. K was at Harrison's and they had a brisk skirmish across the river with rebels, and as they believed, wounded several "Johnnies," as we called them. In this skirmish James Mullarkey [11] was wounded and he will probably carry the ball lodged in his arm to his grave.

On the same day Co. H was at Penny's Ford. Co. H and the rebels fired at each other for a time, and then struck up an agreement not to shoot at each other any longer, as the pickets on both sides wanted to go in swimming, and it was dangerous to swim under existing circumstances. Both sides agreed not to shoot at the other and a general swim followed. Collins Willey [12] of Co. H swam out to a shallow spot in the middle of the river and met a Johnny Reb and there the two boys, as naked as the day they were born, visited and chatted like two old women at a gossiping tea party. It was a novel visit under peculiar circumstance, and they both enjoyed the novelty and cracked many pleasant jokes, and each laughed as gaily as a school girl just emerging from a school room. The uniform of each was on opposite shores and no one could tell from the color of the skin which was Reb nor which was Yank. Yet these men were deadly enemies, and twenty minutes previous would have been pleased to have shot or killed each other. Such were some of the peculiarities of this middle river visit.

The next day, September 4, the regiment got orders to report to General [George Henry] Thomas. He had no mounted men with him to do his scouting. But where was General Thomas? He was fifty miles away. While we had been skirmishing and scouting and apparently accomplishing nothing at all, only to make show, the main army had crossed the Tennessee River some thirty or forty miles below, and already had possession of a large scope of country on the south bank, and we had orders to join them and do the scouting in a far more dangerous and hazardous country.

The regiment recrossed Walden's Ridge and camped with Companies A and B that night, the company all being together again. The regiment had been in the service just one year today, and were now in the midst of one of the greatest campaigns of the war.

On the fifth the regiment marched south all day down that narrow valley walled in on either side by the lofty picturesque mountains, and we bivouacked at night near Jasper, a beautiful little valley town.

SEPTEMBER 7, 1863, CAVE SPRINGS, ALABAMA

On the morning of the sixth of September the regiment arose from its camp at Jasper in the Sequatchie Valley and after breakfast continued its march down the valley. Jasper was only a little village of about three hundred inhabitants, situated in a coal, iron, and other minerals region of Tennessee.

As we wound our way down the valley it widened out until its mouth brought us into the valley of the Tennessee River at Bridgeport. Here the Nashville & Chattanooga Railroad crossed the Tennessee River on a great railroad bridge. Several spans of this great bridge had been destroyed by the rebels to prevent our crossing or ever using it for railroad purposes. We found the railroad repaired clear down to the bridge and a large force working at the bridge to repair it, but they had a great job on their hands. The army had all crossed the river on a pontoon bridge. On this light, frail-looking bridge great army wagons drawn by six mules are drawn to safety and great artillery wagons drawn by six large powerful horses are crossed. As the heavy teams cross, the boats sink to within a few inches of the top rim, but rise again as soon as the team reaches the bridge over the next boat. If the river were wide there would be eight or ten teams on at once but they are not allowed to keep close together for fear of sinking the bridge. As I stood on the shore and looked at a team crossing the bridge it seemed to be sinking just in front of the team and rising just behind it. When several teams were on, the surface of the bridge was like the waves on the ocean with the teams all at the foot of the waves. Guards were kept at both ends of the bridge to see that too many did not rush on at once and pioneers were kept on the bridge walking up and down all the time watching every plank, beam, and boat to repair every break, loop cord, or anything that might work loose.

It took three days and three nights of continuous marching across that bridge to cross the Army of the Cumberland with all its infantry, cavalry, artillery, supply teams, ambulance trains, and ammunition trains. They were about all across when the 92d came down to cross. We dismounted and each man led his horse (none were allowed to ride) and before we got across we learned why. We went on single file, each keeping in the centre of the bridge. There was no railing on the side, but none felt giddy because we were so close to the water and about two feet above the surface. In the middle of the river where the current was strong the bridge kept constantly swaying. The rushing water against the pontoon would strain the anchor rope so that it would tighten and slacken and the bridge swayed to correspond. Men and horses found it difficult to keep on their feet under such circumstances, the width of the bridge bothered them more than the

length, and they walked more like men on a sidewalk at midnight returning home from a saloon pow-wow.

Bridgeport was simply a little station just large enough to contain what
hands were necessary to keep the bridge in repair.

After crossing we continued ten miles on the valley road and camped
at night at what was called Cave Springs at the foot of the Raccoon Mountains.[13] Here a stream came pouring out of the side of the mountain. The
opening was large enough to travel right up into the great caverns of the
mountains, but the creek came rushing down with such force that no one
could think of trying to work his way into such a cave. Some of the boys
found an opening to another cave far up the mountain and since I had
never seen a cave I had a great curiosity to enter one. I arose very early the
next morning, fed and saddled my horse, ate breakfast, and got everything
ready to march long before the rest of the regiment were up. I supplied
myself with several candles and matches so that in case I should get lost my
light would hold out until I could find my way to the opening. It was
reported that the cave was a very extensive one with many rooms, halls,
turns, and pit-falls and that it had never been fully explored. One rumor
said that many of the mountaineers were afraid to enter it as one man went
in and never returned and the cave was haunted.

I found the chaplain and several other curiosity seekers adopting my
course and we were at the mouth of the cave before daylight. We all
entered in a group, walking at first erect, then stooping, and finally crawling. Had I been alone when we had to crawl I should have certainly backed
out, for I did not like to leave such a small hole behind. The opening was
crooked and it was darker than midnight blackness, except what light our
burning candles gave us. After traveling along sometimes erect and sometimes crawling, we came to a large room. From this room were a multitude
of other openings. I traveled from room to room, taking great pains to mark
my course so that I could retrace my steps. For hours I traveled around from
place to place, each one with a host of natural curiosities that needed time
to study, but our little band had to hurry as the command would move on
and leave us if we stayed too long. How far we traveled or how long we
were gone I know not, but when we emerged from the cave the sun was
high up in the heavens and the regiment was gone. Our horses were tied to
trees and we mounted and galloped on.

SEPTEMBER 16, 1863, POND SPRINGS, GEORGIA

On the evening of September 13, after about two hours' rest on the Summertown Road, Colonel Atkins rode out from Chattanooga where he had gone to report to General Rosecrans, with orders to establish a courier line and open communications with General Thomas who was somewhere on top of Lookout Mountain way south of us.

Just before sunset the regiment dismounted and began to lead the horses up that awful steep mountain. It was dark before we reached the top. As soon as we did a man was pressed into service as a guide to show us the road, as there was not a man in the regiment that had ever been over the road or knew anything about the mountain roads. A man by the name of Foster who lived at the very summit was pressed in for that service. He was a mountaineer who knew every road and cow path for miles up and down the mountain. As good luck would have it Mr. Foster was, like many mountaineers, a Union man. Co. K was in the lead. Captain Woodcock and his men from that company were taken first to form courier posts. Captain Woodcock made Foster's house his headquarters for the first post.

The courier posts consisted of five or sometimes six men. They were established from two to five miles apart according to the condition of the roads.

The regiment was on this trip to form such a courier line and Rosecrans was in great haste to have the line formed. Darkness, mountain storms, nor anything must stop us until the line was formed. The night set in with the blackest of darkness and the mountain road was very hilly and generally uneven and crooked. It wound in all directions and headway was very slow as we felt our way along in the pitch darkness on a strange but little-traveled road. The battery of mountain howitzers had much difficulty in keeping up and we would stop and wait for it. When it caught up, however, there was no way of sending word up to the head of the column as the road was full of men on horseback and on the side of the road was brush, timber, rocks, gullies, and other dangerous objects to ride over. But, as necessity is the mother of invention, so it was in this case. A telegraph line that we always had with us but never used before was brought into play. After we stood in the road waiting for perhaps half an hour the battery caught up and they cried out, "Battery is up, pass it along." Men farther up the line cried out, "Battery is up, pass it along."

The darkness, the mountain air, and the fatigue stimulated feelings of sleep that I had never experienced in all my life before, and it had the same effect on all the men. Every man was nodding in the saddle. It seemed to me as though I would have freely given a million dollars, if I had had it, for the privilege of setting down and stretching out on the ground and going to sleep. Some of the men did get off their horses and laid down by the roadside while waiting for the battery to come up. When the battery got up we moved on and it was so dark that no one noticed the empty saddles. They lay until they awoke the next day and then they came on foot to the camp. I am satisfied that I was sound asleep in the saddle two thirds of the way, only waking when telegraphing, "Battery is up."

Sometime between midnight and morning our advance was halted by General Thomas' pickets. After a little bother in convincing them who we were, we moved to the general's headquarters and bivouacked for the balance of the night, sleeping in the open air without tents. Companies K and C had all been used up in forming courier posts as we traveled along. Colonel Atkins reported to General Thomas at 4 A.M. and delivered all his letters and dispatches brought from Chattanooga. By six o'clock that same morning a dispatch was passed back over that new line a distance of twenty-five miles to Chattanooga. Captain Woodcock and Captain Hawk[14] had charge of this line.

While it seemed to us like a foolish ride in the dark, yet the successful establishing of that line in such a short time was of the greatest importance to General Rosecrans as it was now evident that the rebels were preparing to give battle, and if they should turn suddenly upon what troops were about Chattanooga the rebels could whip Rosecrans in detail before the troops could be concentrated.

One horse of Co. B fell dead in the road on the night march.

We got up very late in the morning after our ride, and about ten o'clock were in the saddle again. Moving towards the east we went down the side of the mountain into the valley. Companies K and C were left on courier duty and did not return to the regiment until after the great battle of Chicamauga was fought. The regiment then commenced a regular scouting up and down the valley along the Chicamauga Creek or river and found rebels posted at every ford.

On the 14th we camped at Pond Springs after an all day scout. The regiment scouted down the valley to General Crittenden[15] and informed him of the position of our troops. Returning to Pond Springs that night it felt its way back by and along the Chicamauga, and the regiment found the rebels guarding every ford and pass as before. The valley was full of deserters, or men pretending to desert.

A great battle was daily looked for and the only fears were that our troops might be scattered too far down the valley for quick concentration, but we all had implicit confidence in Rosecrans, the general in command.

On our first scout to Crittenden's headquarters he was informed of the fact that the rebels were guarding every point along the Chicamauga. He would not believe it. General Rosecrans sent a sealed letter with orders to deliver it to Crittenden. A corporal and four men were sent with the letter in the night. The corporal reached Crittenden's headquarters at 4 A.M. on the 16th and was refused permission to deliver his message, for Crittenden had left word not to be disturbed in his slumbers. The corporal persisted in delivering his message and was finally admitted and would not leave the general until he got a receipt of delivery with date and time of day. This was fortunate for him as it was an important dispatch. Crittenden did not obey it as he should have done, and Rosecrans afterwards traced that dispatch right home and the receipt was produced to show that it was received. A great battle was hourly looked for and skirmishing and artillery duels were going on almost all the while somewhere up and down the valley.

CHAPTER 5

I Believed My
Time Had Come

Chickamauga, September 19–20, 1863

SEPTEMBER 19, 1863,
CHICAMAUGA BATTLEFIELD, GEORGIA

"No man ever saw all of a battle" is a saying that every officer and soldier knows to be true. The lines were long and the men were concealed in every conceivable manner. The long lines extended through brush, woods, corn fields, wheat fields, across roads, along lanes, and in open fields behind barricades, brass works, earth works, fences, houses, barns, and sheds. Anything and everything was brought to bear to protect the men from the showers of bullets where they were rained at and stormed at with shot and shell.

On Saturday morning, the 19th of September, the great battle of Chicamauga commenced. The regiment was up very early in the morning from the camp at Pond Springs, and was ready for service. Artillery and musket firing commenced in the direction of Chattanooga, but a little to the east. The Union army was fronting principally towards the east and the rebel army towards the west. Chattanooga was towards the north. If the rebels should attack and turn our left flank just a little they could step down and retake the city they had lost.

The firing commenced on the left flank, the very point where we could least afford to lose ground. The infantry had nearly all got positions in line of battle, but it was evident to the common soldiers that the troops were too far south to match the rebel lines. Troops were hurried with all possible speed to the north until the left wing was well supported and the rebel attacks were met and defeated.

The 92d was sent from right to left just in the rear of the infantry lines of battle and then returned to near the centre. General Reynolds' division was fighting desperately.

117

In the morning when the fighting began it was like the sprinkle of heavy drops that preceeds the shower, but as the lines were closed up and they settled together in a deadly conflict the roar of artillery and roll of infantry pouring their deadly rolls of musketry into each other's ranks was like the low muttering of distant thunder. The constant and rapid discharge of artillery from every little knoll and hillock with the corresponding bursting of shells in mid air, was like one constant peal of thunder that shook the earth beneath our feet. The eastern slope of old Lookout Mountain echoed and re-echoed every explosion from every crevice, canyon, and cave. The fighting was dreadful in the extreme and the death rate was enormous. Wounded men came pouring to the rear in great numbers. Each man severely wounded was accompanied by a wheel man; a bosom companion, mess mate, or comrade, bound to see his mess mate properly cared for before he would leave him. The doctors were fairly jumping with work; sleeves up binding up ghastly wounds, sawing off mangled and shattered limbs, and giving chloroform to ease the dying pain of those mortally wounded. Every patriotic chaplain was at the hospital tents noting down the deaths and catching the dying words of expiring soldiers and getting their dying requests in shape to send them to the loved ones at home. Every drummer, musician, and waiter was busy with stretchers carrying and assisting the wounded back to the hospital tent.

Dr. Helm of the 92d, had charge of a hospital tent on the battlefield, and while many other doctors had similar tents and worked nobly, yet, we doubt if ever a man did more or worked harder to bind wounds, relieve suffering, and save lives than did Dr. Helm at that dreadful battle of Chicamauga.

The regiment had not been engaged up to two o'clock on the first day of the battle, but had been somewhat exposed to rebel shells. General Reynolds found that one brigade of his troops had been so long under a severe fire from the enemy that the men were wavering. So many men had been killed and wounded that there was nothing left but a mere skirmish line, and a charge was expected. General Reynolds ordered the regiment to dismount and tie the horses in a thicket of underbrush, then form in line on foot and go in to the battle and fill up the gap caused by the loss of life on the main line. King's brigade of Reynolds' division (the brigade we were to support) was fighting in a piece of second-growth timber. The regiment marched by column towards the front until near King's brigade, when the head of the column turned to the right to get into line of battle.

Just as the regiment was in the shape of the capital letter L, the rebels made a furious charge on King's brigade and the mere skirmish line that was left couldn't withstand the onslaught, and the whole line came at a dog trot pouring through our lines and the rebels at their heels yelling and pouring their volleys after them and into our lines. Thirty men of the 92d were shot in less than three minutes. The regiment was not in line of battle and could not return the fire nor could not be got in line in less than one or two minutes, and in less than that time the rebels would be upon and among us. We were ordered to fall back in haste and form a new line farther back. A part of the regiment had to jump or climb the fence, but there was lively work done and a new line quickly formed.

At this juncture I bought a little dear military experience and came near paying for my foolishness with my life. Just as I jumped the fence to go back with my regiment to form a new line I looked and saw a rebel carrying a rebel flag coming towards us walking in a crouched position to keep the balls from hitting him. I conceived the idea that it would do no harm to stop just long enough to shoot that rebel. I stopped, took deliberate aim, and blazed away. To cap the climax of my foolishness, feeling elated I commenced to reload my gun. This was one of those peculiar junctures in warfare where a minute's time to a regiment is worth the lives of a hundred men. I looked up and saw the regiment almost in line of battle and nearly ready to fire, and I standing between the two lines. I started back on a run, but before I could reach the regiment the whole line opened fire on the rebels and I was directly in front of the Spencer rifle companies, whose volleys never ceased. To take another step towards the regiment was to be riddled with bullets. To run the other way was to run into the jaws of death or the rebel lines. Sure death stared me in the face, and for the first time in my life I believed my time had come and that I would never see another sunset. I was between two fires, two lines of battle, each firing with a possible speed, and neither line could be possibly reached before I would be riddled with bullets. In times of imminent danger a man's mind is a thousand times more active and accurate than under ordinary circumstances. There was one chance that I might escape immediate destruction, and that was to throw myself flat upon the ground with head towards one line and heels towards the other. This would expose the least possible portion of the body to either line. Quicker than a flash I was in the position described. The balls whistled by my ears, over my head, plowed the ground by my side, in front of me and in the rear of me, but not a ball struck me. Yet I believed that I would be riddled every minute and would never get up alive from where I lay. In a little time the rebels outflanked the regiment, and as there were no troops to check them from lapping by and swinging around the flank, the regiment drew off to the new position. I jumped and ran for my position in the ranks as fast as my legs could carry me, having learned the important lesson that the safest place for a soldier is in the ranks and to fight when the ranks fight, retreat when the ranks retreat, and charge when the ranks charge.

SEPTEMBER 20, 1863, CHICAMAUGA BATTLEFIELD, GEORGIA

The reader must bare [sic] in mind while reading these notes that the right wing of the Union army was nearly annihilated at this great battle of Chicamauga, while the center, under Thomas, held its position and beat back the charging rebels at every charge and pushed with great slaughter. The 92d with Wilder's brigade took a position on the extreme right.

We arose early from out battlefield slumbers and tried to get a hasty breakfast of hot coffee and hard tack, but by the time the coffee came to a boil we were ordered on to our horses and to change position. We got on to our horses, holding our half-boiled coffee in one hand ready to drink it or throw it away as emergencies might permit or compel. The regiment was moved out and strung into a long thin line of battle, covering the positions of five or six regiments, the men sitting on their horses in speaking distance of each other in the edge of a wood overlooking an open valley. Nearly half a mile behind us the infantry and Wilder's brigade formed new and solid lines of battle for the coming conflict. Whether these lines in the rear of us were properly formed or not is a question that a private soldier is not regarded as a proper judge on, but I had an opinion for all that, and I give it for what it is worth.

When a regiment goes into line of battle, and there is any likelihood of an attack, it is the duty of the commander to see to it that each regiment has out a skirmish line in front, and then all the balance of the men should be set to work piling up rails, logs, dirt, trees, stones, anything and everything that can catch and stop bullets, and the men should be kept at work until a perfect barricade is formed or the skirmish line is fired on. The moment the skirmish line opens fire the men can get behind their works whether half or wholly completed, then wait until the skirmish line is driven back and the rebels charge. The first fire of the enemy, which is the most destructive, can be received with comparative safety when they spring to their feet, pour out a deadly fire, and charge in turn with almost a certainty of success.

There was nothing to any amount of this thing done. The men formed in open field lines and laid down and rested, as they were very much fatigued, and waited for the "ball to open."

As we sat upon our horses we drank our half-boiled coffee and munched our hard tack. We all felt tired, weary, hungry, and a little cross. Every man, however, seemed to have a consciousness that an eventful day had dawned and thousands of those who swarmed in that valley would "bite the dust" before night.

While moving into our new position, in spite of all my efforts to carry my coffee pot without spilling its contents, and dodge the limbs of trees and the whipping bush, there were a great many little things that attracted my attention. All along our way the ground was strewn here and there with all the instruments of war. Beside nearly every large tree was a gun or two, a knapsack here, a haversack yonder, and farther on a cartridge box and belt. Beside a stone or log would be a boot or shoe with a hole in it, which told its own story: how some soldier was shot in the foot, sat down, pulled off the shoe and hobbled away, out of danger. A gun and knapsack usually lay near the spot. But the saddest part of all was that around among these were the dead bodies of men dressed in blue. These had nearly all been attended by some companion since death had relieved them. They had been laid upon their backs, hands crossed, a block of wood for a pillow, and their hats laid over their faces to prevent the deadly stare. Some of these dead bodies had been visited in the fight by their mess mates after the firing had ceased who built small rail pens around the corpse, and then, the top of the pen they had covered with rails, so that no dog, wolf, or swine could get at the body and devour it. Then, when the battle should be ended, the soldier could go and give decent burial to his mess mate. But no Union soldier was ever permitted to visit that battlefield until the flesh had rotted and the bones lay bleaching in the sun.

We had scarcely got into line of battle when it seemed as though ten thousand axes just across the valley were being vigorously applied to a forest. What the rebels were doing we could only guess, that they were fortifying their position. This chopping was kept up for nearly an hour and a half, when all of a sudden it ceased and not another blow was struck. There were rebel sharp shooters in the valley shooting at us at long range with their minie rifles. We sent out a small band of skirmishers who crawled up close to the rebels and from behind straggling trees and stumps exchanged shots with the rebel sharp shooters, and made it interesting for them. Some of those minie balls were fired and came all of a half a mile and wounded several horses in our skirmish line.

About half past eight o'clock a tremendous heavy column of rebels all in line of battle came silently sweeping across the valley, but to the left of the regiment, and were moving down to attack the front of the infantry under General [Alexander] McCook. Word was immediately sent to the general, who seemed to deny the truthfulness of the report. The rebels moved slowly and steadily, occasionally lying down to conceal themselves and halting to close up the ranks. Lieutenant Colonel Sheets went in person to General McCook to inform him of the coming storm, but the general treated it as unfounded information, and treated Colonel Sheets in a manner bordering on contempt. The rebel column was making slow but sure headway and were headed for McCook's left. Word was again sent to McCook, who appeared not to believe it. The rebel column had gone way past the left flank of the 92d and our position was becoming a critical one. The rebels were nearly behind us but to one side. All of a sudden the rebels struck McCook's left and with a rebel yell they charged furiously down like an avalanche and in ten minutes the surprised lines of McCook's were broken into fragments and sent drifting to the rear with nothing left to stem the tide. This was the signal for a charge along the whole rebel line, and immediately in our front came the rebels in battle array, hurrying to get engaged so that our troops could not be spared to assist where the line was broken.[1] The 92d was strung out into a long thin line, as a skirmish line, and all we were intended for was to fight a skirmishing retreat, so as to properly warn those heavy lines of battle of the approaching enemy. We skirmished as best we could, but as the brush was thick in places and we on horseback and the rebels on foot, they could out travel us in the tangled underbrush. Some of the men and horses were badly tangled at times and came near being captured. We succeeded in getting back to the main lines of battle and then what followed will never all be written. Both armies were now hotly engaged up and down the whole length of the lines of battle, and the whole atmosphere resounded with one constant peal from the rolling of musketry and booming of artillery. McCook's corps was beaten from left to right until it looked upon a band of fugitives completely disorganized and drifting towards Chattanooga, with not a man knowing where three men of his regiment could be found. The whole right wing of the army was destroyed or driven from the field, except Wilder's brigade, which, with their Spencers, resisted the charge and held the rebels at bay.

"Old Pap" Thomas, as the boys familiarly call him, was fighting desperately and he had not lost an inch of ground. At this juncture Wilder conceived the idea of putting through the rebel lines and fighting his way straight down to Thomas. He had five regiments and a battery of artillery. Four of these regiments were armed with the seven-shooter repeating rifles and three companies of the 92d had the same effective gun. The brigade was just about formed when Charles A. Dana, assistant secretary of war, rode up to Wilder and gave positive orders not to do so, but draw his forces off and down upon the Chattanooga road near the city. Wilder was bold and daring and would have succeeded, and the fortunes of that battle might have been different. Dana was a coward and had authority at a time when he should have had no authority.

STILL SUNDAY, SEPTEMBER 20, 1863, CHICAMAUGA BATTLEFIELD, GEORGIA

As Dana's orders prevented Wilder from making any charges into the rebel lines he next turned to do all he could in another direction. He threw the regiments into line of battle to prevent the rebels from hurrying up a retreat and then set to work gathering up artillery, ambulance trains, supply trains, and ammunition trains that had been abandoned by McCook's corps.

The 92d was dismounted and thrown into line of battle along with the balance of the brigade.

When a regiment of cavalry fall in line in the morning each company counts off by fours. Each man goes by a number, one, two, three, or four. In case of a battle and the regiment is dismounted to fight on foot, all those who are number one, two, and three must do the fighting, and all those who are numbered four must hold the horses. By good luck or bad luck I happened to be number four on this occasion and took care of the horses. We led our horses into a deep ravine to keep the cannon balls from hitting them and ourselves to boot. While here I got a chance to see what was going on in the rear of a fighting army.

In a large army there are always a few genuine cowards, men who cannot stand the shock of a battle for a single moment. As soon as danger sets in they turn deadly pale and contrive some plausible excuse to get out of the ranks. They claim to be very sick, or have discovered that the lock to their gun will not work, or they have slyly got a ball down without powder and cannot shoot, or they have a sideache, a headache, backache, a sore toe or lame heel, or some other hocus pocus break down or limp. They have got it bad and it gets worse as the danger approaches. They manage to get out of the ranks, and when once out their coat-tails are soon floating in the wind, or in other words, they skip. When the battle is over these fellows come sneaking back to their regiments with a well cut-and-dried story of how they got separated from their own regiment, how they fell in line with another one and had a hand-to-hand encounter with the rebels and killed more than a dozen men and met with several hair-breadth escapes. While the truth is they skulked away in some wood or other concealed place waiting for the battle to terminate. While such cowardice is ridiculous and is despised by all, yet such cowardice is as much a constitutional defect as it is for some to be born without reason. One is called a coward, the other an idiot. One man is born brave and daring, another a coward and shirk. There is scarcely a company of men by what will have one or two natural-born cowards. Yet from reading history sometimes it seems as though there were no such things as cowards in existence anywhere, only among those the historian hated. But human nature is pretty much the same the world over. Those historians who write up glowing accounts of great battles and victories won and the bravery of the men, have always left untold the manner of cowards skulking in the rear to keep out of danger.

While holding horses in the ravine every now and then one of these cowards from some regiment came hurrying over the hill making lively time towards the rear. There were not many of this number, however, not as many as usual, for all the men in this army were confident of success before the battle would close.

A great many wounded came pouring over the hill, some with help and some without. One hale, hearty, good-looking soldier, a boy about eighteen years of age, came limping and grunting along, wounded in both legs, blood flowing down and filling his shoes. He had been shot but a few minutes before. He came close to where I stood with my horses and I asked him where he was wounded, name, number of regiment, brigade, etc., but I never recorded it and have forgotten that part. He was free to converse and sat down on a stump, but as he did so he took hold of his leg that was shot the worst as he sat down, he cried out Oh! Oh! Looking me in the face his eyes danced with excitement as he cried, "The rebels came yelling right across an open field and we were lying down behind fence, and when they got up close we rose up and gave 'em perfect hell. We were just going to charge bayonets when two balls struck me here, and here, and oh it hurts so!" He was young, gritty, and brave. He told me everything in detail and would get so animated that he would forget all about his wounds. He would have staid [*sic*] longer, but the battle was raging and I knew we were losing ground on the right. I advised him to hurry on towards the rear before his wounds would get stiff and he unable to walk. He took my advice and went on. He was only one of the hundreds who came along. The story of the boy was the story of nearly every wounded man; but the rebels, though badly punished for their charging, broke regiment after regiment until McCook's whole corps was gone.

The regiment soon came back to their horses, and we all mounted. The ambulance trains and abandoned artillery were gathered up and everything started for Chattanooga, the brigade protecting the rear. As we started back we saw sights that but few soldiers ever get to see. The ambulances were filled with wounded until they could hold no more, and many men who were wounded in the head, shoulders, and arms, were on foot drifting towards Chattanooga. There were about one hundred and fifty ambulances filled in this way with no troops to guard and protect them except Wilder's brigade. But the greatest sight of all was the disorganized troops. The woods, lanes, and fields were filled with men all drifting to the rear towards Chattanooga. Generals of brigades, colonels of regiments, and captains of companies were drifting along with the rest, without a single man to command. Ask any one of them where his regiment was, and he would tell you that the rebels charged on them and they fought until the regiment was all cut to pieces, and there was scarcely a man left, and he did not know of any man besides himself. We found no organized troops anywhere except our own brigade, and sometimes men had to be taken from our command to take away batteries. The fact of the matter was, those regiments had stood and fought the rebels desperately and had all been badly cut up, and when the rebels overpowered them they became a confused mass, and nothing more could be done until they got back to someplace of safety and then reorganize. About five o'clock we reached the Summertown Road in the shadow of Lookout Mountain five miles south of Chattanooga and went into camp for the night, tired as tired could be.

>─┼─◆─○─◆─┼─<

As Wilder's brigade was moving back, protecting as far as possible the great drifting masses of wounded men, disorganized men, loaded ambulances, ammunition wagons, and artillery, the wounded men attracted my attention. It was a great curiosity to me to know just how a wounded man felt when he was shot. In the first place a healthy man is very hard to shoot and kill instantly. If a ball passes through the top part of the brain, crashing through the walls of the skull on both sides, he is killed instantly and never knows what hurt him. Instances have been known where the head has been struck, torn open, and some of the brain oozed out, and still the person lived for a time. Occasionally the person injured gets partly or passable well. Such cases are usually in the side or back of the head.

Another place where the men are shot and instantly killed is the heart. But even then the man is not instantly killed, unless the ball passes through and tears open those cavities that hold and pump the blood to the system, or some of the vessels that carry the blood to and from the heart.

Then again, if a ball pierces and severs the main artery anywhere between the heart and base of the brain, he is instantly killed; otherwise you may shoot a man all to pieces, so to speak, and he will not die quick. I once saw a man that was shot from seven different guns in less than a minute. He stuck to his horse and ran away, and the rebels failed to capture him.

When a ball strikes a man in full force he is numbed in the parts struck, and the instant pain is not so great as that would be from a light stroke of a carriage whip. The pain comes on gradually. Sometimes a man receiving a flesh wound in an arm or leg in times of excitement does not know it until he sees the blood coming down the coat sleeve or feels it working between his toes in his boot. Those who are shot or hit with what the boys called "spent balls" experienced the most momentary pain. These spent balls either come a long ways and lose part of their force or are shot out of defective guns, or have not powder enough behind them to give proper force for good execution. These balls usually have force enough to go half way through an arm, leg, or the body, unless they strike something to partly ward it off. The most painful wound that is possible to inflict, so far as my observations went, is to be shot in the knee joint with a spent ball that has considerable force.

The most painful wound I think that I ever saw was a little after noon of the first day's battle at Chicamauga. A ball had struck a man in the knee in such a way as to pass under and strain up the knee pan and got wedged between the knee joints of the large bones, and there lodged. Two of his companions picked him up on the battlefield, took hold of him on both sides just as two small boys would take hold of a larger one to wrestle him down at "side-hold," and walked off with the wounded man. He belonged to one of the infantry regiments. His pain and misery was severe to the last extremity of human endurance. He writhed, groaned, cried, and almost screamed with agony and pain, and occasionally vomited. Other men have had both legs shot away with cannon balls that never suffered the hundredth part of the severe pain that this man did.

Sometimes men get wounded under such peculiar circumstances that the boys, after the battle is over, will laugh at the wounded man.

Reuben Edgar was a mess mate of mine, and at our second position of the first day's fight we were almost side by side, but each of us were behind a small stump, loading and shooting as fast as we could jump into it. Reuben had loaded his gun and rose up to cap and shoot. The stump was small and he rose too high. A ball came just over the top of the stump and struck him full in the breast with a heavy thud as it struck. I heard the ball whiz, heard it strike, and saw Rube tumble over onto his face. A streak of sadness passed over me in spite of the din of battle. Rube made a low, guttural, whining noise and I supposed it was a sort of dying, insensible groan. I blazed away and Rube lay there nearly dead or dying as I supposed. That ball had struck the breast so as to pass over a line of the heart. The rebels began to flank us and word was sent down the line that we were compelled to move back and form a new line. We were just about to start when Rube lifted up his head and in a mournful tone said, "Oh boys, don't let the rebels get me." Two or three boys ran up quickly, raised him up and straight with one on either side in a resting attitude and started off. Rube to his own surprise found that his legs worked as well as ever, and after they had carried him a little way he told them he could walk. They let go of him and Rube took a step or two, stopped, threw open his jacket, vest and shirt to take a look at the wound in his breast. He looked an instant, passed his thumb and finger over the wounded spot, then looked up with sunshine and smiles and said, "By golly boys, it didn't go in." A half-dozen boys gave a shout of laughter right then and there. Rube never heard the last of "By golly boys, it didn't go in."

But after all, Rube had been struck with a pretty savage ball. It struck his leather shoulder belt just over his wadded jacket, and it raised a bunch on his breast bone about the size of a hen's egg. It knocked the breath out of him, and his efforts to regain it were what I supposed to be his dying agonies.

I happened to be looking towards Edward Lent when the ball struck him. It seemed to make a streak of whiz. It seemed as though you could almost see the balls coming, but not quite. The balls made a frightful whiz or screech. I heard the whiz and saw the dust rise from Lent's jacket. The ball struck between the root of the arm and breast, about midway. The ball went crashing through, tearing flesh and splintering bones. Lent turned deadly pale, staggered, and said, "Oh take hold of me." His mess mate, Catling Wilson, took hold of him, held him up, and led him to the rear out of further danger.

When men are first wounded they are nearly as limber as ever, except in the parts shot, but after a lapse of twenty-four hours their wounds are swollen and the man becomes very pale, and he is stiff and sore all over his body, so to speak.

As we were moving back with the ambulances I saw one man that had been shot in the mouth, the ball crashing through the upper front teeth, passing upwards through the roof of the mouth and coming out at the top of the head where the hair parts in every direction. He sat up straight in the ambulance, blood trickling down from both ends of the wound.

In times of battle, or series of battles, if a man complains of being ill he is treated by the men as a sneak, coward, or a "play-off." That is, if he gets ill during the battle. But a wounded man is treated with all the respect and courtesy at the command of the soldiers. A well soldier would almost die for the wounded one, but the ill man is treated with contempt. It is very unfortunate and a disgrace to be taken ill during a battle.

>+◆>+O+<►+◄

Companies C and K were left on the mountain strung out into a courier line. They remained on the mountain five days and then were removed and put into a courier line at the base of the mountain on the east side. The new line extended from Chattanooga to Crawfish Springs, a distance of sixteen miles. Captains Woodcock and Hawk remained with General Rosecrans and in addition to supervising the line, were, to some extent, a part of his bodyguard during the great battle.

Widow Glenn's house was the headquarters of Rosecrans. Captains Woodcock and Hawk and what men were on the courier line were a sort of reserve and they all did good work in carrying dispatches to different parts of the field during that bloody battle of the 19th and 20th.

Each man on that line and more particularly those at the headquarters, saw enough to make a volume of history, but it was impossible for me to gather up what others saw; hence, I can only give some of the outlines of what was gathered from them.

Few persons have but a faint idea of the trials, longings, and anxieties of a general in command of a large army. They are but men similar to all other men and have their hopes and fears, successes and defeats, joys and sorrows.

All the time that those armies were skirmishing and preparing for battle General Rosecrans was uneasy, inquiring after everything, what it meant, how strong were the rebels in front, what did a certain cloud of dust mean? Orderlies were sent in every direction to different parts of the field with orders to this general and that. He was never for a moment easy while thousands of human lives were in danger from a mistake or might be spared with wisdom and caution.

During the battle the south portion of the courier line became exposed and Captain Woodcock was ordered by Rosecrans to take it up and form a new line by another road. The captain hurried off and got to the exposed front just as trouble commenced. The rebels were charging in. One of the videttes was captured, and in the confusion the 92d boys got mixed up with the rebels, but all got away, except the one mentioned. Captain Woodcock re-formed the courier line as directed, and when he went to report to General Rosecrans' headquarters at Widow Glenn's house, it happened to be just at the time when the right wing of the army was crushed. All that part of the battlefield was lost, headquarters and all. The captain knew nothing of the disaster as he proceeded to Widow Glenn's house. Along the way he met great swarms of men drifting back, when presently the bullets began to patter about him. On looking around to take in the situation he saw rebels in front, and back of him were Union officers trying to reform lines of battle. He got out of his dangerous position as best he could. But what troubled him was where could he find General Rosecrans? The captain marched about among those drifting masses in search of his general, but he could not find him. He met General Garfield, Rosecrans' chief of staff and he ordered the captain to report to General Thomas.

It was long after dark when the second day's battle was hushed by the darkness of the night, that the lines of General Thomas and General Rosecrans were found. The headquarters of General Thomas had no house, no tent, no pomp, no show, no anything, nothing but a man, a good man, a noble man, standing erect by the side of a few smoldering embers. All about him lay his sleeping men, stretched upon the ground, completely worn out and exhausted with their long and continued hardships. With great powers of endurance, the general held up when all others were worn out. There stood the man who had so watched, directed, and guarded his lines of battle that they received those tremendous repeated charges of the rebels, slaughtered and beat them all back.

There was no adjutant or clerk to formally report to so the captain reported to General Thomas in person. The captain was completely fascinated with the nobleness and grandeur of that great and good man, for he was received without red-tape, pomp, or show, in a business-like, companionable way. Since he had dispatched for several generals but did not know where to find them, he inquired of the general where Wilder was since one of the dispatches was for him. The general said he would ask his adjutant whom he found lying fast asleep upon the ground. This person would not waken, even with repeated shaking so the general took him by the collar with both hands, raised him up, and stood him on his feet and shook him while standing until he got awake enough to talk.

"Do you know where General Wilder is?" asked General Thomas.

"He was shot and killed today at two o'clock," said the sleepy man and down he went to the ground and slept like a log.

But Wilder was all right. The captain also had a dispatch for General Gordon Granger, the demijohn general. Granger had got on to the battlefield by night of the second day and it was to be hoped that he was sober. When the captain asked for the headquarters of that individual, General Thomas stood in a position so that a little light from the smoldering camp fire shone on his face and as a peculiar smile stole across it he pointed towards a great light over in the distance and remarked that over there by a great camp fire was a great tent in which was General Gordon Granger and his headquarters. The captain started off as directed.[2]

It is a rule in delivering dispatches for the general who receives one to tear it open, take out the contents, and write the receipt of the dispatch on the envelope, giving date and the hour of the day when it was received. As the captain rode up to Granger's headquarters, there was a great log fire blazing up the still night air, around which were standing about a dozen soldiers warming as the air was a little frosty. Near by was a great tent in which was the distinguished general and his demijohn. In front of the tent was a soldier on guard, pacing backwards and forward by the door of the tent, allowing none to pass or re-pass. The guard passed the dispatch in to the general's adjutant who also slept in the tent. The captain took his stand by the fire to warm, holding the reins of the horse in hand. In passing in the dispatch to the adjutant and waking him, some noise was caused, which woke up the wrong snoozer. General Gordon Granger and all the brandy inside of him was very indignant at being disturbed in the night, even on a battlefield. He rushed out of his tent towards the men around his log fire and with a vehement oath, said, "God damn you men, get right away from here."

The men scampered off, except Captain Woodcock who stood there as composedly as though nothing had been said. The angry man then turned on the captain and said, "God damn you captain, why don't you obey my orders and go away from here?"

Captain Woodcock replied, "I am here as an officer on duty, the captain in command of Rosecrans' courier lines, and when you give me receipt for the dispatches I have just brought you, I will go away, but not before. I care nothing for your camp fires."

At this juncture the adjutant handed him the desired receipt, and the captain mounted to ride away. Just then a man lying on the ground, a short distance from the fire, called to him, and said, "Captain, do you know where General Thomas' headquarters are?"

"Yes," replied the Captain, "I am going there, now."

"Wait a moment and I will go with you," said the man, who, when he rode up to the captain's side, proved to be General Garfield of Ohio. They rode along together and chatted about what insults it was necessary to take for the good of one's country.

SEPTEMBER 26, 1863, HARRISON'S LANDING, TENNESSEE

Companies C and K remained on courier duty under Rosecrans and Thomas until December 4, doing courier duty from the famished city to places where there was plenty. One end of the line at times would be feasting and the other fasting or starving by slow degrees. At one end shade trees were cut down for horses to browse, while at the other end there was plenty to feed both men and horses.

After two days' hard fighting at Chicamauga it was decided to draw the army back to Chattanooga, form a new line of battle and fortify every inch of the ground. The armies were drawn off in the night and a line of battle formed in the shape of a horse shoe, with the city of Chattanooga occupying the relative position of the frog of the horse's foot, while the heel of the foot rested on the Tennessee River. But, as there was danger of the rebels going up to Harrison's Landing, crossing the river and coming in behind the army, the 92d was sent up there to guard the ferry and ford and prevent anything of the kind from being done.

On the morning of the 21st Wilder's brigade rode through the streets of Chattanooga and down to the pontoon bridge to cross. As we went through the streets the city was filled with these drifting masses of disorganized men. The pontoon bridge was strongly guarded and no disorganized band of men or single man was allowed to go on to it. The river made a natural scoop net to hold the disbanded men, and the colonels and captains were around among them getting their companies and regiments together. As fast as organized they went cheerfully to the front and took their places in the new line of battle.

Down by the river bank were several thousand wounded men who were able to walk and had walked off from the battlefield and got as far from danger as possible. The river had stopped them and they lay down without a murmur, waiting for such time as they might be cared for.

We crossed the pontoon and started up the river, leaving guards at every conceivable place of crossing.

All our men who had been severely wounded and left in the field hospitals had fallen into the hands of the rebels. Dr. Clinton Helm of the 92d, who had charge of a field hospital, stayed with his wounded men, caring for them, and allowed the rebels to take him prisoner. He could have saved himself and let the prisoners suffer, but he thought more of his patients than he did of his freedom, so he stayed by them and let the consequences be what they might. He was taken prisoner by the rebels, but they allowed him to care for his men two weeks upon the battlefield or field tent, after which time he was marched to Ringold, Georgia with about fifty other Yankee surgeons. From there he was taken by car to Richmond, Virginia. On the tenth of October he was confined in Libby Prison[3] and on the 24th of November following he was exchanged.

The Union army now, as it lay in line of battle around Chattanooga, was in a precarious position. The railroad from the north winds and twists in such peculiar shape that no pen can describe the route so that the reader could get a knowledge of it. The rebels had possession of a section of the railroad from the north and no rations could reach the city either by rail or water. Even the wagon road on the direct route back to the next station north was in the possession of the rebels. Bridgeport, which was the next railroad station towards the west and north, was twenty-five miles distant by the direct road. To reach Bridgeport with wagon trains it was necessary to travel north a long way in a valley, cross a high range of mountains, and then come back down another valley, a distance in all of sixty miles. All the army wagon trains were sent to work hauling provisions to the army. It was feared that the rebel cavalry might get across the river somewhere, sweep down one of those valleys, and destroy our cracker line. We guarded the river closely and patrolled up and down for a long distance. All the well men were strung out into small squads watching and patrolling the river. The rebel cavalry slyly traveled up the river on the opposite side, keeping well back and out of sight until they got way beyond where we were picketing and there they forded the river. They then turned and came sweeping down the second valley back of us—Sequatchie Valley—captured, burned, and destroyed three hundred loaded wagons of our supply train. Wilder's brigade started after them, leaving the 92d to guard the river alone. He followed them, caught up and fought them, and drove them back to their own lines after a long running fight.

The loss of these rations and trains reduced the army to one-quarter rations and the outlook was gloomy indeed. The rations that we got during this period did not seem to be anything. Our living under these circumstances was peculiar and novel. The men who were not on duty along the river would get on to their horses and ride way up into the country for miles and miles away until a corn field could be found, for this season of the year the corn was just beginning to glaze in Tennessee. The horses would be fed all they could eat, a sack of corn gathered and then each man would ride all the way back to camp after having traveled all day and perhaps two days as the distance we had to go for corn kept getting farther and farther. Now we had corn and no bread of any kind. How were we to get breakfast, dinner, and supper? We had no meat to fry, no potatoes to boil, no coffee to make, nor four or meal to make bread from. The corn was too hard to boil and too soft to grind, and we had nothing to grind with if it had been hard and dry. It seemed though that every man had a grater the very moment he needed it. Every house that had a stovepipe in it lost it in a hurry. This pipe would be opened at the seam and spread so as to make a half round instead of a whole. The bayonet was used for a punch, small holes were punched from the inside and then over these rough upturned corners an ear of corn was slid up and down until all the corn was grated into meal. The cob was fed to the horses and with a little browse they managed to live. We baked this corn meal into hoe-cake, pone, and corn-dodgers. Those who were fond of coffee would burn an ear of corn black and throw it, cob and all, into a pot of boiling water and have a cup of coffee for breakfast. As strange as it may appear the men were healthy, fat, and jolly on this corn diet.

John M. King (left) and Richard King shortly after their enlistment in 1862.

John M. King with the Spencer repeating rifle he received after the 92d
Illinois was reassigned as a mounted infantry unit.

Major General William Rosencrans.

Major General Gordon Granger.

Lee & Gordon's Mills at Chickamauga.

Major General George Henry "Old Pap" Thomas.

After the war King married twice. Pictured here is his second wife, Mary Ella Parks, to whom he always referred as "May," rather than call her by the same name as his first wife.

King and his family in 1906 or 1907. Clockwise from the top left are Mable, Nora, Emma, Frances, May, Etha, Bertha, Maud, and Charles. Seated on King's lap is Edward.

CHAPTER 6

Half the Winter in the Saddle

October 1863 – January 1864

OCTOBER 14, 1863, HARRISON'S LANDING, TENNESSEE
While we lay at Harrison's Landing picketing the river, living on cornbread, we would frequently, when off picket, two or three in company, ride out into the country a long distance in search of something else that could be eaten by horse and man. The country for miles had been stripped of everything. Where but a few months before were happy families, now there was nothing but desolation. Everything that could sustain life had been taken without ceremony, whether the owners were loyal or disloyal.

On the fourth of August I rode out a long ways in search of something to eat. At one house we found a woman and two children on the brink of starvation. She wanted advice as to what was best to do. Our men had stripped the house and little farm of everything that would sustain life. Her husband was a Union man in the Union army. We advised her to work her way as best she could to Bridgeport, which was about forty miles distant, and when she got there the government would furnish her with plenty. The government had provided means for all those loyal people who lived in the South who were loyal to the government, so that they could be protected and fed.

On the sixth the four of us boys started on a foraging expedition into the mountains. We climbed up the long zig-zag road to the top and penetrated a portion of the mountain country away back from the usual highways and byways. We found a neat little log cabin which was filled with sweet potatoes and corn. We arrived about noon and gathered corn and fed our starving horses about all they could eat, built a fire, and dug some potatoes and boiled them on the spot. We sat down in the patch to dinner right where the grasshopper had sung and made to and wooed his darling while sitting on a sweet "tater" vine. Our bill of fare consisted of sweet potatoes, boiled yam-yams, and potato pot pie. I told the cook that I would take some potatoes. We feasted and munched and had a jolly time, and yet a fear grains of fear stole over us at times as we were a small band that might be easily picked up by a squad of rebel scouts if we were not careful. They were always prowling about for the express purpose of gathering us up piecemeal. We ate with eight rounds in each gun, ready to shoot at the drop of the hat. Our horses were kept saddled and ate with bridles and all on. We filled our sacks with potatoes and corn and returned to camp after an all-day trip. Our little band had several days' rations ahead. We went on picket that night in full view of the rebels and talked across the river with them.

There was an island in the Tennessee River that had about forty acres of the largest and best corn on it that I ever saw grow, so tall that most of the stalks had to be broken over to reach the ears. The soil consisted of material deposited from overflows with clam shells. After our treaty with the rebels we took a very large canoe that had been burned out of a huge tree, said to have been done many years previous by Indians, and with this canoe we gathered the corn in sacks and paddled to shore. One of the boys, unused to canoe sailing, got his corn aboard then disobeyed orders and stood up to paddle. The canoe upset and the bag of corn and all went down to feed the fish. The boy, fortunately, could paddle his body better than he could paddle the canoe, so he got ashore while the fish got all the material out of which he could make his hoe-cake.

On the 12th it began to rain and it continued with several short intervals for a long time. We were picketing so much of the river and country that our turns to stand as vidette were very frequent. In addition to river pickets we had to picket all the principal roads.

The night of October 14 was the blackest, stormiest night I ever saw on picket. The usual method is to sit on the horse, but our horses were so poorly fed that I stood by the horse's head. I was on the midnight watch with the cold rain pouring in perfect torrents, standing on a main road leading into the country, so dark that in waving my hand in front of my face it could not be seen. I could only stand and listen for noise or footfalls in the mud. The horse seemed to listen all the time with ears pricked up and eyes training into outer darkness. He would keep his head close to my shoulder as if he were afraid I would leave him or get separated from him. A bond of sympathy seemed to permeate the spirit of each of us, horse and man. It seemed as though while we stood there in our dark and stormy solitude that he was my best friend on earth, and as he hitched up to me and put his head close to my shoulder and peered into the darkness he seemed to say, "You are the best friend I have, let us watch that we don't get hurt." At the break and fall of a limb or the patter of a rabbit on the wet leaves he would lift his head higher, throw his ears farther to the front, and strain his eyes into the darkness. Occasionally he would sniff the air to see if he could smell an enemy coming. At the close of our watch when the relief guard came in hearing distance from the direction of the reserve post, my horse seemed to known as well as I who was probably coming from that direction. When once back to the reserve post tied to a tree where there were plenty of other horses he did not seem to care or fear any more danger. It rained so hard that none of us at the reserve post could lie down to rest. We stood around a large log fire and let it rain.

Provisions were growing scarcer and scarcer about camp. Our teams were sent way up east Tennessee for corn, but the distance was so great that the mules ate it nearly all up before they returned, when they unloaded their small loads and started back again. The mule drivers hid some corn along the road so they could have some to feed on while making the long trips. Nearly every avenue to obtain provisions was exhausted. The roads were bad and the continued rains made them worse.

The rebels just across the river had plenty. In our visits with them we learned their usual food as soldiers. Cornbread and bacon were the staple articles. They had sugar and salt, but no tea or coffee. They were cold-water men of necessity. Their food seemed to agree with them and they looked hale and hearty. Their uniforms consisted of broad-brimmed black hats and their clothes had two shades of color. It was all, or nearly all, home-made, butternut and sheep's gray were the colors. The butternut was made from the bark of butternut and walnut trees and was usually cotton goods, while the other was woolen and was a brighter color. In speech they are very slow and measured. The ordinary lively Yankee would utter a whole sentence while they were uttering a single word. The more illiterate use the class of pronouns "youons and weens" for you and we, and "gwine" for going. One Southern lady said to one of our boys one day, "Where are youons all gwine? Weens don't go up North to fight youons. Now there is Captain Hooker with his big regiment came down here and pitched in on our ends. His men are all foreigners for I talked with them and they came from that country youons call New York."

NOVEMBER 1, 1863, NASHVILLE, TENNESSEE

After the regiment returned from its starved-out position to Bridgeport, Alabama, a new supply of horses was necessary, as many of the men were dismounted in consequence of starved and "petered-out" horses. A large detachment of men, a portion of each company, was selected and put under the command of Captain Becher[1] to take the cars and proceed to Nashville for that purpose.

I smiled all over when I found that I was among the number to go to Nashville. I pictured to myself a long pleasant ride of some two hundred miles on the cars. What a pleasant thought! The road in getting back to Nashville ran through a long tunnel in the mountains. I was just "dying to drink in tunnel scenery." We were going to travel way up north to Nashville! When up home in the North, Nashville was so far south that we hardly ever thought of it.

On the fifth of November we went down to the depot to take an afternoon train. We waited till long after dark when we were escorted into some palace hog cars. We accepted the situation cheerfully and all those who did not choose to sit down could stand up. Anybody who wished to could sit down on the floor. We were all cheerful because we were going right up to the city. The train did not start so we told stories till a late hour, stories that would have brought a grin to the face of a cast-iron monkey. One by one we fell asleep, trying it sitting and standing, and the next morning when we awoke we found we had traveled six miles up to Stevenson, Alabama. Here the train halted as the engine appeared to be out of breath. We got out and prepared a scanty breakfast from our almost empty haversacks. The trains went through the regular buntings, backings, startings, switchings, and whistling, and then a very long waiting spell when we were all ordered aboard.

When there is anything else to carry on government railroad cars the only place left for a soldier to ride is where the snow, hail, and frost ride— on the roof. He can ride there if he don't slip off. We did not like to ride on the roof of our own accord because we might slip off, but now if we fell off and broke our necks it would be legally done and if we met with an accident we wanted it to be legal. We soon got aboard and the train was off for Nashville.

I had a great curiosity to know how a railroad could be constructed through a chain of mountains twenty-five miles wide with only one mile of tunneling. We were all on observation cars now, and no extra charge for seats. We had crossed the mountains several times and knew they were fully twenty-five miles wide. We were soon up to the mountains and a small stream of water came running through them with tremendous high bluffs on either side. Sometimes the valley was all on one side of the creek and sometimes on the other, and sometimes on both sides. The creek seemed to have cut the mountain in two. The railroad started up this crooked winding valley, crossing and recrossing the stream. The bluffs were so high on either side that no railroad company could ever think of running a road straight and cutting through them. We ran up this valley following the stream. The scenery along this little narrow valley with its massive high walls of solid rock was sublime indeed. On one occasion the sight was so grand that, filled as I was with emotion and hard tack, I rose to my feet and was just going to repeat something from Shakespeare or the spelling book when the old car tilted, bunted, and wriggled. I lost my balance, fell over and caught the foot plank, and concluded to stick to the board. This knocked all the sublimity out of me and I did not have another dangerous attack of it on that journey.

After a time our valley came to an end. A great spring rose out of the foot of what appeared to be a cross mountain. This spring formed the headwaters of the stream that came up. Here the engine plunged into the tunnel. The speed of the engine was slacked and we went slowly so we could have a good view. But horrors upon horrors! The great volume of smoke from the great freight engine had no chance to escape and it filled what little space there was with the thickest of smoke. We could not breathe it. Every man was soon flat on the cars, face down, trying to get a little fresh air to breathe. It had never entered our heads about the supply of air getting short. We ran out just at the time we were expecting to view the beauties of the great tunnel. I got one good sniff of fresh air, shut my mouth, held my breath, and opened my eyes to take a hasty look. Lo and behold! I could see just as much with the back of my head as with my eyes in front. The tunnel was perfectly dark of its own accord, and the smoke of the engine completed the intensity. The tunnel was a mile and a quarter through and we were glad enough when we came out. The west end of the tunnel came out at the head of a valley running west.

We spent the day and until midnight before we reached Nashville. The night was very chilly and cold. We were all sleepy from being up all night. We were afraid to go to sleep for fear we would roll off. But we would nap it in spite of ourselves. Finally some one discovered that we could lash ourselves to the foot plank with our cartridge box belts. We lashed ourselves to the plank and slept on either side of the slant of the car roof with feet down. One or two guns fell off and were lost.

We reached Nashville a little after midnight, stiff and cold. We built up camp fires and spread out blankets on the ground and lay down to take a good square sleep.

On Sunday evening, November 8, a large number of us went to church just to see how it would seem to go to a meeting indoors once more. The patrols were so thick and had such rigid instructions that it was dangerous for a private soldier to walk the streets either night or day unless he had a written pass in his pocket from his commanding officer. Nearly every man wanted to go down to the city every night to see all the sights, while we should remain. The theaters were in full blast. To avoid the trouble of writing a pass for all the men, a pass for the whole squad was given to one Sergeant Brown. We all went to the theater. There was a very large attendance, and when it broke up our squad was somewhat divided and I lost sight of Brown. I got to one of the four corners of the street and in the darkness I could not tell Brown from any other man. Brown carried the pass and I did not want to part his company. I enquired for Brown, Brown, Brown of all the groups of men that started off, but the right Brown could not be found. Soon everybody had gone away and I was alone. I had lost Brown. I was just starting across the street when a man came running past me in the middle of the street as though running for life. In the next instant three patrols, three Union soldiers, came running after him. They slacked not over ten feet from me and fired at the fellow running. He had no pass and did not want to halt. My hair went straight up. I was without a gun, pass, or Brown. I thought my time had surely come to be arrested or shot, but they only halted just enough to get a steady gun and fire and then ran after the fellow with all their might. My legs were very much in favor of speed, but I was perfectly cool. It was a cool evening. My legs got the best of it some of the time and I was down to camp about as soon as Brown and the rest of the crowd.

We had been living on hard tack and corn pone so long that we proposed to have a white wheat bread feast while here. We bought bread at 10 cents per loaf and ate it clear. They do not have butter in the army. We had white bread three times a day on the table—ground every time we ate in Nashville.

NOVEMBER 20, 1863, BRIDGEPORT, ALABAMA

We were now in the great city of army supplies. There was everything here necessary to feed, clothe, and equip an army. Supplies of all kinds came and went by the train load. Everything was done on a large scale.

On the tenth of November we went down to the great market square and there turned over our old single-shooting guns and drew, each of us, a brand new Spencer repeating seven-shooter rifle. These guns were a new invention and perfect in all their parts. They would shoot seven times in rapid succession without stopping to reload. Seven balls were put in at once and each could be shot out separately. The gun was so perfect that fighting could be done just as well in a heavy shower of rain as in the clearest of weather. The powder could not get wet. The gun could be loaded and thrown into a stream of water and allowed to lay and soak and then it could be taken out and it would blaze away as though it had just come from a powder house. The bore of the barrel was rifled with a gain twist. They shot a slug or oblong ball. They were the most effective and deadly weapon in the service. The Henry rifle shot sixteen times, but they were very expensive and rather more delicate and the ball was smaller. There were only a very few of the latter in the service anywhere. We took enough of the Spencers to arm what there were in our squad and the balance were shipped on to Bridgeport to the rest of the regiment.

We next drew a new supply of clothing. Our old uniforms were well-nigh worn out. The government furnishes every soldier with $42 worth of clothing every year in addition to his monthly pay. He can take more than the $42, but all he gets over is deducted from his monthly pay and if he takes less than the $42 worth the balance is added to his pay.

On November 13 we went down to the great government stock yards to get horses and mules—horses to ride and mules to fill up in our supply train. Here was a great sight. Mules and horses were brought here by the car load, train load, and droves. Many of them were fine-looking animals, but many were unmanageable at home and had been sold to Uncle Sam to get rid of on account of being so vicious. Many of them had never been even "halter broke." It was a good place to send an ugly animal. The army was composed largely of young, active, adventuresome men, and many of them delighted in subduing an ugly horse or mule. Many soldiers sought for that kind, while gentle, true ones there was no particular demand for.

The first thing that attracted my attention was four blacksmiths nailing on four shoes on one mule at the same time. One blacksmith at each foot and all "peggin away" at the same time. I had hardly taken a fair look when the mule was turned loose with all shoes on and another wild, ugly, kicking mule took his place. Everything at first seemed to be in perfect confusion, hurly-burly, whoop and yell sort of pandemonium. Mules galloping about in a large enclosure about which was a high fence. The mules brayed and a band of darkies whopped and yelled and the blacksmiths cursed and swore, and the mule in the stocks kicked and struggled. Upon a closer examination I found that this pandemonium had order and system to it after all.

There was one Mexican in the yard who seemed to be in the height of his ambition. He had a lasso in his hand. It was made of raw hide of great length and strength. He would coil this up, stand at a long distance from a group of wild mules, give a sort of rolling throw, and the lasso would go uncoiling through the air and drop over a mule's head and around his neck with perfect accuracy and ease. As quick as the lasso was around the neck of a mule about a dozen negroes rushed up and took hold of the lasso. The mule would jump and "rare" but was soon down and a large rope took the place of the lasso and the Mexican was off for another throw. The negroes dragged the mule by main strength and awkwardness to the stocks, where a great leather blanket passed under his body and lifted the animal from his feet. Each foot was lashed to a beam and a shoe quickly nailed to its place.

They had another device for catching mules by running them into a narrow lane just wide enough for a mule to squeeze in. A man could walk on an elevated platform and put a halter on any mule he might select. But when the mule got out then the fun commenced. A mule has two characteristics. He wants to go backwards when you want him to go forwards, and he can kick your hat off when you are holding him by the bit. They have great powers of endurance and are very serviceable when once tamed and "broke in."

The horses were all halter broke and were in stables or barns, but many of them were untamed; some were balky, and others ugly.

We got our horses and regular cavalry saddles. We had been using citizen saddles of all patterns. A cavalry saddle is far more preferable since it has a place for carrying blankets and other trappings, both in front and rear, while on an ordinary saddle there is none. Our horses and mules were tied together three in a group and each man rode one horse and led a group of three.

On the second day out on our return trip I was placed on picket on the main road running south. We went into camp early that evening and I took my position before dark. We were so far in the rear of the main army that none of us apprehended any danger from any source and had even forgotten that there was such a thing as a bushwacker existed. We all had new guns and we felt as though one of us could whip a half-dozen rebels and then not have much of a fight. I had just ridden into the road and leisurely taken a position, when two stalwart, hale, hearty bushwhackers came riding up the road armed with revolvers and long-range muskets and riding fleet horses. They were in easy range when I first saw them riding towards me. I was astonished at their bold appearance and could hardly believe they were what their appearance indicated. I took my gun from the saddle socket and told them to halt. They paid no attention to my command only they turned the heads of their horses to the right and spurred them into a trot. I repeated my command and placed my gun to my shoulder to shoot them, and as I did so I noticed the swab protruding from the gun. I had carelessly left it inside the gun as I had no other place to carry it. I jerked it out quickly, but it took just time enough so that the bushwhackers had sank behind a hill out of sight in the timber. I felt cheap enough. Two bushwhackers had ridden in close gunshot of me, had refused to halt, and I had not shot at them even. I had learned a new lesson and had it forcibly illustrated. To be a good soldier while on duty one should be like an Illinois chicken-hunter, who shoots his game on the wing and is ready at all times to shoot in the sixteenth part of a second.

We were six days on the return trip and before we got to Bridgeport we ran out of rations and feed for our animals. On the last day of our journey we managed to get a very scanty breakfast and a very light feed for our horses and then pushed on. We traveled hard all day without dinner and reached the old camp ground late at night tired and hungry when lo and behold! The camp was deserted, the regiment was gone. Here we were on a barren old camp ground with nothing to eat for ourselves, nor nothing to feed our horses, and we had all gone without dinner thinking we would reach camp at night where we could get plenty. There were great piles of all kinds of government rations and forage only a little way from us at the depot. It was all closely watched and guarded by strong detachments of soldiers to see that no one took anything. There was a certain necessary red-tape line to travel to get the provisions and forage. Either our captain in command did not know how or did not want to, or could not get the right color to the tape, I don't know which, but I do know that nothing was got for us. It was rather hard to lie down without dinner or supper in full view of great piles of provisions intended for us, but such was our lot. The men were surly and cross and not a few oaths rent the night air. One little squad went down and succeeded in stealing a part of a box of hard tack. A few got a hard tack supper. The time had now arrived when I believed that that kind of stealing was justifiable. Whether my judgment was right or wrong I went down and for two hours did my best to steal a box of hard tack, but failed. The guards were on the lookout. I came to the conclusion that I was a poor thief and gave it up in despair and went back to our temporary camp and crawled in between two blankets and went to sleep.

The next morning when I awoke and looked about me I found that a span of mules which I led down from Nashville had gnawed their halter straps in two and had escaped tied together. I hunted long, but never found the mules. Some teamster had probably picked them up, shaved their manes and I could not tell which they were, and it made but little difference as they would do government service just as well in one team as in another. It was one o'clock before we reached the regiment. We had gone thirty-one hours without food, fifteen of which were in full view of plenty, but lacked the red-tape to get it. Our trip to Nashville was not all splendor.

NOVEMBER 30, 1863, BRIDGEPORT, ALABAMA

While the regiment lay at Bridgeport on the southeast side of the river on the railroad that runs to Chattanooga—a road we wanted badly, but could not get possession of all the way—great events were transpiring all about us, while the unobserving man would think there were none. The great conflict for the free and unobstructed possession of Chattanooga must be fought out soon or our forces must abandon the city.

On the 20th of November I was on the north side of Bridgeport and witnessed the arrival of the advance columns of Sherman's great and splendid Army of the Tennessee. This army of Sherman's had fought its way down the Mississippi to Vicksburg; was at the siege and surrender of that stronghold and fought and campaigned much, before that time and after, had now joined us for the first time and had marched hundreds of miles to do it, in order that they might take a hand in helping to raise the siege at Chattanooga. The men were supplied with all the rations they could carry at Bridgeport, and they passed on up the river to take their allotted position. Sherman's army was to pass up the river on the north side, go behind and pass Thomas's army in Chattanooga, come down the river, force a crossing, take a position, and be ready for a general engagement. Then with Hooker on the right at the foot of Lookout Mountain, ready to go up and fight in the clouds, Thomas in the center at Chattanooga, with his starved army and General Sherman up and across the river on the left, they were all to sweep down upon the rebels at once and wipe them from the face of the earth. But there was one great difficulty in the way: in getting Sherman's army to place and across the river. If the rebels should get wind of his designs, they would place such heavy forces at all the points where a crossing could be effected that he could not cross. There was a range of hills on the north side and Sherman's troops were kept behind those as they went up. Then there was another difficulty. Some citizens living along the route might steal across the river and inform the rebels of the approaching Sherman. Accordingly every citizen along this route must be arrested. Some sort of "hocus pocus" excuse for doing so was invented.

Quite a large detachment of cavalry was sent up in this region in the night. They were divided into a large number of small detachments. Each little squad went into the near vicinity of a house, fired several shots, and then rushed down to the house, took the man or men out of bed and told them that bushwhackers had fired on them and that the bushwhackers ran in the direction of this house and that they were going to arrest him; that there was grounds of suspicion that he was the chap that was the bushwhacker and did the firing.

Many a poor fellow was suddenly awakened, dragged from his bed half dead with fright, with his hair erect, trembling, nearly ready to fall to pieces, thinking that his time had come and that he would be slaughtered in a few moments. Every citizen was gobbled up in a very short space of time.

Sherman's army passed up unseen and unreported by or to the rebels. The citizens were held a day or two and then told that it was some other fellows that did the bushwhacking. They returned home in ignorance of the true cause of their arrest and will probably die in ignorance of the fact that there were no bushwhackers about at that time. Sherman crossed the river in safety and three great battles were simultaneously fought, commonly known as two battles of "Hooker in the Clouds" and Mission Ridge. It was properly three battles in one, as all were operating under Grant at Chattanooga, who had an elevated position and could send orders by signal flags to commanders of the three armies. The battles were a great victory to our forces all along the lines, but the details belong to history and not so much to the individual experience of any one man or regiment of men.

On account of the mountains, river, and scarcity of forage and the peculiar situations of the contending armies these great battles were all fought without the aid of cavalry with the exception of scouting and picketing. A great deal of the latter work was done by the cavalry, but the hard fighting was done principally by the infantry and artillery.

These victories raised the siege. The rebel army was in full retreat and our army too badly starved to follow. Lookout Mountain was ours, the railroad to Chattanooga was ours. The river was ours to navigate. There was a little steamboat that lay at Bridgeport that commenced to run to Chattanooga and return, loaded to the brim with provisions to supply the starving army. This steamer was loaded at Bridgeport and unloaded at Chattanooga. The distance was about twenty-five miles and the little boat knew no night or day, nor Sunday. It was the busiest and most useful boat in the United States for the time. The railroad was quickly repaired, the army supplied, and the country breathed easier.

While the regiment lay at Bridgeport the paymaster came around and paid off the troops. Each man received two months' pay, or about $26. There was no way to spend this money in the ordinary, legitimate way. It was dangerous to send it home in a letter and there were no reliable express lines. The soldiers were principally young men and had not yet laid aside boyish notions, and to have $25 or $30 each in his pocket, and no store nor grocery to spend it in, no place to purchase jack-knives, jew's harps, and candy, when they needed boots, mittens, and school books worse, was a state of things they were unused to. That money was burning a hole in every boy's pocket. It was frequently taken out to cool. The boys frequently had strong opinions on most every subject, and they were ready to "back up that opinion" with money. Gambling was the result. Again, the old chuck-luck board, or dice and blanket, were the means for betting and gambling. There was a little knoll covered with a few large trees, under which the blankets were spread and the chuck-luck boards run high. Sometimes a boy would go down to the chuck-luck grounds and get broke in a little time. One or two of the boys who got broke went back to their companions, secured their personal friends, and planned a raid on the banker who had won their money. They waited until dusk of evening, and the men stood on each side of the banker. The first time a little dispute arose one snatched the money that was in sight and ran away, while the other pretended he was indignant at something the banker had said or done, and detained him in a quarrel, while the other fellow ran. Several robberies of this kind occurred in rapid succession and the officers in command came to the conclusion to break it up.

Nearly everybody frequented the chuck-luck hill either to play or look on. I was looking on one day when the guards were sent there to arrest the gamblers. The guards came up on a run and the captain in charge ordered the guards to shoot somebody. I do not know who it was because every fellow ran but me and I flew. My coat-tail took the horizontal position of a chuck-luck board and maintained it until I reached camp. There was no one arrested and no one shot and the chuck-lucking went on just the same only more slyly.

DECEMBER 2, 1863, RACCOON MOUNTAINS, ALABAMA

On December 1 I was detailed, along with about forty others, to go off on a three-days' scout under the command of Lieutenant Skinner.[2] We were ready and off by ten o'clock. Our road nearly all day was nothing but cow paths and foot paths, where scarcely a wagon ever was used. We were to scout upon the Raccoon Mountains and in the valleys beyond. We climbed the mountain side in the usual zig-zag way, following the paths laid out by cows that appeared to show as good engineering as those mountain roads laid out by man. It took a long time to reach the top, and we were tired out and out of breath as we had to lead our horses up. When we were up at the top it seemed as though we were in another country.

These mountains have an average width of about twenty-five miles and the length is unknown. They appear to extend well down towards the Gulf of Mexico, but terminate by degrees. Although we were on top of the mountains, yet there were hills and dales, springs and creeks, level and rolling lands, timbered and untimbered spots, but most of the land was timbered, tall pine and oak predominating. This timber was well supplied with game, such as deer, coon, and pheasant.

The mountains were also inhabited by a class of people far different from those in the regions in the valleys and plains below. The men, as a rule, were lazy, shiftless, and poor, and were the fathers of more children than you could shake a stick at. There were no slaves up here except the wives of these lazy "squatters."

Whenever a new house was built and farm laid out, it was done after this fashion. The husband selected a site for a house where an acre or two of ground could be cleared with the least work, near enough to some spring or creek so that his wife could go and come with a bucket of water inside of half a day's travel. A jug of whiskey is obtained by the sale of coon skins at some village way off in the distance in the valley; then all the dogs, guns, men, and whiskey go together, chop down trees, cut logs and roll them up into a square pen, and when the sides are as high as the tallest man's head they put on a roof and shingle it with shakes—long flat board-shaped shingles split from short logs about three feet long. When the house is covered in this way what water does not leak down runs off on the shake. The kitchen, dining room, parlor, bedroom, and dog kennel are all in one room. The spaces between the logs are filled with mud by the more enter-prising and aristocratic, while the poorer classes fill them up with cast-away garments or leave them open altogether. One log at each corner near the top of the house is cut longer than the rest and it projects far beyond and makes a place to hang deer and venison to dry and cure. Deer horns are fastened on the inside on which to hang the rifle, powder horns, and pouches, while the outside is used to stretch and nail up pelts, coon skins and deer hides.

The wife makes a garden alone when she can get no help from her husband, and raises potatoes, corn, and a little cotton. The husband hunts, chews tobacco, drinks whiskey, and talks politics. A little homemade cloth is made from the cotton by the wife, spun and wove in the house and col-ored or dyed out of doors by dipping it into water boiled and soaked in butternut bark. The men and boys have their clothes cut and made from this cloth and the mother and girls from the same piece.

Dresses are usually made by doubling a piece of cloth, cutting a hole in the middle to drop over the head, and then sewing up both sides near the top and there leaving a hole for the arms and sleeves. The hem of the gar-ments hang a little below the knee, and as they seldom wore bonnets, shoes, stockings, or other garments of any kind, not even underclothing, these dresses were not injured by being trailed in the grass while chasing squirrels, nor wading in the mountain brooks or hoeing corn, and the taller the girl grew the less was the hem of the dress exposed. Some of these mountain nymphs were said to be very pretty, but I did not see any of that kind.

Children were very numerous. The mountain air seemed impregnated with prolific zephyrs, and the ages of children would range from nine to fif-teen months apart, except in cases of twins and triplets. These children were a sort of necessary evil to the husband. There were no schools and they grew up in perfect ignorance, and romped and roamed about in the timber wherever fancy led them.

Every "squatter" had from one to a dozen coon dogs. These dogs were kept for the double purpose of coon hunting and fencing. Poor old tumble-down fences surrounded his "patch" and dogs supplied the missing rails. Dogs were of far more importance and value to the squatter than children, hence he paid more attention to them. The dogs were trained and the children were not.

Some of the more enterprising had log houses large enough for a log partition and the high energy enough for a lift which could be reached by means of a ladder. The children and cats could all sleep in the loft, and the old folks, baby, and dogs below. Such a man would have a horse and an ornament in the front yard. The horse would be used for the several purposes of carrying corn to mill, marketing coon skins, and bringing back whiskey and tobacco. Two bags of shelled corn would be loaded on to the back of the poor horse and the squatter would get on top with his gun and dogs would follow by his side, and in this way the old horse would tote the load off fifteen or twenty miles to the foot of the mountains where some stream turned a rickety old mill that ground corn. They never used wheat bread.

The ornament on the front yard consisted of a pole set in the ground, on top of which was a little hand-made house of a better pattern than the one the squatter lived in, with a little door and window for the birds to enter and build their nests in.

These were the "poor white trash" of the South. They were lazy, indolent, good-for-nothing people. Too lazy to care and too shiftless to save. They would bask in the sun and idle away their time. Hunt a very little and rest a great deal. Their food consisted principally of corn bread, coon meat, and poor quality of acorn-fed pork. The aristocracy shunned and despised them. Slaves considered themselves above "dat poor white trash."

We traveled all day on the mountain amid settlements of this class of people and could study their habits and customs and count their children as they rushed out of their cabin to see the Yankees go by. We camped at night and it fell my lot to go on picket.

DECEMBER 4, 1863, BRIDGEPORT, ALABAMA

There was a custom among Southern women entirely unknown to Northern women. It was the habit of snuff dipping. To me it seemed like a horrible and filthy custom. The women purchase this snuff, put it in an ordinary tin snuff box, and carry it in the pocket and when they want a "dip" they take out the box, open it and take a little brush made from hickory sprout cut about four inches long, with one end previously ground or crushed between the teeth until it is crushed into many little splints resembling a very small painter's brush. This homemade brush is dipped into the snuff, wet from saliva, and the fine particles of the snuff adhere to the little splints of the brush. With this they scrub their teeth and gums, leaving the snuff well distributed in all parts of the mouth. When the mopping or scrubbing has satisfied the dipper the brush is laid in the mouth between the teeth and cheek with the end projecting an inch from the mouth. It is put there for safe keeping until used again. Every woman seems to be sucking a stick. They spit about as often as an ordinary tobacco chewer would.

The women of the "poor shucks" used a home-made snuff. They raised their own tobacco, kept it hung up in a dry place, and when the dip got low they broke off some of these dry and brittle tobacco leaves and rubbed them between the palms of their hands until it was as fine as powder; this they put in their tins, ready for the dip.

Some of our boys who were in the habit of chewing tobacco went to a house where there were young ladies and took a sociable "dip" from the box, but they always preferred making a new brush. The girls thought it was awful funny to have a genuine "Yank" dip with them. The girls would giggle and the boys would laugh.

One the second day's trip we came to a house where the proprietor was a man of some enterprise and he had gone into the rebel army as captain with a company of mountaineers. The wife and family were well supplied with honey and molasses—home made. Every man went to get his canteen filled with either honey or molasses. The old lady, wife of the rebel captain, pled with the boys to let her sorghum alone, but they paid no attention to her and jostled about the faucet of the barrel, arguing whose turn came next to fill his canteen. The old lady began to inquire after the general in command. The boys pointed out the seediest-looking soldier in the lot as the general and he gave positive orders to let the sorghum alone. Of course no one paid any attention to him and the canteens were being filled as fast as molasses would run in winter. The old lady finally hunted out the right man, Lieutenant Skinner, and she pled with him to save her sorghum. The lieutenant yielded to her supplications. He walked up to the barrel and with a wink of the eye and a nod of the head ordered the boys in a stern voice not to take *all* that sorghum, and the boys responded that they were not going to take all and kept right on filling. The boys left some sticking to the sides of the barrel when they were finished.

We scouted over the mountains into the valley beyond and picked up a goodly number of deserters and captured quite a number who were home on a furlough, and returned to camp on the night of the third day and found the old camp deserted and the regiment gone. We camped on the same old ground, built up large camp fires and had a pleasant evening talking over our mountain exploits and scenery. John Bond and William Murt-felt[3] were along, both good boys, and each had his peculiarities. Bond had been taught the great scripture lesson of an "eye for an eye and a tooth for a tooth," but he was full of fun and eternally into mischief. Billy had a peculiar awkward turn in many things and was a little peculiar in telling a story. If the story was a funny one Billy would have a hearty laugh at the conception before his auditors could know anything about what was coming. Billy had a conception of a very funny little story. Just what it was about is still a secret as he never told it. But it was probably about some mountain nymph dipping snuff or some adventure in the mountains. Billy commenced in his usual way with a he, he, he, he, ha, ha, ha. Ha-a-a-a-eh! Bond was Billy's principal auditor. He stepped up and gave Billy a nudge with his elbow in the ribs, remarking at the same time, "For God's sake Billy, make signs, make signs, we will understand you better." Billy's mirth was turned to instant indignation and his big fist swung around a circle and Bond was nearly overcome with the concussion. In less time than I can write it both boys were on the war path and each had unlimbered his batteries. Bond had been educated in the streets of Oregon, [Illinois,] and every time he fired his fist at Billy the target was hit and Billy's feet were soon on a level with his head. Billy fell within a foot of a hole filled with water, a hole dug out to form into clay, out of which to build mud chimneys, and now filled with water from the recent rains. Bond was too much for Billy, although the smaller of the two. Bond saw the hole of water and centered his forces on ducking Billy head first into the water. Billy's head was just over the edge on the sure road to the bottom when I caught Bond by the collar and pulled him off. Bond made one desperate struggle to free himself and gave Billy one souse. He begged of me to let him send Billy to the bottom just once. In the course of an hour their angry passions had pretty well subsided and the next morning they were joking each other good-naturedly about the merits and demerits of their fight.

DECEMBER 14, 1863, CAPERTON'S FERRY, ALABAMA

December brought winter—Southern winter—upon us. It froze a little nearly every night and the sky was overcast with clouds nearly every day. Sometimes it would snow a little then rain a great deal, and the atmosphere had a damp cold chill to it much of the time. Occasionally, however, there would be a real pleasant sunshiny day.

Our scouting party came up with the regiment at Caperton's Ferry, Alabama, on the Tennessee River near Stevenson. On the south side of the river was rebel territory where their scouts and bushwhackers roamed at large and on the north side was ours, and "no rebel need apply." We found the regiment in what appeared to be a village of small log houses— houses without glass windows. The regiment had gone into winter quarters, to all appearance. It appeared that a cavalry regiment had previously camped there, and thinking that they would stay during the cold weather until spring, they went to work and built log houses or huts. They were built of small logs or from second-growth timber, logs as large as a stovepipe and larger. The houses were of different sizes and shapes to suit the design of the "architect." They were usually large enough to contain four persons each, with two bunks, one above the other, made of poles for slats. At one end was a door and at the other end a fireplace made on the mountaineer plan, consisting of green sticks split from green timber, each stick of about two feet in length laid up like a rail pen, plastered thick with clay mud on the inside. These chimneys burned nicely and soldiers could cook over them in real Southern style. The door consisted of a hole in one end of the cabin and a white tent cloth hung over the opening, which answered for the double purpose of door and window. Enough light would shine through the white cloth to lighten the room. The regiment that had occupied these houses or huts was not as large as ours and there was not enough to accommodate all of our regiment. But we were equal to the emergency. Believing, like our predecessors, that we would stay all winter we went to enlarging and improving. Additions were built, rude tables made to eat on, cupboards for dishes, poles for bunks, etc., etc. One man of a squad of four would chop down the trees and cut the logs; another would rig some sort of a harness for his saddle horse and "snake" in the logs, while two others would notch and fit the logs to place in the buildings. When the sides were high enough most of them were covered with our tent cloths, and as a rule they made very good roofing and in addition let in the light. Some of them, however, were covered with the "shake." In the centre was usually a short table made after the Fourth of July picnic pattern, only very short, just long enough for two to sit on either side and no room for visitors. During the evenings the men sat around these tables and read, told stories, or played cards.

Many of the men of the 92d were great readers, but there were two great obstacles in the way. First it was difficult to get a great deal of matter to read, and second it was difficult to get proper light for the evening. We had some candles furnished us, but not near enough. I had previously written home and just received a self-instructor German reading book. I fancied that I could graduate from that log hut by spring a thoroughbred Dutchman. But I needed more light. Necessity was the mother of invention and I remembered what I had seen my mother do in the poverty-stricken times of an early day in Illinois. I attended to frying the meat—sow belly—and at each frying I poured a portion of the clear fat into an empty oyster can. From this fat I made what the boys called a "betty," to give the light sought for. I tore a piece of the cotton lining from my coat, twisted it into a wick and buried it in the lard, one end projecting above the surface. This made a fair light, but not brilliant. George Hare (who could speak the German language) and I had a reading and spelling match every night by ourselves, but it was all Dutch. The other two boys wrote letters, read papers, told stories, or played at such games as best suited their fancy. Other boys in other huts were performing in like manner. One boy made phrenology a specialty and could read character almost equal to the best traveling lectures.

While encamped here we got a new supply of the seven-shooter Spencer repeating rifles, all new from the shop. There was enough for the whole regiment, so that those who had old Spencers could turn them over to the ordnance department and have a new and complete outfit. In addition to this we received new cavalry saddles of all different patterns and shapes. There was a vast difference between the two kinds of saddles. A cavalry saddle is made light, out of wood, and covered with raw hide. Wooden stirrups with a great leather toe-pad prevent the foot from slipping through too far. If a man falls off or is shot off his horse his foot can never be caught in the stirrup so as to drag him. There are three straps attached to the front and three to the back. There are times when a well-girted saddle will save a man's life. The citizen saddle was most always found wanting amidst great excitement.

The 92d was now one of the best armed and equipped regiments in the service and it was quite evident that thereafter the 92d would be placed where rebels were easy to get at and we would have an opportunity to use our superior guns.

Chaplain Cartwright laid the cornerstone, or rather corner log of a log church. He proposed to have divine services every Sabbath and prayer meetings between during our stay in winter quarters. Everybody loved the chaplain and would do most anything for him, whether Christian or not. He had a good force of volunteer workers at his log structure, and working with the chaplain with ax and levers. Fellows that could hardly utter a full sentence without a string of oaths were assisting and would swear just out of the hearing of the chaplain, while withholding in his immediate presence.

DECEMBER 25, 1863, BROWNSVILLE, ALABAMA

A soldier is like a cog in the wheel to a great machine, there is a power somewhere that sets it in motion and whenever started he must go, whether he wants to or not, whether the machine is guided by a wise man or a fool, it is go he must.

The 92d broke up camp on the 18th of December and passed nearly half the winter in the saddle and camping nights in the open air, all of which time the ground was either frozen or saturated with sleet and melting snow. To ride all day over muddy roads or in a snow storm, rain storm, or in a damp, freezing and thawing atmosphere, then camping in the open air at night, is more of a task and strain on a man's power of endurance than one could easily imagine. The 92d always watched the lay of the country, and where timber could be found by traveling several miles farther we always went to it, to camp, knowing full well that a little protection was better than none. Second-growth timber was always preferred to tall timber. The small trees made a heavier and thicker foliage overhead, and were more convenient to tie the horses to. When once a camp ground for the night was selected each man found a tree to tie his horse to. Water and feed was the next duty then wood for a fire to cook by. Rails always made the best camp fires and the easiest to cook over. The Southern fields were all fenced with old-fashioned rail worm fence. The slaves could split rails and lay worm fences, which was the height of their skill in fence building. If there was a fence near, it was carried immediately into camp by the men; each little squad bringing in a pile large enough to do for the night, just the same as a farmer's son in Illinois brings into the house at night the night's wood as part of his chores. Each little squad then built a camp fire out of rails; not a large hot fire, because no cooking could be done over such, but a long narrow fire, the length of the rails. Water for coffee is brought and set over the fires, resting on the burning rails. Salt pork is fried in a sheet-iron frying pan. Hard tack is dipped into cold water and then fried in the fat left after the meat is cooked. A rubber blanket for a table cloth is spread upon the ground. Four tin plates, four tin cups, and a knife and fork (if they were not lost) completed the table furniture. Four men sat around upon the ground and ate fried meat and hard tack and drank coffee. But for the sake of variety in the meal some of the hard tack was fried in the fat. Some of it was fried more and some less, which was considered pie and cake. That which was fried hard was cake and that which was soft was pie, apple, peach, or cream, as best suited the imagination of the soldier. After supper each man's plate and cup sometimes got a cold water rinse and went back into his haversack ready for the next meal. Beds were then made upon the frozen or wet ground with a rubber blanket. The next morning the horses were cared for, the same meal repeated, and on we went.

For a long time during the severest winter ever witnessed in the South, the regiment was floating about with no particular object in the movement, like a ship at sea without compass, rudder, or keel. With all the light of subsequent events and "after knowledge" it is almost impossible to find the slightest traces of any sensible object or design in all the movements made; we were after no enemy, but simply traveling from point to point, receiving orders from some headquarters high in authority, but mighty low in wisdom.

On the morning of the 18th of December we reluctantly abandoned our snug little log huts and marched under orders from Bridgeport; camped at night; waited all next day for our teams to waddle through the muddy roads and catch up. We camped the second night at Bridgeport and then crossed the Tennessee River on the pontoon bridge to the southeast, being the third time the regiment had crossed the river here, traveling in that direction each time. We camped that night in a peculiar valley of the Raccoon Mountains, called Hog Jaw Valley. This was the point ordered to and we thought perhaps we would stay awhile and we began to fix up quarters a little. We had just begun to get comfortably situated when we got orders to go to Huntsville, Alabama. Huntsville is about one hundred miles west. Accordingly after a two days' tarry in Hog Jaw Valley, December 20 we retraced our steps, recrossed the Tennessee on the pontoon bridge, and camped at night on the old grounds, deserted only four days previously. From here we passed slowly on our journey for Huntsville. There was a large tract of country here shaped like a flat-iron. The point was Nashville, Tennessee. Two railroads branch out from there and form the two sides of the iron-shaped piece, the one on the right striking Huntsville, and the one on the left Stevenson. Another railroad from Memphis came to Huntsville, running east on through Stevenson, forming the broad end of the flat-iron spaced tract. The roads on all of these three lines were in our hands and the great armies were distributed along some portions of these roads for winter quarters. In our journey to Huntsville we must cross the broad end of the flat-iron, one hundred miles in width. The broad end of the flat lay in Alabama and the north end in Tennessee.

On the 23d we started early, passed through Stevenson and traveled twenty-five miles to make seventeen, and camped at night at Bellefonte. This town, with the exception of two houses, was deserted, notwithstanding it was a county seat. The court house was burned, but the jail was yet standing. We started early on the 24th as we had no feed for our horses. About ten o'clock we came to a field of corn by the roadside and we stopped and fed our horses and gathered corn from the field for that purpose.

We camped at night in the Tennessee River Valley, having passed two nearly deserted towns, Scottsboro and Larkinsville. A few live hogs were seen along our journey, and some men fell out of the ranks and the hogs "fell by the wayside" and sprang upon the points of bayonets and brought forth several hundred pounds of pork. But some of the hogs "fell among thieves" and the colonel was ready to "spring up and choke them" but they hid the pork away and the colonel called up the officers that night and lectured them like a Dutch uncle for lack of discipline; but the boys cooked and ate the fresh meat all the same. It was Christmas Eve and to eat nothing but sow belly and hard tack on that evening would never do.

As we sat around our camp fires that night we talked over old times on Christmas Eves in days gone by, when we were converts to the Santa Claus theory and used to hang out stockings by the windows at night so that the great lover of children could come down the chimney while we were asleep in our little beds and fill them with the choicest of presents. We wondered what they were all doing up in "God's Country" as we called it. If we were to hang up our stockings that night the most we could hope for would be to get the stockings back.

Christmas came and we were again in the saddle. About noon we came to a little railroad town called Brownsville. Colonel Wilder met us here and we gathered around the depot and called on him for a speech, but speech making was not his forte; he said enough, however, to show that he appreciated the esteem and respect the men all had for him.

Colonel Wilder had received a lot of eatables for a Christmas dinner for his regiment, sent by their friends from Indiana, but the regiment was not there, so the colonel gave the provisions to the 92d and we spread them out and had a Christmas dinner sitting on the ground "way down in Alabama."

While we sat upon the ground eating the choice victuals prepared by the kind-hearted people of Indiana, the clouds were deepening in the west as though a great storm would soon be upon us.

DECEMBER 30, 1863, HUNTSVILLE, ALABAMA

Winter traveling, when the weather is cold, damp, and chilly, dulls the intellect of the soldier so that he observes less, and even the diary is very brief and incomplete.

The central idea of a soldier is to make himself as comfortable as possible. When a man in Illinois gets out on a cold day, or is caught in the cold, chilly rain and spends the day he manages with extra exertions to weather the storm with but little apparent waste of his vital powers. He goes to a comfortable home at night, takes a good square meal, sleeps in a warm bed in a house sheltering him from the storm. The waste of a man's physical powers are quickly restored and he does not mind it much. But with us it was different. We were always in the storms, exposed to all the moistures from the atmosphere during the day or ground during the night. There was no chance for the vital energies to rest where the waste could be restored. A sensitive man can easily detect in himself the lack of energy and the lack of appreciation of the new scenes, the odds and ends of different classes of people in a different climate. The soldier centers his weak energies on keeping his clothing as dry as possible, plans how to make the best bed he can, how to cook and get the best meal he can, and how to care for his horse so that he will hold his flesh. All other subjects are but secondary affairs and many soldiers overlooked many things that under more favorable circumstances would have been scrutinized with much interest.

After finishing our Christmas dinner we proceeded on west and camped a few miles to the east of Huntsville, Alabama. To my notion it is by far the prettiest city we have found in the whole South thus far. A large beautiful spring bubbles from white quicksand in nearly the centre of the city and forms a creek. This spring has a little dam. The water falls upon a wheel and the wheel is attached to pumping apparatus which forces the

water to all parts of the city. We passed through the city and camped on the
west side, and at once proceeded to fix up our camp, thinking that now we
could spend the winter in this place.

On Sunday many of the men had a curiosity to go to church in
Huntsville. Many of them watched and heard preaching and singing with
female voices just as they used to at home, but something seemed new and
rare with us now.

We had not heard from home in a long time. The mails were not running regular. I wrote a letter home more for amusement than anything else,
as there is not much chance of its ever getting there.

The country all about Huntsville had what might be called an unlim-
ited supply of corn. The cotton fields had largely been planted to corn with
an eye to feeding the rebel armies. The crop was an unusually large one and
had not been gathered. The country all about was cut up into large plantations and the small fry or poor white trash had all been crowded back on to
the hills and mountains. Each plantation looked like a village. One large
stately mansion for the owner, one good business office for the overseer,
and the balance were log cabins for the slaves and barns and stables for the
horses and mules. The log cabins were nearly every one of precisely the
same pattern on each plantation. One overseer would get the plan of a
cabin and build them all on the plantation alike. They were simply log
houses about 16 x 20; one door, about two windows and a great fireplace
at one end. There was sometimes a loft overhead. The negroes were paired
off in some sort of married relation, performed by a negro minister, without license or record. They remained together as husband and wife until the
master saw fit to sell the husband or wife and then they were separated and
the one left behind could marry again. Whenever a planter wanted to raise
a little extra money to send his own daughter off on a wedding tour, he
could sell a husband or wife to be shipped to the New Orleans slave market for the purpose of raising the necessary funds.

Huntsville was a healthy location and raising negroes for the slave market was a very lucrative business. A young negro, old enough to be taken
from his mother, was worth about $500, while a full-grown healthy negro
man was worth $1,500, and if an extra good one with a kind disposition he
was worth $2,000. Women were worth from $800 to $1,400, according to
their capacity to work and raise their children. All these various points were
carefully weighed and considered in getting at the value or price of the
slave. These different points were as carefully considered by Southern

planters as they are among breeders of short-horn cattle, Norman horses, or Berkshire hogs, in Illinois.

To estimate what a man is worth in Alabama they estimate his personal property and real estate—slaves and land.

The Southern slave driver collects his slaves into log prisons, locks them in until he gets a load and then ships. He does not drive them loose into a car like the Illinois man does his hogs and cattle, but he handcuffs them into squads, from two to a dozen in a squad. One man's hand is locked to another, and another and another, etc. When they arrive at the New Orleans market they are again imprisoned, fed well, washed, combed, and barbered up in the best possible manner. Their clothes are brushed, shoes blackened, and the driver then goes among them, looks them over carefully, makes everyone stand erect, cheer up, walk lively, and put on as young a look as possible. The driver looks each slave over and places the youngest age upon him that would be possible to make a purchaser believe, and then tells the slave that that is his age. And he further tells him that if any man asks his age to always give that age, and if he fails to do it he will tie him to the whipping post and flog him till the blood runs. When the buyer comes and looks them over, inquires for the age and the driver gives it, and then if he inquires of the slave he gives the same age the driver did and sticks to it. When the whole batch is closed out the driver goes back for another cargo.

JANUARY 1, 1864, ELKMONT SPRINGS, TENNESSEE

We remained four days in Huntsville and fixed up our camp with stick and mud chimneys for a stay, thinking we had traveled about as much as would be required without any apparent object, but we were doomed to disappointment. The holidays were not over before we were again in the saddle traveling north.

During our short stay here we were out of salt. Accordingly Co. K, under the command of Major Woodcock, was sent out to forage for salt. To forage for anything in the army was to go and hunt for it, and it made no difference where it was found or who claimed it, we took it. Sometimes this was called confiscating, and sometimes foraging. Some of the boys said that they were glad we had the two words foraging and confiscating, for they never intended to steal a thing as long as they were in Dixie, because they found anything they wanted. All they had to do was forage or confiscate it. Under this version of terms I feel warranted in saying that the 92d had not a thief on the muster rolls.

The major, with Co. K, went out in search of salt. He had word from some source that on a certain large plantation there was a quantity of salt. When he arrived at the plantation he was met on the portico by a young lady, who greeted him with as much feeling as though she had met her father. She was a Northern lady from Massachusetts, and had come down there previous to the war to teach school, and after the war commenced she could not return. For her own personal safety she had feigned to be a rebel in sympathy and had as a consequence fared well. She longed to hear from her own native land and would gladly return if an opportunity offered. She hastily told the major her story and asked him if it would be possible to get a letter home. The major told her to prepair [sic] one and he would be post boy and see that it reached its destination. At thus juncture the old planter came upon the scene and the major told him that he had been sent there for salt. The planter declared that there was no salt on the plantation and gave his word as a Southern gentleman that there was none. The school teacher joined in with the planter and gave the major "particular fits." She told him that she was ashamed of him and all of his men for coming around to private houses, ransacking the plantation, hunting for what did not belong to him. She gave the major a good sound scolding in a similar way, all in the presence of the planter, which pleased him much. The lady stepped into the house and into her own private room and prepared a letter, while the major and his men went from building to building in search of salt. The planter declared in the most positive terms that there was none. All the buildings had been searched except one little ash house, which had the door locked. The planter unlocked it to save the door and there sat several barrels of ashes. The men were just leaving it when one man ran his hand down deep into the ashes and brought up salt. The old planter was crestfallen enough and begged the major to leave him some of it, but it was all loaded into wagons. The planter pretended that this was all he had, although the house had not been searched. The teacher came upon the scene and told them to search no more for there was no salt in the house nor chamber. The major proceeded to the chamber and there found a room well stored with a large supply. While this was being removed the teacher slipped her letter into the hand of the major, at the same time giving him tongue lashes as a woman only knows how, all the while they were in the presence of the planter. At her request enough salt was left to supply the wants of the family for a long time. When the major returned to camp a proposition was made to raise money, take the lady from her exile, and send her home, but a move ahead broke up the project.

On December 31, the last day of that year, in the midst of a cold, sleety freezing rain, the 92d broke up camp, got into saddle and again was on its winter ramblings. We camped that night on a thick wood in the great Huntsville Valley, eight miles north of the city. We camped on Judge Hammond's plantation. It was a bad night to camp out. The rain turned to snow and it froze and got colder rapidly. It was New Year's Eve and watch night, and many of the men watched until midnight because they dreaded to lie down to sleep upon the wet and freezing ground. Many of the Christian soldiers knelt in silent prayer by their own camp fires as they were wont to do on those holiday nights at home in watch meeting. It snowed during the night and the timber looked as though the ground was well strewn with logs. Each man as he lay under his blanket looked like a log covered with snow. It was New Year's but it was hard to believe that it was really a Happy New Year.

After breakfast several companies were ordered to scout for horses and mules that day and to continue traveling in a northern direction and be with the regiment at night. It was very cold and freezing rapidly. The streams were bridged with ice, not strong enough to bear up our animals and consequently in crossing numerous streams our horses would break through and the ice would cut their legs until they bled. They soon got so they seemed to dread a stream of water whenever we approached. We went from plantation to plantation, searching every barn and stable for horses and mules, and whenever we found one that was serviceable we took it without ceremony, except Captain Smith gave to each planter a voucher that he got so many horses and mules or both, and years after the war is over, if the planter proved that he was a Union man he could get his pay, and if not his pay was sacrificed. Most every one we got horses or mules from were genuine rebels, except two. They had every appearance of being Union men and did not seem to feel bad to lose their animals, because they believed the government was in need of them and that in due time they would get their pay. But the old rebel planters looked blue enough to see their stock going to replenish the army of their enemies. Sometimes they would get word of our coming and send the darkies into the timber with their horses. But the Southerners were not cunning. They were unused to snow, while our men were all used to it, had hunted some in Illinois and tracked the deer through the snow. When we came to a barn or stable if there were no horses or mules we looked for tracks in the snow and easily followed the trail and found the horses tied to trees in the thick timber. We caught several bunches of horses in that way during the day, and the planters did not get any voucher for them, as they had in all such cases declared they had none. That night we arrived in camp with sixteen horses and mules.

We camped that night at Elkmont Springs, a Southern watering place at a mineral spring. It is just over the state line in Tennessee. It was a summer resort for Southerners, and in winter it was almost entirely deserted. One family left to take care of the buildings. Some of the men camped in these empty buildings and some out of doors as usual. I tried camping in a building that night, and never tried it again on a cold night. I learned a new lesson that night in camp life. I lay within a few feet of a large blazing fire in the fireplace, and although I was in a pretty good building I could not keep warm. I would begin to shiver in an hour after lying down, notwithstanding I had all my clothes on and blankets over and under me. I would warm before the fire, lie down and try again, but I could not keep warm. Those who slept out of doors on the frozen ground slept comfortably, while those in a house shivered all night. The secret was this. Those who slept on the ground with one or two blankets under them never have not a particle of cold wind rising to carry away the heat of the body, while those who sleep on the floor of a house when it is a little elevated from the ground and no tight walls underneath, the cold air is constantly rising up through the floor and carries away all the bodily heat, and the floor sleeper is shivering in a short time, while the ground sleeper is warm and comfortable. Several men froze their hands and feet during the day. The weather grew colder and colder with regularity.

JANUARY 10, 1864, PULASKI, TENNESSEE

On the second of January, at Elkmont Springs, after a bitter cold night we hovered about our camp fires until twelve o'clock noon before we again took the saddle. During our night's camping here, one negro boy, an officer's servant, who went into the fields to get corn and fodder for the officer's horse, being unused to and unacquainted with such cold weather froze both arms and both legs so badly that all had to be amputated.

The second of January was cloudy and cold and the weather settled down colder. We camped at dark at a place called Prospect, Tennessee. We lingered about our camp fires the third until noon, and again wandered along without any particular object or place to go to, except to keep going, like a lot of wandering gypsies telling fortunes.

We crossed Elk River on a pontoon bridge just completed. Troops were scattered all along our route. Many regiments were re-enlisting, as their time had nearly expired for which they had enlisted. It was feared that the army would be greatly reduced in the spring on account of the fact that a very large number of troops would have completed their three years' term of enlistment in the spring. To obviate this difficulty the government had offered all those soldiers, whose time was so near expired, $300 each as a bounty if they would re-enlist, and in addition to this each soldier might have a furlough to go home and spend a portion of the winter with friends and have free transportation both ways. There were many regiments that accepted the offer, being a few in each who would not re-enlist, and these few were left behind to look after and take care of the traps and luggage, while the balance went home and had their fun. These remnants of regiments were scattered all along here and there and everywhere.

We camped that night within eight miles of Pulaski, Tennessee. On the fourth we managed to get within half a mile of Pulaski. It was very cold and a "winter's fog that will freeze a dog" set in. It was too cold to travel farther. We were frozen in, or frozen out; we could hardly tell which. Our clothing was prepared for a warm climate and we had arctic weather. Had we been dressed in furs and robes for overcoats, such as is used in arctic regions, we would not have thought much about the cold. But here we were wandering about in ordinary clothing and the thermometer reaching seven and eight degrees below zero. We had traveled until the cold prevented us from traveling more, and the ground was frozen, so we could get no mud with which to build the mud and stick chimney. We managed to get our "pup tents" staked down so that they would keep the snow off from overhead when it snowed; but these had no capacity for warmth whatever. There was from six to ten inches space between the eaves and the ground, and one or both gables were open. To live out doors and keep warm under such circumstances drafted upon a man's skill of doing well with but little or nothing. We stayed here eight days waiting to freeze to death or get a chance to ramble about. While here the coldest days of the winter passed over us, and during the eight cold nights that we were here I never slept cold or suffered with the cold during the night any more than I had on the first shiver on entering a bed in a cold room at home. But I do know that I was an exception to the general rule. Every night there was a constant stirring of men crawling out of their blankets and raking up the camp fires at all hours of the night. They would stand around these fires warming one side while the other was cold, nearly freezing. Then the cold side would be turned to the fire and the warm side would soon get cold. They would stand about the camp fires and get as warm as they could and crawl under their blankets again. It was not unusual for some to get up and warm several times during the night.

Self-preservation is the first great law of nature and I determined to preserve No. 1 to the best of my ability. There was no mother to care for me now. Every man had the simple duty of taking care of himself or freezing to death, and if his choice was in favor of the former it meant business. My bunk mate and myself went out into a corn field and loaded our horses with corn fodder—leaves stripped from the stalk and tied into bundles. The slaves strip it off in the fall, tie it into bundles and make little stacks of it all through the cornfields, and it stands there until needed for feed, when it is hauled in. We packed our horses with this fodder and carried it to camp. We took this fodder and carefully packed it on the ground in the tent and made our bed on top. Only one blanket was necessary for the bottom sheet and the rest we had over us. We buttoned our overcoats together and made a blanket cover of them also. We slept with all our clothing on except our hats. We covered up our heads and lay "spoon fashion." We each kept open a little breathe hole to get air. No cold air ever comes up from the ground, and after a few moments we were as warm as two kittens in the chimney corner; and to tell the truth, I do not know that I ever slept warmer at home. There were many others who took much pains during the day to provide sleeping places at night. All such were tolerably comfortable.

There was another thing during this cold spell that attracted my attention. We had considerable fat meat while here. A negro, Ben by name, had been employed as company cook, and his cooking was so poor that the men preferred to cook for themselves. Ben himself came near starving to death on his own cooking. I had a nice skillet of lard left after frying meat for dinner. On one of the coldest nights Ben came and wanted the lard. I asked him what he wanted to cook with it. He replied that he wanted to eat it. I gave him a pint of lard and he ate it clear without any other kind of food with it, and then wished I had some more for him. I asked him if he was in the habit of eating lard. He said, "No, only when it is awful cold like now." I discovered that my own appetite was becoming daily more keen for fat meat, fatty food. Fat meat that I could not eat all heretofore I now had a keen relish for and ate large quantities. By a little observation I found that all the men ate their fat meat with a relish and scarcely a scrap was ever cast aside. We all took food in large quantities. I had read in a book when a boy that men who went into the arctic regions frequently drank train oil. The thought almost made me sick at the time, but now I thought of it and really felt as though I would like a little of it myself. Nature tries to overcome all exposures of the body and build up where it is weak. To keep the body warm, fatty substance seemed to produce the most heat, and our appetites were changing in that direction.

Those regiments that were allowed to remain in camp stationary had built the mud and stick chimneys and arranged by many devices little houses of different patterns, all using their tents for shingles. These little kennels with a bright blazing fire in one end were quite comfortable, but the useless roaming orders of the 92d debarred us from such privileges.

JANUARY 16, 1864, HUNTSVILLE, ALABAMA

On the 11th of January, while at Pulaski, Tennessee, the weather moderated, became pleasant, and the next day, the 12th, we again took to the saddle and were off. But where were we going now? We were like the tramp in search of work. He got a job of moving a pile of stone from one point to another. When the job was completed he went to his employer and enquired, "What next?" "Move them back," was the reply. We had traveled north from Huntsville to Pulaski, and now we could go back, so back we went. We were three days on the journey, traveling over the same road we went up on. We established a permanent camp on the east side of the city of Huntsville, about one mile out, in a beautiful grove.

Although we were in a beautiful country, yet there was something wrong among the regimental brigade and division commanders. The army was undergoing a reorganization. Army officers are not unlike politicians, where each is ambition and want to get to the top, or as near as possible. Each colonel wanted to be promoted to brigadier general, and each brigadier general wanted to be promoted to division general, etc. Each commander wanted the best armed and equipped regiments and more of them. Many of the officers, although their motives were concealed from the men to the best of their ability, acted on the general principle of self-promotion first and save the country afterwards. There were a few noble exceptions to this rule, but the number was not astonishingly large. Human nature is the same in war as well as in peace. To secure a promotion it is difficult to tell how much an officer would secretly sacrifice to accomplish his ends. There was no voting or discussions among the soldiers on these promotions or re-organizations. Soldiers had nothing whatever to do with it. There were simply cogs to a wheel in a great army machine. These changes were all subject to appointment by the general in command of the whole army. And such a general in such a time is besieged like a new president appointing a new cabinet and other officers. All that occurred in this stretch of time among officers will never all be written or known, but there was wrangling and hard feelings and jealousy and sourness all around. It was apparent to the dullest soldier.

We had scarcely got our camp fixed up comfortably when the colonel ordered on a line guard around the regiment. What it was for was hard to tell. We had not had a line guard before for ten months.[4] Every soldier was a prisoner. No man can go beyond those walls without a permit from the man who superintends the prison. The wall that encloses the prison is a wall of soldiers with loaded guns in their hands with instructions to halt any man who attempts to pass in or out, and if he does not halt to shoot him of course. To keep up a line guard takes about one-fifth of all the able-bodied men in the regiment. The line is kept up night and day, through sunshine and shower, snow or rain, heat or cold. Every man has to take his turn in standing on line guard. The object of such an order was received as an insult by the men. It was regarded as utterly useless. There were heavy picket lines way out beyond, which were kept up by each regiment furnishing part. All the regiments were inside the picket lines, and our guard line was regarded as the sourness of some disappointed officer somewhere in command. General Crook had command of all the cavalry forces lying about there and his name was cursed on every hand. The effects of keeping up such useless line guards are far-reaching and the results are never all known. When a hundred men are kept up and out in all kinds of weather, night and day, in weather well calculated to breed coughs, colds, consumption, rheumatism, fever, and all diseases that flesh is heir to, it may be more easily understood why the men of the regiment felt indignant. None of the members of the 92d ever felt that way in standing picket in any kind of weather, because there was a necessity. But a line guard there was no more use for than there was in greasing water that it might run down hill. Men felt that they had come to fight the rebels and not waste their health in standing on a useless line guard to please the fancy or whim of any officer of either high or low rank.

The first night the guard was put on the very old nick was to pay. Shortly after dark a dog came trotting along and the guard told him to halt, and the dog did not obey orders and the soldiers blazed away and then another fired at the tail of the rapidly departing dog. A rabbit crossed another fellow's best without halting and it was fired at. Another fellow treated a mouse in a similar way. To add mischief to the fracas some fellows threw a bunch of cartridges into a camp fire and then hid. Every time one exploded it cracked as loud as a musket, and the ashes flew, and the charcoal danced all about. The colonel got mad and called up more guards. I was one among the new levy of guards. About half of the regiment was now guarding the other half. Strict orders were issued against shooting, but in spite of all that could be done some fellows would crawl out of their tents and dump cartridges into the fire and then quickly get back to the tent before they commenced exploding. In a few minutes there would be an uproar in a camp fire and no one dared go near it. There would be a general chuckle all over the regiment. Patrols were sent all over the camp; guards watching for parties throwing cartridges into the fire, but no one was caught and every now and then the firing would break out in a new place. It was long after midnight before the men would give it up. After they had expressed their contempt for such orders in that way they all yielded as cheerful obedience to the order as circumstances would permit. As men in the army lose all individuality they have nothing to say as to what they will do or will not do. They are all subject to the order of some one or two men, and it makes no difference how foolish or absurd an order may be, or how narrow a gauge the officer's mind may run on, his orders are all binding and must be enforced. To openly refuse subjects the soldier to severe punishment, sometimes with death and every form of disgrace.

CHAPTER 7

Bang Up Against
a Whole Brigade

January – April 1864

JANUARY 25, 1864, SWEET WATER, ALABAMA

We stayed in our new camp at Huntsville for nine days. In the meantime the weather became fine. On January 23d we received orders to take the saddle for a long scout. We knew this meant business. We did not break up our camp, but left a few men in care of all extra luggage. We traveled west on a parallel line with the Tennessee River, on the north side. Some of the time we were close to and some of the time far from the river. We passed through Athens about eight o'clock in the morning of the second day.

Athens was naturally a beautiful town, situated on the Nashville & Decatur Railroad, about fifteen miles north of the latter. The beauty of the business part was spoiled as the heart of the town had been burned. It was reported that when General Turchen[1] first entered the town with his brigade the rebels fought him on the streets and the citizens fired from the windows at the Yankees. After the rebels were whipped and driven out the burly Turchen is reported to have said: "Boys, I suts mine eyes for shust one hour. I sees nothing." When he opened his eyes again the city was on fire and hopelessly ruined. The detached buildings in which families dwelt were not fired.

As soon as we left the picket lines about Athens we were on disputed ground, over which bands of either side roamed at will and a fight might come on without a moment's notice. We rode hard all day, still keeping in a westerly direction, meeting no rebels, except here and there we ran down some rebel who was home on a leave of absence. Our presence was a surprise to them and sometimes at first sight a rebel would break for tall timber, but three of four men on horses would soon bring him in.

We camped at night in a little crossroad town called Rogersville. We had the bulk of the old Wilder brigade of mounted infantry, every man now well mounted and armed with Spencer repeating rifles, and we felt bold and confident and were not afraid to meet the rebels anywhere, in fact longed to meet them. A good solid picket line was put out for the night and the troops camped with all proper precaution. The officers of this brigade were very good on this point. It would have almost been an impossibility to ever get a surprise or ever have driven us into an ambuscade when on the march, as both sides of the road were scoured with an advance guard before the main columns ever passed. This was always done over every inch of the ground that the command traveled over. And more than one ambuscade was avoided that might have swept us from the face of the earth.

On the morning of the third day we were up and off early, and traveled rapidly in the same westerly direction. The 92d had the advance of the brigade and Co. I was on the advance guard. About noon the advance guard came to a crossroad which led down to the Tennessee River to Bane Bridge Ferry, about one mile distant. At the four corners was a rebel cavalry picket post. As soon as Co. I came in sight shots were exchanged and Captain Becker ordered the charge and away went Co. I charging after the rebels at break-neck speed, firing as they ran. The regiment galloped on after Co. I to back it up if it should meet more than it could attend to. In the mile race to the river, Co. I wounded several and captured three and drove the rest around behind a bluff fronting to the river. In the river was the ferry boat, which hurried back with its load, and on the other bank stood rebel General Roddy's[2] command behind trees and in trenches, ready to shoot the first man who came to the river's edge. The rebels that had been chased could not re-cross, but by getting under the bluff it would compel us to charge down the narrow valley at the foot of the bluff exposed to the volleys of Roddy's whole command on the other shore. At first it was thought that we could make a quick charge, take them out and hurry back and get from under the fire from the other shore, but a second thought brought the sensible conclusion that the game would cost more than it was worth. We got up close enough to shoot all their horses, exchange a few shots across the river just for fun and then left them to their fate and went on. The advance guard was then enlarged to three companies, I, F, and B. The latter being my company I had the fun of being on the advance and was really anxious to get a hand in, but before night I had all that kind of fun I wanted.

Our little episode at the ferry had warmed our blood a little too much. Every man felt keen for a fight. We rode rapidly to the front and traveled too fast, and did it unwittingly. We were nearly two miles ahead of the command. While we were hurrying along the road we came bang up against a whole brigade of rebel cavalry coming towards us. We wanted them to break and run so we could chase them and they wanted us to do the same thing, and before we knew what we were about we were engaged in one of the hottest battles that I ever saw. The rebels were stubborn and would not budge an inch. A large force of dismounted rebels got into a log house, log stable, and other outbuildings, knocked the chinking out and took deliberate aim. We all dismounted from our horses and sent them back with every fourth man as horse holder. This came near being a fatal mistake as we supposed the command was right at our heels, when in reality it was nearly two miles behind. We crawled up within close gunshot range of the house and barn and peppered away at every one we could get a sight at. We little deemed of what our real situation was. The firing from the house was rapid and accurate. We had to keep concealed behind fences and trees to keep from getting hit, as every rebel had a dead rest and good aim through the crevices in the log house. Nearly the first shot took Captain Smith[3] of my company through the arm. He cast his eyes down to the wound and paid no more attention to it except to occasionally snap the blood from his fingers that came trickling down.

Back of the house was a little hill and a ravine beyond. All of a sudden a yell rose from the ravine. At the same instant a roll of horses' hoofs mingled with the yell, as a great [rebel] cavalry charge came sweeping over the hill, revolvers in one hand and sabers in the other with full ten times our number. It was an awful moment for us. Our company was surrounded and the rebels were moving closer to us while Co. F was far in the opposite direction. Each man was now considering where the horses were but as one [Union] man saw our company through the trees he assumed we were making our retreat and cried out, "They are retreating" while he started to run, looking back as he started. At the first step to retreat he ran square against Captain Smith, whose practical eye and clear judgment had taken in the whole situation at a glance. Captain Smith was a hero in such an emergency. He raised his scabbard and struck the boy a stinging blow, and at the same time he cried out with one of his most determined and strenuous commands for "every man to stand to fight. I will chop down the first man that breaks to run." In my opinion that command saved the day for us. It sent a thrill of courageous gladness to every man's heart. The only thing we thought of was how much we could shoot. Co. F came to our side and pumped with all their might and Co. I from every tree, stump, or brush did its very best. It was not a volley but a continued roll from our repeating Spencers. By the time they got to Co. I the horsemen were so well shot off and wounded that the line faltered, reeled, then turned and fled, and we poured it into them until every horseman was either killed, wounded, or over the hill and out of sight. Our gun barrels were hot with such rapid shooting. We all stood erect while breaking the charge, and the fellows from the house were shooting at us all the time, taking deliberate aim, but we were so excited over the charge that we paid no attention to them. They hit and badly wounded some of our men, but the chargers did not hurt one of us.

There was a flock of sheep just behind us, between us and our horses. The sheep were stampeded and rushed head long down among our horses and stampeded them also, and in spite of all the horse holders could do they ran pell mell, carrying riders that stuck to the saddle and leaving those who fell off, and strung our overcoats, blankets, canteens, and saddles all along the road for a mile or two. The brigade heard the shooting and, seeing the stampeded horses, thought the rebels were just behind. Although their own horses were nearly stampeded, yet they jumped off them and formed in line of battle in a field on the run, and instead of being frightened at the commotion every man was keen for the fray. This line of battle was formed the quickest of any in the history of the brigade. But our continued fire at the house, still a half a mile ahead of them, told them of their error, and they gave three loud cheers to nerve us on, that aid was near. We next concealed ourselves and continued the fight with those in the house and stable, and other buildings, which were full of rebels, and there were many on the outside and behind. There was a large squad behind the house that took turns in shooting from a certain corner. They loaded behind the house and came in turns to the corner to shoot. I lay down upon the ground and rested my gun on the bottom rail. It so happened that every rebel who came to that corner to shoot exposed his whole body to my view. I drew a bead on every fellow that came. The first was a captain who came to look. I fired six shots in rapid succession and then my gun was empty. I rose up on to my knees to fill the magazine when a rebel spied my position and took a center shot. The ball entered a rail just in front, went through and pushed a sliver against me and stopped with the point of the slug ball pointing through but lodged. I got down quick. Just then the command came up keen for a fight, and they could not wait to shoot but charged across the garden and fields. The rebels turned and the whole command poured their continued roll of musketry at them as they ran. The rebels ran on foot and horseback pell mell through the woods over the hills, leaving everything in our possession. It was now nearly dark and I, for one, felt as though I had all the fight I wanted for one day.

JANUARY 30, 1864, COURIER POST, ALABAMA

After the battle of Sweet Water we took a look over the field to gather up the wounded. We found that we had killed fifteen rebels, captured twenty, and wounded about thirty more, making a total loss to the rebels of sixty-five to seventy-six, while we had less than seventy on the advance that did most of the fighting. Our three companies had six men wounded and none killed. Mr. Colehour of Co. I had just returned to the regiment, as he had been home recovering from a wound received at Chicamauga. It seemed to be his lot to be hit whenever shot at. The dead rebels lay scattered about here and there, but mostly around the log house and where the charge was made. I had a curiosity to see how things looked at the corner of the house where I had six splendid shots, and after the charge was over I went back by way of the house corner, and to my astonishment five men lay there, three dead and two mortally wounded. Captain Ingraham of the 4th Alabama Cavalry was among the number. He lived near Huntsville, and was known as a decent man and well liked by his Southern neighbors. One of the wounded rebels I really felt sorry for, notwithstanding the excitement. He was shot through the lower part of the abdomen, the ball passing on through the body, tearing the intestines, and leaving an opening through which they had protruded. When a man is wounded in that manner he will not usually live longer than from ten to twenty-four hours. On seeing this poor fellow so painfully and mortally wounded I hoped that it was not a ball from my gun that hit him. There were so many of us shooting that no one could tell who did the execution. There was only one thing that I felt certain of and that is that I shot once at Captain Ingraham and five times at others at the same corner. Lieutenant Colonel Wyans,[4] who led the charge and was in command, was killed in the charge. On his body was found marching orders. He had been directed to form a junction with those who were trying to cross the Tennessee River at Bane Bridge Ferry, and with them they were to attack Athens the next morning at daylight, where he was informed that a column of dismounted men, with artillery, would aid him—the last mentioned column—to cross the Tennessee River after dark, immediately south of Athens, the three columns striking Athens at daylight.

By means of these marching orders taken from the dead body of the rebel commander we were in possession of the rebel attack on Athens. In order to get the benefit of this information we must proceed straight back to Athens. Just how far it was back we did not know, only that we were two days' travel west of it. In order to reach Athens in time for the rebel raid on that town it would be necessary to travel all night and all day, and then we could quietly slip down to the river, capture the ferry boat after the rebels had all got over and away, and then go and take in the whole command at one fell swoop. Colonel Miller,[5] who was in command of our brigade decided upon that plan. We gathered up all the rebel wounded and carried them to rebel-sympathizing friends, left the dead to bury the dead, and started back. We were all very tired and our horses much jaded, but we knew there was no time to spare. We traveled all night, stopping only for supper and breakfast. While eating breakfast Phillips[6] came up with us coming direct from Athens. He left everything so quiet there that he could not believe that there was any danger of a rebel attack at that point. He succeeded in convincing Colonel Miller that there was none and again we counter-marched, going now west again towards Florence. We had not traveled long when a courier from Athens brought us word that the rebels had struck Athens at daylight and captured the town and done all the damage they could. Again we marched towards Athens. We reached there too late to do any good. The rebels, not being co-operated with and learning of our presence west of there, hurried back to the river and recrossed. The opportunity of bagging them had been lost. Had we continued as we first started we would, without doubt, have bagged the whole force.

By this means we had spent two days traveling backwards and forwards, like the horse in the fable that starved to death between two stacks of hay, not knowing which to choose.

It might be well to state here to those not acquainted with war that it is the most difficult thing in the world to ascertain what the enemy is doing and what he is going to do. The officers at the head do all the planning and directing, and the soldiers who do all the fighting under that plan don't even know where they are going or what the intention of a raid or scout is for, nor where it is going nor when it will return. This is done so that if a soldier is captured he cannot tell anything about it if he wanted to. In order to get information in regard to the enemy it is almost guess work.

After receiving the news by courier of the attack on Athens, we proceeded back to that point and thence to Huntsville, where we arrived in a two-day march. The cars arrived the same day from the north in Huntsville, for the first time since our stay in this region. We lay in camp one day and received orders to march to Triano, a little town on the Tennessee River directly south of Huntsville. This little town is located in a splendid corn region, where we could spend the balance of the winter and obtain plenty of feed for our horses. It was ten miles from Huntsville to Triano, and as there were no telegraphic lines up, a courier line was established to take its place, and for the first time in my life I was turned in to a post—a courier post.

FEBRUARY 5, 1864, COURIER POST, ALABAMA

When the regiment reached Triano it went into permanent winter quarters. It was January 30 when the regiment reached Triano.

There was a courier line immediately established between Triano and Huntsville, and five other men and myself were established as the middle courier post between the two points. This was to me the pleasantest winter spent in the South. We were outside the picket lines and were at liberty to form acquaintances and learn more of real Southern life, views, habits, and customs than any other time during our whole stay in Dixie. We established our headquarters on Madkins' plantation. We took possession of an unoccupied log house built for the habitation of slaves. There was a large fireplace in one end, and we arranged or made our beds in the other, and constructed a rude table in the centre. There were six of us and we took turns about cooking and turns about carrying dispatches. Each man would cook for one day, and then the next man a day, etc. We were numbered off one, two, three, four, five, and six. When number one started off with a dispatch, number two saddled his horse and was ready for the next, while all other horses could remain unsaddled. We galloped briskly to the next post, either north or south, as the case might be, until we reached the other post in that direction and gave it to a man with saddled horse, who galloped briskly on, while we could ride leisurely back; talk with negroes, or hunt game, such as ducks, wild turkies, rabbits, or take in a fat "porker," if we could get within rifle shot of one. We always carried our guns and were in some danger of bushwhackers, but were fortunate in not being fired on, although there were quite a number of deserters, rebels, and other mysterious fellows beating their way through swamps and timber.

Our scouts were picking up deserters, rebel soldiers, and scouts almost daily, and these were all sent over the line, not as dispatches, but were sent through under guard of the couriers.

If there was but one rebel prisoner we would put him on one of our horses and take him through in that way. But we always took the precaution not to put a bridle on the horse that the rebel prisoner rode, and tied the halter strap firmly to the saddle on the horse we rode. By this precaution the rebel could not make a quick sudden dash and get away. If there were a squad of three or four prisoners we rode on horseback and the prisoners went on foot. Two couriers always went for guard if there were more than two prisoners. If a prisoner happened along at meal time we sat him at our table and we all dined together and talked about the war as though we were the best of friends; told stories and joked as freely as though there was no war nor any trouble. Prisoners and deserters were sent over the line almost daily. The courier post next to Triano would bring them to us; we would take them to the post next to Huntsville, and the latter post would take them to the provost guard in the city. The latter would hold them until a car load had been gathered up, when the whole would be sent north under guard to some Northern rebel prison, like the one at Chicago.

The planter on whose plantation we were on, Mr. Madkins, was very kind and sociable to us. He was what is known as a "Southern gentleman." He was a fairly educated man and well read and posted in Southern politics, and had given an only son to the rebel army, who was shot and killed at the battle of Bull Run. He was a rebel in every sense of the word, but knew enough to hold his tongue when the Union army was all camped around him. He was wealthy, owned a large plantation well stocked with negro slaves. Many of the "young bucks" had left on the approach of the Union army, but the women, children, and old negroes stayed and waited for developments.

While Mr. Madkins was pleasant and affable with us, we could not draw him out on anything pertaining to war or slavery. He would slyly turn the tide of conversation on to other matters and would dodge a conversation on those topics. He was a great talker and was at our cabin much of the time, anxious to talk and joke with us and seemed to enjoy our company. Finding our efforts all in vain to draw him out on the war question, I stated to him one morning that I should really like to get his views on the war and subject of slavery. I told him that I expected that we held wide and different views, but wide and different as they might be, if he would express them to us and maintain them with all the best arguments at his command that none of we six on that post would take the least offense from anything he might say. Each one of the six men pledged his individual honor to that effect, but we all agreed not to talk on those topics when any other soldier was present aside from the six who had made this pledge. He was perfectly willing to open up under these circumstances, having perfect confidence in our word. It was a good thing that we were all on our individual honor to take no offense, for had it not been for that more than one hot argument would have broken up in a row.

My first set-to with him commenced about nine o'clock in the morning and lasted until night, stopping a short time for dinner. I had found a posted Southerner and he rather surprised me with his arguments. I had never heard any Southern views coming directly from the lips of an educated man who believed what he said and could give plausible reasons for the faith that was in him. We both agreed on one point, that slavery was the ultimate cause of the war, and we got right down to first principles. Was slavery right or wrong? He held that it was right and I held that it was wrong. He went to the Bible for proof, and in my opinion he got the best of the argument, but I did not tell him so, you bet. He was a Christian and read the Bible much, and was very familiar with every passage from Genesis to Revelation that touched on the subject of slavery. His Bible was brought in for proof, and there it was in black and white. He quoted from very many chapters of different books, all tending to support the slavery principle. Among some of the chapters quoted from were Exodus, twenty-first; Leviticus, Deuteronomy, fifteenth; Job, seventh, and Second Samuel, eighth, and many others. The church North and the church South had divided on the ground of slavery, one claiming the institution to be divine, the other that it was not. The only point that I was able to make a Bible argument on was from the eighth chapter and twelfth verse of Matthew:

"Whatsoever ye would that man should do to you, do ye even so to them."

I held that he could not obey that command and hold another man as a slave. He interpreted the meaning like this:

"Whatsoever ye would that man should do to you (under like circumstances) do ye even so to them (under like circumstances)."

That is: "do by your slave as you would like to have your slave do by you, providing the master and slave had been born under reverse circumstances."

This proposition I thought staggered him a little and I made the biggest handle I could out of it. But that the old Bible sanctioned slavery in some form was too evident for me to try to reasonably deny, although I had heard the opposite preached all my life. We were two radical opposites. I had been reared in the abolition school and it was a part of my religion, and I wouldn't sanction slavery if all the books and Bibles in the world upheld it. He had been reared in the slavery school and believed that slaves were held in a divine right, and it had been ground into his very nature. Books had been written to counteract the effect of "Uncle Tom's Cabin" and circulated far and wide among the educated. One of their books had quoted every passage in the Bible on the subject of slavery. Mr. Madkins had a copy and gave it to us to read, and we nearly all read it. We found in Mr. Madkins an able advocate of their "peculiar institution" and it took close reasoning to keep even.

FEBRUARY 16, 1864, COURIER POST, ALABAMA

While in the ranks a soldier has but little opportunity of gaining information of Southern sentiment, but our new field of couriers, isolated from the large commands, left us among the citizens with an opportunity to learn much that had heretofore escaped our notice.

After the pledge to Mr. Madkins to allow him or his family to talk their real sentiments to us when no other soldiers were present, they all seemed to have the most implicit confidence in our word and the whole family visited our quarters frequently, and entered into conversation on any and all questions of the day with the utmost freedom. Mr. and Mrs. Madkins had a little daughter about ten years old who was very pretty and bright. The parents almost worshipped her. As young as she was she was a little rebel. On one occasion her father had been up to Huntsville and returned. He came over to our quarters to tell us the news from the city. France was hesitating whether to acknowledge the Southern Confederacy as a nation or not. A report had reached Huntsville that day that France had acknowledged the Confederacy. Of course this was bad news for us, but good for the rebels. Mr. Madkins related the news to us while his little girl was standing by his knee. She saw from the smile on her father's face and manner of delivery that the news favored the South. This little childish female rebel commenced jumping up and down crying, "Goody, goody, goody, goody, goody, goody, oh, I am so glad." It brought the red to every one of our faces, but we had pledged ourselves to take no offense for speaking their true sentiments pro and con, so we swallowed the little girl's demonstrations as best we could and said nothing, but it was a hard pill to take.

Mr. Madkins kept a teacher to instruct his children at home. This teacher was a very interesting little schoolmam [sic] by the name of Maggie

Scott. She belonged to the F. F. A.—First Families of Alabama, and had been well educated. She had not adopted the filthy habit of the common and poor people of the South, that of dipping snuff. She neither dipped nor would for a moment associate with those who did. Here was a natural division line between Southern aristocracy and the more common people. Maggie was very sociable with the boys of our post because we were educated, and nearly all the educated people of the South belonged to her class. Maggie was very ladylike and our courier boys put the best foot foremost when in Maggie's presence, and kept up the dignity of the occasion.

We had some difficulty here. Men would steal out of the camp nights in small squads and go to private houses and pillage and steal generally and then tell the citizens that they belonged to the courier post on Madkins' plantation. Some of the citizens were so enraged at us that they would have waylaid us or bushwhacked us if they could have got an opportunity. They went to Mr. Madkins about it but we had so completely won him over to the belief that we would not do such things that he took our part and reasoned with them for some time before he could convince them to the contrary. He finally came and told us all about it. These nightly visits were so frequent by jayhawkers[7] from camp that we had reasons to believe our cabin was watched a few nights by citizens to ascertain whether we went out and returned or not. We all slept at night without picket or guard. It was dangerous, but we were never molested. We carried dispatches both night and day as they happened to come along.

I got awfully scared one night while out with a dispatch, but did not like to tell anyone at the time for fear some one would laugh at me. I was galloping along the road one very dark night, riding my little cream-colored horse, a horse that I thought as much of as a man can well think of a horse. The road was partly skirted with timber and fenced on either side with a high old-fashioned rail fence. My horse had a keen eye and seemed to examine every object we passed, but was not foolish or scared at shadows. All of a sudden he slackened his pace and raised his head so high that his ears were almost in my face. He saw something, but I did not. The most I feared was an ambuscade or bushwhacker. My gun was quickly jerked from the socket, cocked, and ready to pump eight rounds into an enemy. My horse was nearly frantic with fear, and in spite of rein and spur ran sidewise across the road to the other fence. Close to the track that I was formerly on I saw a white object. I prodded my horse with both spurs and when I got even with the white object I was about to pull the trigger when

I thought of the story of the boy in the barn, scared at a white pillow in a swing. I withheld my fire. My horse had reached that point where he wanted to go with all his might and I pushed on the reins and let him go. We annihilated space and left the scare behind and never knew what the scarecrow really was.

The negroes were delighted to have "Linkum men on de plantation." Madkins had a large number of slaves and they had to work hard and did not know the value of a friend or how to appreciate one. They were used to the lash, kicks and cuffs, and hard work. They came to us with presents of corn bread cooked in the most approved plantation methods. We accepted it all, but did not eat it all. Some of them were tidy and clean, while others were not, and their bread bore evidences of the difference. We preferred to cook for ourselves and generally did so. We were all friendly with the slaves and inquired all about their servitude; how they liked to be slaves; would they like to be free; did their overseers whip much; and a thousand and one questions of this nature were asked. They were delighted to answer such questions and wanted us to ask more, and flocked into our cabin to tell us of their hardships and trials and tell their experiences. Men soon become tired of any medicine when taken in overdoses. We were taking overdoses of negro hardships. We wanted a rest, but the poor, ignorant things had but little knowledge of propriety. When it came supper time the cabin was so packed that there was scarce room to cook or move about. They were so friendly we hated to kick them out. About the second or third time this nuisance occurred one of the boys we called Dick was cooking. He gave the rest of the boys the wink, as much as to say he would "clear the shanty." He filled one hand with metallic cartridges, a stick in the other, and with a great back log for the fireplace elbowed his way up to the fire. He raked open the coals from the back log, and as he laid it on managed to drop his handful of cartridges in the hot sinders [sic] and buried them deep in the hot ashes with his stick. He then elbowed his way back, the little "nigs" and the old "nigs" filling up solid behind. It was chilly and they were fond of a good fire. We were telling funny stories so we could have an excuse to laugh, for we knew what was coming. Presently a cartridge exploded with a loud crack, sending ashes all over the shanty. The darkies blew the ashes from their faces and stampeded for the door. We shouted with laughter. After a moment's fright and run they got over their fright and laughed too, thinking it was a good joke. They settled back to their old positions not dreaming of any more. One old negro thought it was "de poppin' of a peanut." But all of a sudden the second, third, fourth, and fifth went off in rapid succession strewing the hot ashes and sinders all over the darkies and over the floor. They ran hurly-burly, helter-skelter for the door, old negroes over younger ones and the little ones scrambling with all their might, as each additional bang of a cartridge sent a fresh cloud of hot ashes gushing through the room. Every negro was as pale as a sprinkling of hot ashes could make him. A more perfect stampede was never witnessed. By the time the last cartridge exploded there was not a negro in rifle shot of the cabin. We could never get a negro in the cabin again. Occasionally one would peek in at the door, grin, and run away.

MARCH 1, 1864, COURIER POST, ALABAMA

On February 19, 1864, we received orders to break up our post and report to the regiment the next morning. We spent the evening previous to our departure with the family of Mr. Madkins. It was the pleasantest evening that our little band had ever spent in company with Southerners. They were educated and refined people and knew how to make us feel happy and comfortable in their presence. Their friendship was of a genuine nature and not of that affected kind that we so frequently see among Northern people. While we differed so widely on the slavery question and their interests and our interests were at actual sword points, and although their friends and our friends were being slaughtered daily somewhere along our lines of offence and defence, yet we had tested their friendship in more ways than one and we had confidence in them as being true to their word with us. There were many little incidents that tested their sincerity. I will give one.

On one occasion a great many army trains were passing the house going into the country to load up with corn. There was a small guard in advance, and when the long train had got nearly past, the head of the train stopped suddenly, and a man came riding back as fast as his horse could carry him. Mrs. Madkins was standing on the front porch looking at the train. Thinking that a force of rebels had struck the train and were in the act of capturing it she ran across the yard to where I was and told me she believed the train was being captured by "our men" and wanted all the boys of our post to come right over to her house and she would protect us and would not let "our men" hurt one of us. We appreciated her kind regards for us, but had we heard a single shot up in the direction of the head of the train we would have quickly mounted and poured Spencer bullets into "our men" at the best rate we could pump.

During our evening visit the sitting room and parlor had great blazing fires in the fireplaces that gave a cheerfulness that is never witnessed in our Northern stoves. Negro waiters were in the background, so to speak, to minister to the slightest wants. Maggie, the Southern schoolmam, attracted fully her share of our attention during the evening visit. To one of our number Maggie related in detail her trial of ups-and-downs on the slavery question. She said there were some things about slavery that did not seem exactly right. When a man servant and woman servant had been given in marriage for the owner then to turn around and sell the husband or wife and shipping her or him away to the New Orleans market for sale and retaining the other, thus separating the husband and wife, the children from the parents, and using the money perhaps for a wedding tour of a son or daughter of the white folks, or in other words, to destroy one family to make another; to destroy and send the deepest pangs of sorrow into one family to make another happy. This did not seem right, yet as she read her Bible she found that slavery was practiced and sanctioned by the inspired men and she could not see but what it was all right, but it did not always seem so. She had read "Uncle Tom's Cabin" by H. B. Stowe, and "cried like everything" when she read it. She was almost persuaded to be an abolitionist, but when the war came, when Alabama voted to go out of the Union and joined the Confederacy, all her friends and all her interests were in Alabama. All her sympathies went with the fortunes or misfortunes of her state.

We went to our quarters late that night and the next morning after an affectionate farewell we reported to Colonel Atkins' headquarters. We were ordered to form a new line between Triano and Moorsville, two small towns on the Tennessee River, about ten miles apart. Our line had been running north and south, Triano to Huntsville, and now the line was so changed as to run east and west. We were again on the middle post and had to ride five miles either way to reach a post where any other soldiers were located. We established a post in the office building of a large plantation that was under the charge of an overseer by the name of Huddleson. He belonged to a lower grade of Southern society to what Mr. Madkins did. His wife dipped snuff and had two sisters with her and they dipped snuff too. They were uneducated and they all had a languid, soft, flat appearance, sauntering and lazy. Mr. Huddleson had just enough education to partially keep books, count money, weigh produce, and divide bacon among the slaves.

Our new post was regarded as a far more dangerous one than the other. The Tennessee River lay only a little way south of us and there were no pickets along its banks, while just across the river the rebels roamed at will. If a small band should cross in the night and come upon our post they would take us all in while we lay asleep. The second or third night we got word that some rebels were crossing, and we kept up a watch all night. After that we slept every night without a guard and were never molested. At our plantation office was a large trunk full of books. A young Southerner had lived on the plantation and had been sent to a Northern college. When the war broke out he enlisted in the Southern army and joined his fortunes with that of his state. The books left in the trunk were all first-class and Webster's Unabridged Dictionary was among the lot. A part of our boys were reading nearly all the spare time they had, and the balance played cards and other games of amusement. There were two good beds in the office and one good table. We could write, read, or play cards, as best suited our taste.

On the plantation was a pack of bloodhounds used for the double purpose of fox hunting and catching runaway niggers. Huddleson was in our office frequently telling stories and was very fond of card playing. He told us many stories about fox hunting and our curiosity was aroused. We wanted a fox hunt. Accordingly we left two of our number in charge of the post and all the rest mounted their horses for a fox hunt. Huddleson brought a large cow horn all dressed down very thin, and placing it to his lips blew it, producing a loud and shrill blast. The dogs seemed to come from every direction, each dog baying with all his might. It matters not where the dog is, the moment he hears the horn blow he leaves all else and goes bellowing in the direction of the blowing horn. We galloped about the fields in real Southern style, the dogs striking many trails; but Mr. Huddleson called them off from each trail, professing to know from the zig-zag manner of the trail that it was a rabbit. No fox trail could be found; finally the dogs were let loose on a fox trail; and two or three were quickly run down, caught, and devoured by the dogs.

There was an abundance of corn all through this whole section of country, a thing never known in that section before. "Cotton was king" and this was a cotton-growing state. But there were laws passed by the Confederate Congress, and by some of the states, that a certain percent of the crops planted must be of some grain that was used for food. The South had depended on the Northern states for their food while they raised the "cotton and de cane." The old fields that had been nearly exhausted in the culture of cotton, when planted to corn yielded abundant harvests. The yield was very great. But the armies designed to be fed on it did not get it all. Train load after train load was gathered by Yankees and eaten by Yankee horses. The corn and fodder for the whole cavalry command of our army was gathered in Alabama, to winter on, and saved thousands and tens of thousands of dollars in the pocket of Uncle Sam.

APRIL 1, 1864, COURIER POST, ALABAMA

On March 16, while yet on the courier post, a courier rode up with two dispatches. One was for me and the other must go on. What could it mean? A dispatch for me! I was no officer. Upon opening the large envelope it proved to be the appointment papers of a corporal. The boys all stood looking on. As soon as the contents were made known they made all kinds of fun of me and we had lots of army jokes at my expense. A corporal is the lowest rank in the whole line, and no soldier is ever proud of being a corporal. Most any soldier would rather be a private than a corporal. Each one is required to wear two V-shaped stripes on each arm to indicate his rank. But the corporals of the 92d seldom wore the stripes. They usually cut them off until Colonel Atkins issued a general order to compel every corporal and sergeant to wear the stripes to indicate his rank. The pay is $2.00 per month more than that of a private, which makes a small inducement to accept. The corporals are appointed by the colonel from a recommendation of the captain. The army regulations have tried to give some dignity to the office of corporal by preparing a sort of commission of statement of the appointment, prepared with elegance and style, partly written and partly printed on parchment. But with all the spread eagle on parchment volunteers have no exalted opinion of the rank of corporal.

It was now seed time in Alabama, and planters were beginning to prepare the fields for cotton and grain. To look at farm implements such as were furnished the slaves for preparing the ground was fairly obnoxious to a Northern farmer. A good plow is the great pre-runner to good crops in the North, but such plows as they had in Alabama were too rude and simple to be worth even a description. In fact there were no two exactly alike and yet there was a sameness to them all. About the only object the plow manufacturer had was to get something that would root. There was really no plowing done, it was rooting. If the head of a long-nosed hog were to have handles attached and chained fast to a small log it would give as good an idea of an Alabama plow as anything I might describe. There was no plowshare nor mold-board, only what could be made in a rooting shape, with a band of iron on the edge to keep from wearing out the rooter. A mule, or yoke of steers or oxen, were attached to these rooters and driven across the field from side to side. The drivers were wenches and negroes, each plow making a little rooted furrow. Everything depended on the hoe in planting or clearing of weeds. The hoe too was a perfect slave-killer. A huge piece of iron with a hole in which to insert a rude handle. It was estimated by some that the South was fifty years behind the North in agricultural implements. It was my belief that one good active man in the North with our system of agricultural implements would farm more land in a much better shape than fifteen well-worked slaves would with their implements.

There was much cotton in northern Alabama that stood out all winter and was not picked until spring, and some of it was not picked at all on account of the presence of the two armies on either side of the Tennessee River. While the cotton picking was progressing slowly on some plantations I visited them to see the wonderful cotton-gin about which I had read and heard so much but never saw. It has been said that the invention of the cotton-gin was a great benefit to a whole human family. Being such a wonderful invention I had an idea, or expected to see a large complicated machine, large in dimensions with cog wheels, belt wheels, numerous springs and devices that ordinary men could not understand. But when I stood and looked at one in operation it looked like the simplest little thing in all creation. It had two revolving journals fastened in a frame about the sixth of an ordinary fanning-mill, and looked a little like one. It sets up high in the second story of the barn or gin-house, and from the tail end where chaff comes from the fanning-mill comes the fiber from the cotton seed. It is perfectly white and to look up in the tight part of the gin-house where this cotton is blown into it looks as if it were snowing a fearful storm, and when a darkey has occasion to open the door and walk into the cotton room he comes out looking like a man who had been out in a snow storm.

CHAPTER 8

We Suffered a Terrible Slaughter

April – June 1864

APRIL 12, 1864, RINGOLD, GEORGIA

Springtime had come and orders were daily expected and a forward movement commenced. [On] April 3, in obedience to orders, the courier line
was disbanded and the regiment was in the saddle traveling in the direction
of the old battlefields about Chattanooga and the Lookout Mountains. We
started in a driving rain. We passed through Huntsville and there met a lot
of recruits for the 92d just down from the North. They all wore a flush on
their faces, the like of which had entirely disappeared from the faces of the
92d. The contrast was so marked that every recruit looked as though he
were brim full of chicken pie and had been wintered in his mother's band-
box. As we had no extra horses for them they took the cars for Chattanooga and we floundered on through the mud. We retraced our steps,
traveling over the same route traveled some four months previous. Bridgeport had that same desolate look and the atmosphere gave off the odors
from the remnants of the dead mules that lined the valleys that branched off
there. We crossed the Tennessee River here on the pontoon bridge again
for the eleventh and last time. We passed in full view of the rugged heights
of old Lookout Mountain where Hooker fought his famous battle about
the clouds, and then climbed the same mountain and down into Chattanooga and on to Rossville, and then to Ringold, Georgia. Here we were
at the front again. The railroad that passed through Ringold Gap—just the
other side of the gap—the rebels held possession of. We could go no further in that direction until the whole army should be concentrated, and
then force our way down.

    We went into camp in a peach orchard that had been used as a corral
for mules. The continuous rains and continuous tramping of the animals
had made it a pond of slush. Why such a place was selected for a camp was

not for privates to know, but we were there all the same. The recruits came up and were overjoyed to be at the end of their journey. They thought they had been buffeted about and treated in a very bad manner and now they were among friends and all was lovely. It was about three o'clock when we settled in the mud to camp, and the recruits stood around telling very lustily their hardships and experiences while on the cars and in camps trying to get to the front. The old soldiers listened to their stories but kept at work filling slush holes with dirt, leveling down mounds and staking down tents, and fixing places to sleep. None were idle except the recruits, whose tongues ran on as though nothing ought to be done until all their experiences had been told. The sun began to sink behind the mountains and the air was damp and chilly and a little frosty. By this time the old soldiers had their tents erected and some prospects of a comfortable night's shelter. The recruits began to inquire which tents they should sleep in that night, and were told of course they could sleep in the ones they had erected. As they had erected none they had no place as yet to sleep. Then they inquired what they would eat for supper, and were told whatever they had a mind to cook and prepare. A sober, thoughtful look came to the face of every recruit. They had all left good homes in the North where they stepped into their father's house at night and were sheltered from the cold, and sat at tables well supplied with provisions, cooked by the skilled hand of a mother or sister, and slept in a bed that kept them dry, comfortable, and warm. But now before they could step into a house of any kind for shelter they must erect it in the mud, and before they could eat they must cook it, and before they could sleep they must not only make but arrange a place for a bed. The old soldiers had all been at work, every man, arranging for himself or in unison with another, had prepared everything for himself, while the recruits had stood around waiting as though they expected some substitute for a mother would perform all such work as was customary at home. Then they went to the orderlies for information on what to do and were told to erect tents to sleep in if they wanted to where the ground was staked off so that their tents would come in line with the others.

As I worked about my camp fire getting supper I selected one recruit whose ground was staked off close to my own tent and watched his motions and expressions of face while he experienced his first lesson in actual soldier life. He was a fine-looking young man about nineteen years of age. He came down the company street walking with the sergeant, carrying his tent cloth under his arm. The sergeant staked off the line for him to build to and there it was a perfect mud hole like all the rest. As soon as the ground was staked off the sergeant returned to finish his own tent and the recruit stood and looked at that muddy spot as though he did not know what to do. Presently a thoughtful cast spread over his face and he sat down on a little bog of dirt. His tent cloth lay across his lap and his elbows were on his knees and his chin placed in the palms of his hand, and there he sat facing the mud hole. Presently tears came into his eyes and then began to course down his cheeks one after another in rapid succession, but there was no sobbing or sighing. He sat there apparently unnoticed until dark, when he got up and with a heavy heart began to prepare the best shelter that his inexperienced hands could erect. He slept that night supperless, after learning the great lesson in army life that "The Lord helps those who help themselves." This was a sort of breaking in.

New recruits, as a rule, were very poor companions at first for an old soldier to chum with. Fresh from the luxuries of the home table they were naturally dainty when brought face-to-face with hard tack, sow belly and coffee, and these too prepared in a rude way with rude cooking in utensils that were in no danger of being worn out with scrubbing and cleaning. A recruit would sit down to such a meal prepared much better than the recruit could think of doing it, yet it was not anywhere near what he had been used to at home. He would, nine cases out of ten, turn up his dainty nose as he had frequently done at his mother's table. A fond mother would bear it and try to please, but an old soldier would not bear the first wrinkle of the upturned nose. In nearly every case where a recruit tried to chum with an old soldier the union was dissolved about the second or third meal. About the first time the nose went up their friendship went down and the recruit was requested to cook for himself and by himself. Of course he never scowled at his own cooking, notwithstanding he did the poorest known to the service. After a few weeks of horrible fare these recruits made the most companionable chums that any soldier would wish to be with. They were good men and made good soldiers, only they had a lesson of hardship to learn and this is the way they learned it.

APRIL 20, 1864, RINGOLD, GEORGIA

While the regiment lay in camp at Ringold some of the most important events occurred to some of the members of the regiment. The muddy camp was soon changed to one of beauty. Walks were laid out, evergreens set out, and when General Elliott[1] in company with General Thomas came to inspect the regiment he boasted to General Thomas in the presence of some members of the regiment that he had the cleanest and handsomest camp of any regiment, infantry, or cavalry in the Army of the Cumberland. Thus with industry and energy the filthiest spot was changed to the cleanest and handsomest. Although the camp was very fine and the weather grew milder, yet everything seemed to be out of luck here. The officers got into trouble among themselves, the men were mad at the officers, the pickets were shot on their posts by rebels, an attempt was made to dismount the regiment, a cavalry officer from the Potomac wanted to take our Spencer repeating rifles from us and arm us with the single-shooting short-range carbine pop gun, Colonel Sheets and Major Bohn resigned and went home, and it rained porridge when our dishes were wrong side up. Every member looks backward on this history with anything but pleasantness. To give a full detailed account of all that occurred is not altogether pleasant. Our greatest troubles were of a domestic nature.

We had all become used to the mounted service and every man preferred it to the dismounted or infantry service. During the winter and early spring months the army was undergoing a reorganization in regard to brigades, divisions, and corps, and commanding officers from the eastern armies were sent to the western, and generals from the west were sent to the east. General Grant went from west to east, Kilpatrick[2] from east to west, and other officers made like changes. There was a chance for promotion too among the brigadiers and colonels, and not one was ever known to let a good opportunity slip to "come up higher."

Colonel Atkins was found to be human and was not unlike the good people at home who are always ready to be sacrificed in a good cause and will smilingly accept the office of pathmaster, school director, town clerk, supervisor, or even the office of county clerk, judgeship, member of assembly or congress, and occasionally one will consent to be governor. So it was with Colonel Atkins. If the government wanted to sacrifice him as brigadier instead of colonel, of course he was ready to be thus sacrificed. Of course there have been many who had no such desires and were called good little boys by their mothers and died young. None of them ever found their way into the army.

It appears from the best information obtainable by a private soldier that General Bayard, who commanded a division of infantry, had a brigade without a brigadier, and the brigade would be a strong and good one if the 92d could be dismounted and attached to that brigade. It was also talked, rumored, and believed that in case the 92d dismounted that Colonel Atkins would be promoted to a brigadier. Whether this was strictly true or not it was believed and talked among the men. It was true, however, that the colonel did recommend and urge the dismounting of the men, and had it not been for the opposition of all the officers of the regiment and general dissatisfaction of the men, it would have been accomplished. An excuse or pretext was necessary for dismounting and in due time it was presented. It was represented at headquarters that the regiment was becoming demoralized and getting worse from day to day. Colonel Sheets opposed the measure. An order had been prepared for our dismounting. The quartermaster of the 10th Pennsylvania Cavalry came for our horses, but Colonel Sheets being in command at the time refused to give them up. An inspection of the regiment was ordered and Generals Thomas, Elliot, and Girard[3] came and inspected. It was claimed that Girard had the order in his pocket for our final dismounting, but upon inspection of the men, their guns, their dress, their camp and all were pronounced the cleanest and neatest. The men had as fine and soldierly a bearing as any regiment in the whole Army of the Cumberland. This took the starch entirely out of all efforts to dismount. This attempt was unfortunate, however, in several particulars. It created some hard feelings and bitterness that did not wear away for a long time. At a meeting of the officers of the regiment every officer except two voted against dismounting.

Trouble did not come single-handed. General Judson Kilpatrick, from the Army of the Potomac, came down and took command of our division of cavalry. Kilpatrick was a good, brave, dashing cavalry officer, but he had graduated at West Point and of course knew of no gun that was fit for cavalry to fight with, only the kind laid down in the school books at West Point. The Spencer repeating rifle was not laid down in those books, and of course in his judgment the Spencer must be laid aside for the little short-range pop gun. The 92d could hold more rebels at bay with their Spencers than any three regiments in the whole brigade with their pop guns. But as the officers and men had such a high opinion of the Spencer the general was not stubborn nor arbitrary. He was willing to give them a fair trial. After the first fight, when the 92d got under fire where the work was interesting, the general learned a new lesson and thought as much of the Spencer as any officer or man in the regiment.

At Ringold is a range of mountains running from the northeast to the southwest called Taylor's Ridge. It is properly a continuation of the

Allegheny Mountains. On the southeast of these mountains the rebel army lay in camp, and on the northwest the Union army was concentrating with the centre at Ringold. At Ringold was a gap called Ringold Gap, through which the railroad had been constructed that ran down to Atlanta. From peaks on the mountains the rebel camps could be easily seen, and the rebels could overlook our camps in a similar way. Troops were daily concentrating, and the army about here was swelling and growing larger every day, all under the command of General Sherman. The time was drawing near when the whole army would break through the gap, scale the mountains, and fall like an avalanche upon the rebel hosts. The cavalry guarded every little cow path over these mountains for miles up and down the ridge, and trouble along the picket line was almost a daily occurrence. The rebels being well acquainted with every cow path, peak, and hiding place, they had the advantage. It was nothing unusual for a rebel with a field glass to mount to some high peak and examine our position thoroughly. Picketing became more and more dangerous every day. Additional forces were frequently called for during the night, and men sound asleep in their tents in camp would be called out in the dead hours of the night to go and strengthen some of the most dangerous outposts the regiment ever guarded.

Colonel Sheets and Major Bohn both resigned and returned home. Colonel Sheets resigned on account of business reasons, and Major John H. Bohn tendered his resignation on a surgeon's certificate of disability.

AFTERNOON, APRIL 25, 1864, RINGOLD, GEORGIA

When I wrote the next passage in my small diary I felt fortunate to have the life in my blood to grip my pen and mark the paper. We suffered a terrible slaughter at the hands of the rebels. On the 22d day of April, camped near the village of Ringold in northern Georgia, sixty-two men of the 92d were detailed for picket duty and placed under the command of H.C. Scoville. I was one of that number. Each company of the regiment had contributed a few of its men to make up the sixty-two; my company contributed six including me. We were ordered to go down the valley, away from all commands, eight miles away from all our other forces and there remain for two days and nights. We were to guard a little path, over the Taylor's Ridge mountain. This little steep, rugged path, known as Nickojack Gap or Nickojack Trace rose from the valley, wound its way in a zig-zag course around huge rocks, knolls, and broken cedars until it reached an altitude half a mile up. This path was so steep that a horse could not climb it, although there was a report to the effect that a rebel once did lead a horse over it. Our command of sixty-two men was divided into four or five bands of about twelve in a band or squad. These squads were so arranged as to guard paths, roads, and passes in several directions from a central point. Lieutenant Scoville located himself with a squad at a central point, with another squad as a sort of reserve to assist in case of danger or attack. Nickojack Gap was the farthest point from camp on the mountain, and we guarded it with the knowledge that it was rather the most dangerous. The lieutenant placed his reserves on the road immediately opposite the gap. I was put in a squad of twelve to go to the top of the mountain in the gap. The mountain was only about two rods wide on top at this point, and then tumbled off at a steep descent either way.

We had been on picket all day and night of our first day and all day and nearly all night of our second day, without trouble or alarm. But about four o'clock in the morning, before it was light, E. M. Elliott, one of the three videttes at that hour, crept quietly down behind some rocks where the other nine of our squad were lying around some smoldering embers, and told the one there whose duty it was to remain awake—told him in a whisper—that a large force of rebels were deployed in line of battle, and were ascending the east slope of the mountain to attack us. He could hear the low command of the rebel officers on the still night air, the breaking of sticks under their feet, the occasional rolling down of a stone as it would be torn loose by some rebel pulling himself up those steep mountain sides. Elliott re-took his post as vidette and awaited his fate. The men were all quickly and quietly awaked except myself—I was overlooked. I had been up nearly all night and had been relieved but a little while, but I had gone sound asleep. There was no time for reflection and no plan for retreat was made, but every man prepared for fight, getting in good positions behind stumps, stones, ledges, and trees. With the light of afterknowledge we could see that it was a mistake for twelve men to square themselves to fight with a great army, so to speak; but fight was all the boys thought of and it was all they prepared for. When the rebels got within range of our rifles they were not over two rods apart. The other eleven boys nearly all fired at once and repeated with their repeating rifles. A long line of rebels sent immediately back a tremendous volley.

The first crack of the musketry caused me to jump to my feet while still in a sound slumber. I grabbed my rifle, chambered a ball, and was ready to shoot. I could not tell what was the matter nor where I was. I could see flashes and sparks and hear the rattle of musketry all about me but not a man could I see. The fighting was being done on a plane of nearly ten feet above where I stood. While thus trying to collect my scattered thoughts from sleep, one poor fellow cried out in a loud voice not over thirty or forty feet from me, "For God's sake, don't shoot me again! You have shot one of your own men; Oh! Don't, don't, don't, don't shoot me again!" His cry was so pitiful, yet loud and piercing, it made my hair stand on end and it seemed to raise my hat off my head. I could not help it; I did not know who he was or to which side he belonged. Neither do I know now. But there was no time for pity. The musketry rolled on but only for a few moments. At this juncture a man came to the edge of the rocks and set his gun down by his side as though his work was completed. He seemed to come from the point where Elliott belonged, but it was too dark to tell the colors of his uniform, notwithstanding he was not more than fifteen feet from me. I had to look up to him and he down to me. I strained my eyes to see who he was, and he did the same towards me. My gun was at my shoulder, finger upon the trigger, but I dared not shoot because it might be Elliott. In a moment he drew his gun to his shoulder and pointed it at me and remarked (over his shoulder) as he did so, "Lieutenant, these are Yanks down here." But I had the drop on him; my gun was already at my shoulder and I fired first. All I knew about it was he did not shoot at me and I was too close to miss.

In another instant a long row of heads presented themselves in full view. In another sixteenth part of a minute we would be shot down or captured if we continued to fight longer. Since I had just been appointed corporal and was second in command of the squad, I cried out in a loud voice, "Fall back!" This was my first command as a corporal in action. Every man obeyed on the instant. The sergeant who had the command had got so worked up in shooting at the rebels that he had forgotten to give the command, although it was apparent to him and every other man that we had got to go or surrender.

We ran down the mountain rapidly and the rebels poured their volleys after us, having captured one, killed one, and wounded one and shooting one of our men through the arm as we went down. We could not follow the zig-zag path in the dark, especially on the run, while volleys were being fired at us. I came to a perpendicular precipice on the run; I did not see it until I was at its edge. Too late to stop, I fell, and as I fell my gun slipped from my hand and I never saw it again. I struck on my side and it numbed me so badly I could not stand until I had rolled and rolled down, down the mountain and made many attempts to stop myself. Our horses were tied to the trees at the foot of the mountain; we mounted and rode off.

We had gone but a short distance when we met a part of Lieutenant Scoville's command coming to our assistance. We halted to form in line and fight a retreat. We had no more than made the proposition when the pickets on the valley road fired. In an instant a roll like thunder of horses' hoofs came dashing up that valley road.

On to the reserve post they dashed and never halted for anything. Scoville and the remainder of his little band were running for dear life with rebel cavalry at their heels. It seemed as though rebels were on every hand.

Fighting was now out of the question; it was a scramble for dear life. The rebels were ahead of us in the road that led to camp, driving Lieutenant Scoville and his band into a trap that none of us knew anything of. At the foot of a little hill the rebels had stolen a position in the rear during the darkness of the night and had built a horse-shoe barricade that could not be seen until you were in it. Lieutenant Scoville and his squad all ran into the trap of course, and were all either killed or captured. While the rebels were running Scoville into the trap, we were keeping along the foot of the mountain as fast as our horses could run, wishing we could reach the road along with the lieutenant. But as soon as he was captured they turned upon us. They were ahead of us and we were now completely cut off. Some of our boys tried to dash through their lines and reach camp. Some succeeded and others were captured and shot in the attempt. I had no gun and resolved to hide as a last resort. There was one deep gorge coming down the side of the mountain. At the foot of this was underbrush. I ran my horse into that but dared not stay with him for fear he would neigh for the other horses and thus disclose my hiding place. I tied him hastily to a small bush and climbed up the side of the mountain, keeping under the small cedars as best I could. I felt decidedly ridiculous in my new position. I had lost my overcoat, haversack, hat, and gun and did not know but what I would lose my horse and even my life before I got out of there. But I determined to hold bravely on to my new position. I heard the finishing shots that I have since learned killed Willie Hill, Joural O'Connor, and William Cattanach,[4] all of whom were shot after they were captured. Willie Hill was shot near a house. A lady has told us she saw a rebel take a gun and put it against his breast and shoot him after he had surrendered. Cattanach was captured at the trap and a rebel lieutenant by the name of

Pointer shot him twice with his revolver after he had surrendered. He had life enough in him to tell his own story before dying. These things I have all learned since the massacre. O'Connor was shot after he had been taken a mile back.

The rebels left the valley. A large force of blue coats came down the valley road in fighting trim under the command of Captain Smith—as good a fighting officer as the 92d had. It made me feel glad from the top of my head to the ends of my toes. I was badly demoralized and scattered by this time. My coat was in one place, my gun in another, and horse in another. Word had gone in ahead of me that I was among the killed. One man got in who saw me fall and saw me attempt to get up and fail and he knew I had no gun. It was taken for granted that I was killed or badly wounded.

I got into camp about the middle of the afternoon. I had been without breakfast and dinner and was covered with dirt and dust. When I rode into camp in my scattered condition as a whipped corporal, without a gun, coat, haversack, or hat and even my hair had stood on end and tried to get away, one of the boys who first saw me called my name out with a loud cry and at once nearly a hundred men gathered around me, took me off the horse, carried me through the company grounds on their shoulders, shouting for joy.

Elliott, at the picket post, was captured.[5] Out of the sixty-two men there, thirty-three were captured, killed, or wounded. Of the six of Co. B I was one of the two survivors.

APRIL 26, 1864, RINGOLD, GEORGIA

Ten dead men were picked up of the 92d, after the Nickojack slaughter, besides several who were mortally wounded. One sergeant who was with Lieutenant Scoville, while riding at the top of his horse's speed right towards the rebel trap, had his horse shot and he fell full length in the middle of the road, throwing the rider head-over-heels rolling and tumbling into the corner of the fence by the roadside. The rebels were right at his heels riding as fast as their horses could carry them. Notwithstanding his bruises and hurts, the sergeant lay motionless. The whole rebel force rode within three feet of him and passed on. As soon as the last rebel got past he jumped up and cut across the fields to the timber and got away. He was the only man with Scoville who did escape.

At another point higher up the valley a squad of rebel cavalry struck a small post of our pickets and a race followed. Our boys got a fair start and the rebels made a desperate effort to catch them. One rebel was on a very fleet race horse and he "let him out" and rode right up to our boys, their horses not being fleet enough to keep out of his way, but the boys would not surrender to him and demanded that he surrender to them or they would shoot him off his horse. They compelled him to throw down his gun and revolver and stay with them. This was all done while their horses were running as fast as they could and the rebels in force close behind. Our boys stuck to their prisoner and carried him into camp.

O'Connor and Cattanach were both left for dead and were both shot after they had surrendered. Lieutenant Pointer[6] of a Tennessee regiment, was the contemptible coward who did the shooting. He shot two or three others of the 92d, finishing them on the spot. O'Connor lived twenty-four hours and said he was captured in the trap; was dismounted and the guards sent back with them made them run. O'Connor had on a pair of new high-topped cavalry boots. A guard stopped him and ordered him to pull them off and deliver. He did so and got behind a little. The rebel hurried him to catch up. O'Connor was short-winded and could not keep on a constant run and told the guard so. At this point the work had been completed above; and Lieutenant Pointer rode up, flushed with excitement of shooting several of our men whom were prisoners, drew his revolver and plunged a ball through O'Connor. The ball passed through his abdomen, and O'Connor went down and was left for dead. The lieutenant and guard galloped on to catch up with the balance. O'Connor was picked up by the force that came down the valley under Captain Smith and conveyed to camp. He told this story while writhing in great agony and he died just twenty-four hours afterwards.

William Cattanach was a young man only just old enough to enter the army and was a new recruit. He was robust and healthy; in fact he was a perfect picture of health; fair skin and red cheeks and was the best-looking man in the regiment. Cattanach was the first man the cowardly Pointer shot. There is no doubt but what Cattanach's fine appearance attracted the villain's attention as the contrast between a copper-colored Southerner and Cattanach was so great. At the first shot the ball passed under two ribs. Then Cattanach threw up his hands and begged for his life but a coward and villain knows no mercy when he has the advantage. He shot Cattanach again, which brought him to the ground. The ball passed through the lungs and he continued to breathe, the air passing in and out of the ball hole as he inhaled or exhaled his breath. Men of great vitality do not die easy and although it seemed as if Cattanach's wounds were enough to have killed him on the spot, yet he lived on with slight hope of recovery. He was brought to camp, his statements made and sworn to under oath. I took turns in sitting up with him and caring for him nights. His wounds were festered and he was feverish. He had much troubled sleep and horrible dreams disturbed his rest, dreams about the rebel barricade or trap in which he was caught and shot. He almost jumped out of his bed in great excitement trying to make "old Jane" jump the barricade. When the regiment and the whole army moved out, Cattanach was sent back to a hospital. Word shortly after came that he was dead, but just where he was when he died or where he was buried no man of the 92d could tell.

The whole Nickojack affair had created the most intense excitement among the men of the 92d and troops generally. Men killed in fair fighting is acceptable, but to kill a prisoner of war causes the utmost excitement and men could be heard to mutter everywhere that shooting prisoners is a game that two could play at.

The boys who caught the rebel on the run were first into camp and as they knew nothing of how the rest of us had been served, and they had met with no loss, their run to save themselves and their novel mode of capturing the prisoner they brought along was regarded as a laughable joke all around. But when the news first arrived of the great havoc along the picket lines, the officers anticipated the feelings of the men, and immediately caused the removal of the new prisoner to some parts unknown to the men of the 92d. This was a wise and timely move, for no sooner was word brought to camp than the real truth was distorted and exaggerated, and the wildest rumors were afloat. It was believed by some that the rebels had shot every man captured and all had fought, practically, under the black flag, neither giving, nor receiving "quarter." Acting under such a belief, a rush was made to the place where the new prisoner was supposed to be held, to have him give an account of his position, but no prisoner was to be found. The 92d never had treated a prisoner in a cruel manner; but under the circumstances, had this prisoner been on hand at that critical moment, he might have been an exception to the rule. Little knots of men all about the camp were discussing the butchery of the morning and it seemed to be the settled conclusion of every man that the 92d would never take another prisoner.

On the afternoon of the 24th the regiment held a solemn funeral with ten corpses at the altar while three others were either dead or dying and would need burial the next day. Chaplain Cartwright preached the funeral sermon, in the open air, while the regiment stood around with uncovered heads. The sermon was very touching as those asleep in death were among the best men of the regiment. Great tears rolled down the sunburned cheeks of the kind-hearted chaplain and there was not a dry eye in the audience.

After the usual military ceremonies, three of the bodies were sent home for burial and seven coffins were lowered into seven newly made graves and the men returned to talk of avenging the wrong done by the rebels.

APRIL 30, 1864, RINGOLD, GEORGIA

The next day after the Nickojack slaughter I was sore and stiffened up from my bruises and hurts received while on the break-neck flight down the mountain. I was relieved from all duty until I might recover. While I was sore bodily I was also sore mentally. I said nothing, but there were the facts. The other boys who were hurt had been injured with rebel lead in action and I had not. Their wounds were honorable. They had received them in action face-to-face, but as for me—good Lord! I was not wounded. I was only bruised and hurt, and I had received my bruises too in a way that is not laid down in the books where "good little boys" and "brave soldiers" are described. I had received my injuries while charging down a mountain under fire to a new position where no rebels were supposed to be in line of battle. I had received them while my back and coat-tails were both point-ing in the direction where the rebels were in line of battle shooting. This was really too much! I had never read in all the books of brave men and good boys a similar occurrence. I did not like the way it looked. I had never been chased off the picket post before, and I felt as though our side was the one that ought to do all the chasing.

The picket posts were still maintained at Nickojack, and the picketing down that valley and in that gap had become a sort of terror in the minds of many, yet not a man flinched. The men did not mind meeting the rebels under fair circumstances, but here there was no fair show. The men scat-tered out into small squads, seven and eight in a place, miles from any con-siderable forces to fall back on, and every man realized that in case of an attack there must be a long run before a large force could be reached.

The slaughter had taught us a new lesson. "Necessity is the mother of invention." There was nothing to prevent the rebels from gobbling a portion of our pickets the same way every night if they should choose to try. Accordingly, every night our pickets held their position until after dark, when the whole line drew back a mile and a half under the cover of darkness, and at the first streak of light from the eastern horizon they all moved back to their old positions. Rebel scouts and spies were prowling about nearly every night to get the new arrangement and spring another trap, but they were unsuccessful. The most rigid and yet dangerous precautions were taken. If a man approached a picket from any direction but the one agreed upon, after dark, he was to be shot without halting. There were some laughable occurrences that happened immediately afterwards, notwithstanding the danger.

Reubin Edgar, of Co. B, was on picket one night and was standing as vidette at the foot of the mountain beside a thicket of brush. Just as it got dark word came to the reserve post that the rebels were near and about to make an attack. The pickets all drew back in haste for the night position, one mile and a half, but forgot to tell Rube to come in. Rube stood at his post for several long hours after he knew it was time to be relieved, but no relief came. He did not know what was the matter. He listened and listened to hear some faint sound of a foot fall at the reserve post and the coming of the corporal's guard to relieve him, but not a sound could be heard. He knew that something was wrong, but what to do was the question. He reasoned the matter to himself very carefully as he was in a critical condition and his life he feared was at stake. If he went back to find the pickets in the night and they were in a new position he knew they had standing orders to shoot without halting. It would never do to go back. If he stayed on his post and rebels came along he would not dare to shoot and run back, as he would run into danger that way; and if he let them capture him the rebels might shoot him as they had other boys, or he might be taken as a spy and shot. Just what to do under the circumstances was a stumper. He finally concluded to lie down in the brush and go to sleep, as the rebels would be less liable to find him and there would be less liability of being shot if found. He lay down, forgot his fear, and fell asleep, and awoke the next morning at the chirping of the birds after a good night's sleep and rest.

There was much trouble and more or less excitement every night down the valley, and new levies of men were taken from sleeping couches and sent down during the dead hours of the night.

Nine days from the night of the slaughter I had recovered and was again on picket duty in the famous old Nickojack Gap. Every possible precaution was now taken to prevent another surprise. The road was heavily barricaded with rails to prevent another dash without warning. After dark we moved back about two miles up the valley to a position along the north bank of a creek. Captain R. M. A. Hawk[7] had command of the pickets, and he caused a strong barricade to be built on the north bank of the stream. Behind this eighteen men were posted with orders to shoot without halting anyone who came to the opposite bank of the stream. My little squad established a reserve post in the rear of the captain's squad, and every two hours I went up with two men and relieved the two videttes who had stood two hours. Long about midnight, or later, there was a gun fired off by some unknown person higher up the stream than where my picket stood. Who did the firing we did not know, only it was probably either an accidental shot of some prowling rebel or he had seen some object that he mistook for a Yankee and fired at it. I had just gone up to relieve the two men and saw that the shot was outside of our picket lines. I waited to see if any rebels came or made any dash, but all was still and quiet. While everything was still, yet every man had his gun cocked ready for dash. Every man had a position ready to shoot. If the rebels came they would probably come on a dead run. As soon as I became convinced that there was no attack I started back with my two relieved men. When we had got within range of the reserve post we were startled with the command "Halt!" given in an excited tone. I realized that something was wrong. As no one spoke I replied with all the mildness and indifference I could command, "Returning of relief guards." Some one said, "Come on." We walked down then to the reserve to inquire why they halted us, as we supposed every man there knew that that was our route to travel to and from our videttes. We were surprised to find nearly every man trembling, not with fear of rebels, but with the thoughts that they came so near shooting us without halting. The moment the stray shot was heard every man sprang to a position behind a rail fence that fronted in that direction. Every man had his gun pointing through the fence ready to fire if an enemy came. We were the first objects that they saw through the dim moonlight approaching. The sergeant told Captain Hawk in a low voice that he would shoot us without halting. The captain knew the position of our post, and although he believed we were rebels coming he said, "No, halt them first." The sergeant urged and begged for the privilege of giving the order to fire without halting, while the whole eighteen Spencers were turned upon us. All this was done in a low whisper, but Captain Hawk firmly refused to allow the sergeant to give the order until we were halted. The word "halt" came as described above and the timely reply prevented the volley, and we were saved from being riddled with bullets from the guns of our own men. I felt that my life had been spared by the good judgment and coolness of the captain, and I ever afterwards regarded Captain R. M. A. Hawk as a warm personal friend.

MAY 2, 1964, RINGOLD, GEORGIA

On the 29th of April, 1864, we were aroused from our slumbers at one o'clock and ordered to saddle up and prepare for a reconnaissance. We were on our way by two o'clock, and we traveled quietly along the road with scarcely a word spoken. It was very dark and it was the time of night when men sleep the soundest. We soon came to our last picket post at Ringold Gap, which was kept up and maintained by our infantry. The post was strongly fortified and maintained by a strong army, so to speak. We were soon on dangerous ground and as we rode silently along we listened every moment to hear the rebel "halt!" and the crack of his musket. We had not long to wait before the word "halt!" rang out on the still night air with a pure Southern twang, a twang that cannot be described but must be heard to be appreciated. The "halt" was almost instantly followed by three cracks of rifles and the whiz of three balls passed close over our heads. Charge, and a general rush for the rebel picket post followed. We did not charge far before we ran sprang against an impassible rail barricade, and we could proceed no further until a number of men dismounted and tore a hole through so our horses could pass. This gave the rebel pickets a chance to get a little start, and, although many bullets were sent after them none were brought down to our knowledge. Whether or not they got away with whole hides was regarded doubtful.

We were now in an unknown region of country. None of our troops had ever occupied it before. We moved on rapidly from barricade to barricade, and every time the rebels stopped to fire we charged on them, sending volleys after the skedaddling pickets. We took no prisoner that day as the men were determined to avenge Nickojack. We drove them from point to point, and all the while our engineers were taking observations and the lay of the country, mapping it all out, every road, path, stream, hill, valley, or mountain. The country was divided into hills, mountains, and valleys, and wherever there was a hill or mountain it was very short and abrupt, and where there was a level it was almost a perfect water level and very beautiful. We finally drove the rebels back almost to their camps, where we found them in strong force. Of course we would not attack them there, as we were only scouting and prowling around to get a knowledge of their country and the position of their armies. We turned and went back over the same road we went out, and quite a large force of rebel cavalry followed us and tried to annoy us on our return. One force of rebel cavalry got behind a range of hills and galloped on until they passed us unseen. They took a position on a sharp hill to our left and as we came back they annoyed us quite a little with their well-directed fire. It would never do to leave the rebels there shooting at our columns as they passed back. They must be driven from the hill. The 92d was thrown in line and ordered to charge the hill, and away we went across the valley pumping Spencer balls as our horses galloped towards the rebels. We never halted until we reached the top and the rebels were going down the opposite slope and we were sending bullets after them to accelerate their speed.

While here one of those scenes which represented Southern lawlessness and recklessness to danger occurred, which but very few, however, possess.

A rebel officer rode out on the beautiful valley which our troops had but a few minutes passed over, and looking up to us as we stood on the hill we had just taken he began to curse and swear at us. He was within a long musket range of us riding on a fine black horse, his side towards us. He rode on a slow walk, making every taunting remark that he could think of. He called us damned Yankees, and said that we could not shoot worth a cent, that we had not a marksman in the whole damned Yankee crew. He told us that we could not hit a barn at short range. We were shooting at him and doing our best to hit him. He laughed, "Ha, ha, you damned fools, that ball was too high; that was too low; that went way over yonder." And so he went on in that reckless way. We were shooting while in the saddle and no accurate shooting can be done at long range from the back of a horse, as the horse is never perfectly still so that a steady and accurate aim can be had. About a half-dozen of us got off our horses and down by a stone fence and took accurate aim. We got in some two or three shots apiece when the fellow gave a quick hitch in the saddle, stuck spurs in his horse, and was quickly out of sight. He got at least one hole in his side, but the distance was so great our balls lost much of their force before reaching him. We returned to camp with no further trouble. The rebel papers reported their loss at twenty killed. The 92d lost three. One killed and two mortally wounded.

Nearly every day some members of the 92d were under fire from the rebels while on picket, the scout, or march, but on the 20th there was not a member of the regiment shot at. Three days after our whack at the rebel pickets we moved out a second time; this time with more men and a better knowledge of the country. The whole cavalry division went and was backed by Baird's division of infantry. This made an army of considerable size. Our regiment had the honor and all the trouble of leading the van. We soon struck the rebels and charged after their pickets. We soon found long barricades, behind which were large forces of rebels to support their pickets. We drove them from barricade to barricade, and the fighting was so general that other regiments were brought up and we continued to drive them. Kilpatrick waited to drive them fast enough so as not to check the steady march of the infantry. After the 92d had driven the rebels from three barricades, charging every time in front, the rebels leaving five dead men behind the third, then the cavalry were given the lead.

General Kilpatrick had recommended that the 92d give up their Spencers and take the short carbine and saber in their stead, but he had yielded to see the Spencer tried.

The cavalry had not driven the rebels very far when they found them strongly posted on a hill behind a strong barricade and an open field in front. This brought the cavalry to a halt. They could not dislodge them as they were too strongly posted.

"Now, by God," said Kilpatrick, "let us see what the 92d can do here with that peculiar gun of theirs that they cling to so tightly."

We were ordered to take the hill. We had a hard job on our hands, and it would take some effective work, so we dismounted, as we could do double the execution dismounted. We left our horses and wheeled into line without losing a minute's time. Before we had our line scarcely formed the rebels opened on us from the hill. We gave one long continued yell and started on a run up the hill, pumping one continuous roll of musketry on to the barricade, raining the leaden balls on to those rails like hail stones on a roof. No rebel dared raise his head to shoot again and we were in perfect safety. The rebels saw at a glance that they only had a minute to decide between surrender or leg bail, and they chose the latter and ran down the south slope of the hill faster than we could up the north slope. This was done in the presence of Kilpatrick and all the cavalry. Kilpatrick was ever after as warm a friend to the Spencer as any man that carried one. After the cavalry saw us pass over the barricade then they came up and chased the fleeing rebels, and we took breath and waited for our horses. We drove the rebels clear into Tunnel Hill, where they had large forces encamped. Their tents were torn up and hastily loaded into wagons and sent back to the rear, and their whole forces drawn up in line of battle. We brought up several batteries and shelled their lines with artillery and kept them in commotion for a time, then we all drew back and on through Ringold Gap to camp again. The loss to the regiment was only one man wounded, but the rebel loss that morning was considerable. We had no means of knowing how much.

MAY 11, 1864, SNAKE CREEK, GEORGIA

The troops began to concentrate about Ringold, and a general forward movement was being arranged for. The army was in splendid condition and the sick and extra baggage were all sent back for storage, and troops were daily pouring in, and it looked as though all the Confederacy could not check them when they once started. The construction train was clear up to the picket line on the railroad, where it passed through the Gap, and a force of men ready to repair the railroad as fast as the army should capture the country from the rebels.

On the fourth of May I was again on picket down in the dangerous valley at Nickojack. At night we withdrew as usual about two miles back, and that left us in the near vicinity of Hooker's corps of twenty thousand men,[8] which had just moved in, and we felt as though we had plenty of backing. During the night we heard a considerable noise in the direction of Nickojack Gap, but as we had all withdrawn two miles up the valley we had no one there to get hurt. The next morning at the earliest signs of light we went cautiously down and took our position at the Gap, and we found that the rebels had been there during the night with the evident design of capturing our pickets, but finding us away they dare not venture up the valley.

Hooker's corps was composed of New England regiments, or "down-east Yankees." These men all had their peculiarities, which, of course, differed from Westerners and Southerners. Every man seemed to be a trader, a sutler, or tinker of some kind. Nearly every man had a little box, bag, or basket in which he had something to sell, or took to fix something with. Every man would have a consignment of some kind of goods such as could pass through the mails.

On one or two occasions the 92d rode through the camps of Hooker's corps, composed as it was of these genuine Yankee soldier boys, and the road was lined on either side with them, and every man appeared to have something in his hands, or hanging on his arms to sell. It seemed as though the whole corps was made up of peddlers ready to cheat the South of their Confederacy. These goods consisted of pens, penholders, tobacco, tobacco pouches, diaries, rings, watches, tooth brushes, combs, watch chains, jack knives; in fact every trinket known to the small Yankee trade.

While the genuine Yankee delighted in peddling, the Southerner despised a peddler. The Southerner would consider himself grossly insulted to be called a peddler, while a New England Yankee would be tempted to desert his picket post for an hour to sell a nickel's worth of thread to a ragged negro. Officers were said to hold their rank in proportion to their ability to peddle.

On the seventh of May the whole vast army was called up early, knap-sacks packed, tents loaded upon wagons, extra luggage all previously sent to the rear, and everything rigged for march and fight. The cavalry pulled out early and the whole army followed. The central forces went through Ringold Gap and pressed their way straight down the railroad for Dalton, while the cavalry went down on the west side of the mountains, past Nick-ojack Gap to one farther south called Gordon's Gap, where we crossed the mountains followed by thousands of troops whose numbers none of us knew but little about.

Sherman's army was so strong or great that it might be called three armies known by three different names, as they had all operated previously in different fields. There was the Army of the Tennessee, commanded by "Bird's Eye" McPherson, a general whom all the men loved for his gallantry and bravery. Then there was the Army of the Cumberland, commanded by "Old Pap" Thomas, the hero and savior of Chicamauga. Then there was Hooker's corps, of New England Yankee peddlers. Added to this was Kil-patrick's division of cavalry. All these forces consisted of Sherman's army starting out to cut the Confederacy in twain and crush its armies sent against us. We felt perfectly confident that we could thrash the life out of the rebels in any general pitched battle, but yet we knew that small forces of ours would in very many cases get badly used up by the rebels unless we used great precaution and not get singled out from the main forces. These forces could be divided into two or three parts with safety, and while two armies were fighting a heavy battle in front the third could be making a flank movement in conjunction with the cavalry, and secure a new position in the rear of the rebels, and thus compel them to retreat from a strong position in front.

Two of these armies went straight down the railroad and at Tunnell Hill the rebels fought, but were quickly whipped by our infantry and driven on to Dalton, where their great natural fortifications found nearly the entire rebel army in line of battle. Here was some hard fighting and our troops could not dislodge the rebels, but Sherman had expected it and had sent all his cavalry to Creek Gap, some twenty miles south and west. We were the flankers, and we traveled for two or three days skirmishing with rebel cavalry, all the time in the hearing of the cannonading in front of Dalton. We kept to the west of a range of hills, and our movements were not discovered by the rebel generals until we entered and took possession of Snake Creek Gap, an easy pass where our troops could approach the rebel railroad at Resaca, some ten miles south of where the rebels were fighting our forces.[9]

We entered the Gap on the tenth of May, after a hard day's march and some skirmishing, and the cannonading above at Dalton ceased. We had entered the Gap but a little while when regiment after regiment, brigade after brigade, and division after division of infantry came streaming through, and battery after battery came rolling and lumbering along. We were now south of the main rebel army, and the fact that the fighting had ceased above at Dalton had a significance that we did not appreciate. They were changing position and would soon be concentrated against us. Our troops moved in to line of battle as fast as they passed through the Gap. We were along with the cavalry and were in front of these great lines of battle, pressing the rebel skirmishers back so they could not see what was going on. The rebels at first were few, weak, and timid, but they hourly grew more bold and stubborn. A pitched battle and stubborn fighting might now be expected to commence any time. We were skirmishing lightly almost every hour somewhere along our lines.

MAY 14, 1864, RESACA, GEORGIA

Marching and fighting was as much an every day business as plowing and harrowing is with a farmer in seed time. "Seed time" in war had come with us and men could travel and sleep anywhere. The weather was warm and it was the fighting season.

As strange as it may appear the men felt better and enjoyed better health when marching and fighting every day than they did when lying in good camps idle with nothing to do. There was less discontent. The men were more friendly and sociable and seemed bound together with stronger ties of friendship when under fire from the enemies's [*sic*] guns than when not so situated.

We entered Snake Creek Gap on May 10. On the 11th a small detachment moved up in the direction of Resaca, a small station on the railroad in the rear of the main rebel army. Our scouting party found rebels and had one horse shot and four men of the 10th Ohio captured. We camped that night behind strong barricades in line of battle. We all knew that as we were in the rear of the rebel army if they withdrew their whole army and turned upon us that they would strike hard and would come to crush us. At this time we had less than a third of Sherman's army at our back, while two-thirds were fighting the main rebel army some twenty miles north of us at Dalton. If they should withdraw from Dalton in the evening and travel all night under cover of darkness they would be in our front in the morning with force enough to nearly annihilate what force we had unless we did some fearful hard fighting.

We were up at four o'clock on the morning of the 12th, ready for an attack if one was made. We ate our breakfast and the regiment started out to see if rebels were near. Before we had got out of musket shot of our infantry we struck the rebel cavalry and a fight ensued. We drove the rebels three miles, skirmishing hard all the time. Towards night we drew back and the rebels followed up, skirmishing all the time. At dark we returned to our position in the lines and we found that large numbers of infantry had arrived during the day and our forces were greatly enlarged. It was now a certainty that the rebels were concentrating on our front and that Sherman was concentrating his army here for the general engagement. A great battle must be fought right here, or within a short distance from where we then were.

The next morning, Friday, May 18, Kilpatrick took his cavalry and started out on the same road leading towards Resaca. The 10th Ohio Cavalry was in advance and they soon struck the rebels, and a brisk fight ensued. The rebels were obstinate. The cavalry charged, but a deadly fire checked them and Kilpatrick was shot from off his horse. His aides carried him back in their arms, while the general bled profusely from an ugly wound.

Colonel Murry, of the 6th Kentucky Cavalry, was the next highest in rank among the cavalry regiments, so the command of the division fell to him. Atkins was then given Murry's place and took command of the brigade. Murry was a gallant officer and a good commander. There was a stubborn nest of rebels up the road and the 92d must be put up there dismounted, and with their repeaters clear the road. We were quickly in line and up we went to "find the man who struck Patrick," or Kilpatrick. We had no trouble in finding them and we drove them too, but not very far. We came to a fence with an open field in front, and it seemed as though we had gone far enough. It seemed as though we could smell the rebels in large quantities near at hand. Sharp shooters were blazing away at us from trees. Some lashed themselves to the timber, concealed by the foliage. We lay down in line of battle behind the fence, directing shots at rebel "coons," when all of a sudden there came a heavy line of battle over the hill in our front—a line of rebel infantry—and opened fire on us. Had we all been standing erect with no barriers in front when we received their volleys they would have killed a great many men of the regiment, but as it was only a few of our men were hit, and we returned a continued volley that was ten fold more severe. Every man was behind a fence with a good rest and could take accurate aim, and it told fearfully on the rebels. In a few minutes the whole rebel line was compelled to retreat or hide behind trees, stumps, and logs, and none dare raise up to shoot. The trees too were cleared of sharp shooters. We held the position for a time when an officer came and ordered us back. As we went back we soon discovered what had been going on while we were fighting. Sherman's infantry had been drawn up in long lines of battle just behind us with artillery on every knoll and hill overlooking the fields where fighting might be expected. These lines were drawn up double and behind the first was a second line of battle, and behind that again was a third. Everything was in readiness to either advance or retreat as the fortunes of battle might require.

All successful generals are always prepared for advance or retreat on the eve of battle. Those steady lines advanced just across the field where we fought, and just as they turned the brow of the hill behind the "ball opened" and did not subside again for two days, except after dark. The lines were extended and advanced, and the fighting extended farther and farther to the right and left. Cannonading was increasing every hour and the fighting became general. The cavalry was placed on the flanks to prevent the rebels from swinging around either way to get in the rear of our forces. We were sent to the right flank and were soon fighting with rebel flankers. Some of the time we were fighting, some of the time scouting, and some of the time lying still waiting for orders.

At one time while waiting for orders and not exposed, Captain Smith took out his watch and we timed the explosions from the firing of artillery. Sometimes the firing was as low as ten cannon shots to the minute, and at other times it would run up to forty per minute. The average was twenty shots per minute with the artillery or cannon. This was equivalent to twelve hundred shots per hour. The rapidity of musket shots could no more be estimated or counted than the rattle of hail during a hail storm. The fighting was tolerably steady and continuous with now and then a sudden outburst of an extra volley when some portions of our armies made a sudden charge to take a battery or hill.

The average rate of headway of our armies was about a mile a day. The rebels were hard pressed at every point and reserve forces were everywhere in line of battle ready for disaster in front. But few, if any, occurred, and every time there was a chance to get the advantage of the rebels with fresh men, Sherman always had them ready to throw right in.

The country was rolling and covered more or less with timber of all kinds and sizes. Point after point was taken from the rebels and their whole army driven back by inches, so to speak, they leaving many of their dead and wounded in our hands. But our armies were not doing all this without pay. Large numbers of men were being brought to the rear every moment. Some on stretchers, some led, some carried, and some walking erect and alone. Those killed on the instant shot were left until it was more safe to get near them and care for the dead. Hospital tents were hastily erected all along in the rear of our armies, and the wounded gathered in like sheep into a fold. Doctors, chaplains, stewards, drummers, fifes, and band men went to the hospitals, took off their coats and went to work. There was plenty of work for all and none need be idle.

The remedies used on such occasions were not quack medicines, salves, plasters, pills, tonics, and bitters, but were of a simpler nature and no magic cures in any of them. They consisted in lints, bandages, and plasters to draw wounds together, water, knives, and saws.

Most chaplains were very kind and used to catch the dying words and last requests of those who expired, and took charge of their little keepsakes and sent them to friends as directed by the dying, in company with their last requests and parting words, as they stepped across the great river of life to where no pickets ever say "halt."

MAY 18, 1864, ADAIRSVILLE, GEORGIA

The second day's battle at Resaca was a hard day for both sides, the battle raging furiously all day, and we had gained at many points; still the rebels kept themselves well fortified with all manner of temporary works. The fighting continued until late in the night, when it gradually ceased until all was still except the groans of the wounded and dying. But after the fighting had ceased at night there were but few of the fighting soldiers who had been steadily in line of battle that heard a groan after they once lay down on the ground to rest. The strain upon the whole system of men when in battle is very great and wonderfully exhausting. Sleep comes quickly to the soldier the moment he lies down, and his slumber is so deep and heavy that nothing but a shake or rattle of musketry close at hand will rouse him. Groans and pleadings of the wounded and dying are rarely heard by any except by those whose duty it is to stand a couple of hours on the skirmish or picket lines during the night.

The third day's battle was not so severe as the second. The artillery were the principal weapons brought to bear and the musketry was almost quiet by spells. During the third day the 92d was sent down the Oostanawla River to ascertain the condition of the fords and ferrys. This little river ran from the northeast to the southwest. Our right wing and the rebel left wing rested against the river, but the rebels picketed the river from the south and east side and we passed down the southwest side. We passed down the river some ten or fifteen miles, visiting every ford and ferry, and were fired at and exchanged shots across the river at nearly every point. We passed on until we arrived at a town called Rome, Georgia. Here we found Wilder and Minty with their forces of cavalry which we joined, and all returned that night and reached the vicinity of the battlefield about midnight.

About ten o'clock at one of the ferrys we could distinctly hear the low rumbling of wagon trains traveling south on the opposite side of the river. Sherman was informed and artillery was placed in position and shelled the country across the river in the direction where the road was supposed to be; but in the darkness of night firing is more or less guess work. The rebels did not reply and the rumbling continued.

On the morning of the 16th Resaca was vacated. The rebels had crossed the river during the night, destroyed the wagon bridge and railroad bridge after them, and were now in full retreat. Although the rebels had destroyed the railroad bridge during the night our pioneer corps and construction train were the next day working at a new bridge. The rebels went ahead and burned the old bridges after them and our constructors came and built new ones, and almost if not quite kept up with the army, so that supplies came to arm, feed, and clothe the men.

Pontoon bridges were quickly laid in several places and the whole army was crossing as rapidly as possible and was close on the heels of the retreating rebels, and hot skirmishing was kept up for days. We soon passed Calhoun, the next station south, nearly deserted, and camped that night near Adairsville.

The next morning, May 18, we entered and found what had once been a beautiful little village, but now hastily deserted with furniture standing in the houses, dishes upon the shelves, and everything in readiness for the home and comfort of families.

The rebels were skirmishing hard in our front and nothing but infantry were allowed to do the fighting in the centre. We lay at Adairsville all day and camped there at night. I saw the most troops that day that I ever saw in one day in all my life. Very few people have but a faint idea of the vastness of seventy-five thousand or one hundred thousand men in an army. No man ever saw all of Sherman's army in one day. It is very doubtful in my mind if Sherman ever saw one-half of his army during any one day. Our regiment took a position that happened to be fortunate in having a good view of the main road both up and down for a long way. Three corps out of the five or six that were with Sherman came down this road, and our regiment had the opportunity of playing that we were general inspectors. The road was full all day, four men abreast as close as they could walk, occasionally interspersed with artillery, and it took from early morn till long after dark for this vast army of three corps to pass, all moving on a steady walk. This was exclusive of ammunition trains, supply trains, and baggage trains, which were several times longer than the army itself. From the best estimates that I could make I thought I saw fifty thousand troops that day.

While at Adairsville there was one dead rebel that attracted my attention, and I stood and stared at that ghastly corpse for some time and meditated upon his probable fate. He was a man of medium height, square shouldered, well formed, muscular, and robust. A musket ball had pierced his breast, tearing through his vital parts, which of course destroyed his life. He lay down upon his back upon a board near the front door of a dwelling, his hands folded across his breast where some friend had probably placed them. The sun shone full in his face and his eyes had a peculiar stare seen only in the face of the dead. The flesh had not yet begun to decay as he had not been dead long. As I gazed upon his face deep meditations flitted through my mind in spite of the marchings of the hosts in highways and heavy skirmishing at the front. It is unnecessary to place thoughts in print that soldiers may think, because if all such should be published it would fill columns in untold numbers. The flies were eating at his face and I wondered why he did not wake and brush them away. I was about to do it myself when I thought he was a dead man and turned and left him, knowing that in due time proper persons would gather up the dead that lay thinly scattered hither and yonder, and bury them. What could be said of this one dead rebel would be similar to what might be said of thousands that met similar fates.

We camped that night at Adairsville.

JUNE 1, 1864, ADAIRSVILLE, GEORGIA

Sherman had whipped the rebels badly at Resaca, and they were now in full retreat going south, keeping along the railroad, leaving station after station behind them. We had started from Ringold and had taken the station in rotation: Tunnel Hill, Dalton, Resaca, Calhoun, Adairsville, and Kingston, and still the rebels were retreating, fighting our advance guard as hard as they could to save themselves.

To feed, clothe, arm and equip, and keep up with the waste of war, furnish hospitals for the sick and wounded for such a vast army as Sherman's was a task that but few persons can wholly conceive of, that too while marching into an enemy's country while every man's hand was against us. It would take several train loads per day to furnish all the needed supplies. How could that be done when every inch of railroad had to be fought for and captured after everything had been destroyed that fire could burn? It had to be captured foot by foot and mile by mile and then rebuilt. Then, too, there is another difficulty. The road all lay in the enemy's country where every man was ready to assist in ditching a train and destroying bridges and trestle work. The road that supplied this army hung by a slender cord, so to speak. Over two hundred miles of this road ran through Tennessee, every mile of the distance in the enemy's country, and it had to be guarded and patrolled the whole distance day and night. We had now added on to nearly a hundred miles more, all lying in a country where rebel bitterness was keen and vindictive. Rebel scouts, bushwhackers, spies, and deserters were prowling around the country, all centering their plans of mischief on the railroad, ready to pounce upon and ditch a train any moment.

Rebel cavalry commands frequently sent detachments out to travel in a great circle, coming in across the railroad many miles in the rear of our armies. These bands nearly always had a wagon or two in which they carried torpedoes for ditching trains. These torpedoes were made of cast iron about the size of a two-gallon jug and shaped much like one. When they came to the railroad they would dig a hole just deep enough so that the opening of the jug-shaped torpedo would come to the under side of the rail. In the opening of the torpedo was a tube-shaped concern something like a tube to a gun. This cap lay tight against the under part of the rail and when the locomotive came bounding along, the natural spring downwards of the rail would explode the cap and torpedo just as the engine was right over it. The engine would be lifted clear from the track and strike on its side in the ditch and the cars would telescope and pile up. The rebels would come out of some hiding place and pillage the wreck, carry off what they wanted, take prisoners of what men were not killed in the wreck, set fire to what would burn, and travel off with their booty. A wreck of this kind occurred about the time the army reached Kingston. Sherman then sent all the cavalry that had been under Kilpatrick to patrol all the railroad that had just fallen into our hands and to scour the country for miles on either side, to hunt down and capture all rebels, deserters, bushwhackers, and all men of doubtful repute. We much preferred to remain at the front, but we had a work assigned us of vast more importance to the welfare of the whole army than anything we could do at the front. We went back and scoured the country in every direction up and down that road from Dalton to Kingston, and farther south as the army advanced.

Every possible precaution to protect the rails and road that could be thought of or invented was taken. Every train had what might be called a guard car, next to the engine. It was an ordinary car made over, with heavy three-inch, hard-wood-plank sides, with loop holes about breast high all the way around to shoot through. The top was also a level platform with a low hard-wood-plank railing all around and a small howitzer, all mounted. In spite of all precaution the rebels would sometimes get to the road and try to capture a train, but unless they used the torpedo they were frequently beaten off by the fire of the guards from their traveling little fort. Another method the rebels had of capturing a train was this: They would find a position near a curve and tree up the track, and just as soon as the train rounded the curve the engineer could just have time to save his train by reversing his engine. Some concealed rebels would spring upon the track in the rear and take up a rail, which cut off the train and prevented them from going either way. A fight between the rebels and the men in the guard car would be ensured. If the rebels were in large force with artillery the guards would surrender, but if it was only a small band, or even a few hundred, the boys seldom surrendered, but bravely fought to save the train.

Patrols passed in small bands over every foot of the road several times a day, and at every stream where there was a bridge of any importance there must be kept a man on guard night and day. In addition to the guard there was a small force of from fifty to one hundred men comfortably quartered in a strong little stockade. The most of these stockades indicated the very best philosophical engineering. Ordinary fortifications are built on a hill where they overlook the greatest expanse of country, but these little stockades reversed this general plan. Their location was such that they could not be seen until one was within musket range. They were built of logs set in the ground like fence posts, only much higher and close together with loop holes to shoot out of. A musket ball cannot penetrate, but a cannon ball could. Now, if the stockade was on a hill the rebels could come up within half a mile of it, plant a battery and shoot right through it, and the artillery would be so far away that the men in the stockade could not shoot back with their muskets and they would be compelled to surrender without shooting, and the rebels would not lose a man. But by having it concealed behind timber and hills the rebels could not get within sight with their artillery without getting so close that the men in the stockades could pick off their gunners with ease. Twenty-five to thirty or one hundred men in a stockade properly located made such a stubborn little nest of Yankees that no rebel commander ever cared to capture one of them because the game cost such a price that it paid better to let them alone. The stockades were so situated that the men could shoot any man who put foot on the bridge.

The inhabitants all along the line of road had deserted their homes, but after the armies had both passed on farther down they came skulking back, and many of them that wanted work were employed as track hands, repairing the railroad, and if they showed a willingness to work they were kept at it, but those who did not were watched with suspicion.

Sherman banished the newspaper reporters from his army the same as St. Patrick in an early day banished the toads and snakes from Ireland. In this, history has been robbed of many events that are both historical and instructive. But the annoyance of newspaper reporters was a positive harm in more ways than one. We will give one illustration, while driving the rebel army from point to point.

One of their keys or books to their signal service was left behind and one of our men found it and it was turned over to our signal service. Our men were experts at the business and soon learned to read their signals, and men were kept on duty reading their signals and interpreting them to the generals of the army. From this source our generals could get a pretty correct idea of what was going on in the rebel camps all the time. One day one of our shells burst in the tent of rebel General Pope and killed him. Our signal corps saw the news pass over the rebel signal line and read it two or three miles distant and transmitted the information to General Sherman, who knew of it about as quick as the rebel commander did. A newspaper reporter was present and he telegraphed the news home to his paper and also told how they got the news. It was published, and a copy of the paper found its way through the rebel lines to the rebel commander. The result was that the rebel signal corps changed their key, and news from that source was all cut off after that. This was only one of many similar cases.

CHAPTER 9

Where No Man
Ought to Go

June – September 1864

JUNE 24, 1864, KINGSTON

On the first of June the regiment was still guarding the railroad and patrolling the country in every direction to prevent a raid upon and destruction of the railroad.

There was a patrol station on the valley road on the south side of the Etowa River, while on the north side ran the railroad, and troops were scattered about in camps. The valley road was a thoroughfare on which in time of peace there was much travel. At the bridge where the road crossed the river we had a heavy force of pickets. If a heavy force of rebel cavalry should dash up quick they might drive our pickets away and capture the bridge and cross their forces before we could get force enough there to hold it, or have time to burn it to prevent it falling into their hands. To prevent such a surprise a patrol was placed upon the valley road beyond, to the south, and for a distance of five miles. The patrols rode up and down, up and down, night and day. It came my turn to patrol this road in the night. Four of us on our horses rode to a certain point five miles down and then rode back again; turned around and rode back to the point down the river and then returned as before and continued all night. If we met anyone we were to first halt them, and if they showed any signs of fight we were to shoot and then return to the bridge as fast as circumstance required. It was midnight, or a little after, and the sky was overcast and dark. We were riding silently along the road where it was skirted on either side with dense forests. Everything was as silent as the grave, save the low tread of our horse's hoofs in the road. There were four of us—E. A. Irvine, Wm. Doty, Joseph Norton,[1] and myself. Our eyes were constantly strained, peering into the dark expanse in front of us, and our horses were examining every object, their ears standing to the front to catch every sound, and sniffing the air with their nostrils.

In this way we strode along the dark vale not knowing one moment what the next would bring forth. Presently our horses began sniffing the air, their ears stood farther to the front and their heads raised higher and higher at every step. There was not a word spoken, but each of the four men cocked his gun and brought it to his shoulder with finger on the trigger. Irvine and I were riding in front. By the time our guns were at our shoulders Doty and Norton were at our side, forming a small line of battle of four men. By this time our horse's heads were trained so high that their ears were almost in our faces. At this juncture we could just glean some of the outlines of an object in the road just in front of us. We stopped short and Irvine cried out in a loud voice, "Halt! Who goes there?"

"C–c–c–c–ci–citizen."

"Advance one for examination. If more than one comes we will shoot without further notice," said Irvine. A man on an old cream-colored horse rode up, dressed in the ordinary garb of a Georgian, trembling like an aspen leaf in a summer breeze. He was so frightened that it was with the greatest difficulty that he could speak at all. We examined him carefully to see if he had a revolver, bowie knife, or any other deadly weapon, and then we asked if there were any rebels along the road over which he had passed, assuring him that if he lied to us or deceived us that we would shoot him the moment we discovered the deception. He declared that there were no rebels down the road to his knowledge. We placed his horse between Norton and Doty, and one of them held to the rum strap and we took him along to the end of the route and returned to the picket post and gave him over to Captain Smith, who was in command there. As we strode along the road the old fellow made up and told a very sleek story, telling us that he had been to a certain town where there were rebels and found out all about the number and positions etc., and was now returning to give the information to General Sherman. We had no means of knowing whether he was giving us "taffy" or not, but without doubt he was an old citizen rebel sympathizer who was out prowling around nights to find some easy approach to the railroad where a rebel raid could be easily made, and the railroad destroyed and the trains ditched. We never knew what became of him after we turned him over, but he probably was considered as a prisoner of war and sent along with others to some prison encampment.

The regiment frequently moved from point to point, up and down the railroad, so that rebel bushwhackers and scouts could not tell of our whereabouts. We moved back up and stopped for a day or two on the

Resaca battlefield. Blackberries were ripe, and all over the battlefield the berries were growing as if human blood had fertilized the soil. The first time I passed over the field in search of berries I passed by long rows of new dry earth where large numbers of men who had stood shoulder to shoulder in line of battle were now lying shoulder to shoulder in their silent and shallow graves. There I saw a shoe standing on the heel. My curiosity was aroused and I touched the toe of the shoe against the toe of my boot, and the shoe fell over filled with a human foot. The shoe was filled with a decaying foot and the stump of a decaying human limb freshly parted at the ankle joint from my touch, was just at the surface, and the whole body lay beneath a thin covering of earth without box or coffin. The color of the gray pants was the only sign indicating on which side he had fought.

After a great battle where thousands of men are slain the men are buried without box or coffin, and the weary men who perform the work have their energies so completely exhausted in the previous struggle that they dig very shallow graves and put a thin covering of earth over the departed. It is but a common occurrence to see a hand, a foot, and some-times a head peering out after a hard rain.

At another place in an earthen breastwork of earth where our infantry had charged a hill and taken it, and while under fire they had hastily thrown up earthworks to shield themselves from rebel bullets, and everything was piled in that would stop bullets, including the dead bodies of the rebels who were killed before leaving the hill. In this embankment lay a rebel body with one arm hanging out nearly ready to drop off. In spite of all the hardships and cruelties of war I could not be so hardened that such sights didn't cause a sense of horror to creep over me, and I turned away and sought for locations where no men were buried. The whole atmosphere of the battleground had an appearance of desolation; a sort of a deserted spot where no man ought to go.

We returned again to Kingston and the scouting and patrolling was kept up. It was hard to teach our recruits that they were in constant danger when outside of our picket lines. They could not realize the necessity of keeping together and always having their guns in their hands when there were no rebels around or heard of by the citizens. When they went to a house they would scatter out, one in one place and another somewhere else. One would set his gun in the corner while he went into a smoke house, or would leave his gun in the smoke house while he went into the house, or would set his gun in one room while he sat down to a meal in another.

A scouting party had been sent out with several recruits along, and while they were at a house a band of rebel cavalry dashed unexpectedly down upon them like an avalanche with their swift running horses. The boys who were together successfully fought a retreat, but when they got on to sound grounds again they found three of the recruits missing, who were probably wandering about the plantation with their guns anywhere but in their hands, and were easily made prisoners. The sixteenth part of a second behind time on occasions like this would cost a man his life and the same sixteenth part in advance would save it. The recruits were all good, well-meaning boys and we regretted their loss very much. Justus C. Norton was from our company and he had a brother Joseph who had been with us from the start, who regarded the capture of his brother as equivalent to death or worse, as he probably would starve to death. His fears were well grounded, as [Justus] died a prisoner of war in Florence, Alabama in November following.

Heavy cannonading was going on daily at the front in the direction of Atlanta, showing that the rebel army had halted and were making a stand and determined to fight every inch of ground. The cannonading could be heard all the way from ten to fifteen miles distant, according to changes in the atmosphere. Sherman's army was pressing the rebels at every point and the fighting was regular as the days came and went.

JULY 20, 1864, RESACA

Every horseman or cavalryman who has a good horse falls in love with him, as the horse will be a true friend to the rider on fair treatment, and on thousands of instances a good horse saves a man's life, and a poor, half-starved animal is just excuse enough sometimes in eminent danger to let fast-riding rebels ride up and take the rider's life or take him prisoner. I had a good horse and regarded him as my best friend. I loved him and he was a splendid rider, easy of gait and full of life. He never trotted but always racked instead; a gait that was rather peculiar to him and very easy for the rider, and made it a real pleasure to ride.

While on picket one morning and my horse eating his oats from the green grass at the foot of a small bush to which he was fastened, his foot became entangled in the halter and he was thrown to the ground with considerable violence, dislocating the stifle joint (the joint of the hind leg analogous to the human knee). When he arose again he could not use one leg. To the country this was not much a loss, but to me it was great. He hobbled into camp and the horse doctor—Dr. Spoon—called, and he gave assurance of his ultimate recovery. Several active days were spent with the horse when the order came "Back to Resaca again." Rebels were expected, and away we went and the horse must be left behind. I was ordered to turn him out as a "petered-out horse," abandoned, as of no more use to the army. I could not desert the horse so easy, I found a woman who agreed to look after him and care for him, and away we went. But my affections were left with my horse, so to speak.

On Sunday, July 3, we reached Calhoun, and that evening Chaplain Cartwright announced to the regiment in his usual way, but canvassing, that he would preach in an old church there. Accordingly we all gathered after a long day's march and a hasty supper and listened to a good affectionate rough-and-ready sermon given on the fly. Chaplain Cartwright had a faculty of having successful meetings under difficulties, difficulties under which some ministers would have sunk into forgetfulness. Then would be the time when he would rise the highest in the minds of even those given to profanity and infidelity. It was not uncommon to hear a profane man remark after such a sermon that "that was the damndest best sermon he had ever heard."

July 4, the great national day, was spent on the road to Resaca, and fixing up camp after we got there. Wild rumors were afloat that rebel bushwhackers in considerable numbers were prowling around. Scouting parties were sent out in all directions.

On the sixth of July scouts returned from Dallas and reported that guerrillas had torn up the track and burned a loaded train of cars, and that a rebel spy was caught in our camps at that place and was taken out and hung to a tree after a short trial before a drum-head court-martial. On the ninth another set of scouts from our brigade returned, bringing twenty-eight of the rebel train burners besides killing some in the capture.

The citizens came into our camp daily, trading berries for sugar, coffee, tea, etc. Old coffee and tea drinkers of the South had been so completely blockaded that none of these articles could be had at any ordinary Southern country store, and they would give a large amount of berries for a small amount of coffee or tea. Most any man preferred to drink less tea and coffee and eat more berries, and this made trade in that direction lively.

My horse left at Kingston was uppermost in my mind and I was begging, almost, for a pass to go down in the cars after him, and then I could lead him back. The officers refused on the ground of extreme danger of one man returning alone on a lame horse, as the country was so beset with prowling spies and bushwhackers. At last I conceived a plan by which I agreed to make connection with the patrols and come all the way back with them. A large band of well-armed patrols passed up and down the railroad several times a day from station to station a little in advance of every train. We had men stationed in stockades at regular intervals, whose duty it was to guard bridges and patrol the railroad. It took a great many men to do this over a long line of railroad, but it was the only way the road could be kept open, so thick and troublesome were the spies, scouts, bushwhackers, and cavalry raiders. I was granted a pass on this plan. I boarded the first train, took my seat on top of a box car, where soldiers most always rode, with gun in hand. I made a good mark for some lurking bushwhacker to try his hand at a man on the fly. So frequent had the trains been captured or ditched that every engineer, fireman, brakemen, guards, or passengers, if any were aboard, were on the closest lookout for danger or a lurking enemy. No man ever knew what moment he would be the target of a sharp shooter or receive a shower of balls from some cavalry raiders. I reached my destination without any mishaps and I left the train with the full satisfaction that I preferred to take my lot in line of battle fighting as a soldier than to take my chances as a train man, not knowing what moment one might go into the ditch with no power to prevent it. I found my horse much run down and lame, but able to walk around. There were troops stationed here so I waited till morning to start with the patrols. I stayed at the house of a citizen that night and we spent hours in social conversation talking about the war, the North and the South, and comparing the customs and ways of one with the other. The husband and wife were both illiterate and knew but little of the ways of the world, but from all outward appearances they were on a par with their neighbors of that section of the South. In the evening the husband brought in an armful of pitch pine cut and split into bits about eighteen inches long and the size of a broom handle. As the darkness of the evening approached the wife drew the two "handirons" of the fireplace together in such a way as to leave a V-shaped place where she placed one end of the stick of pitch pine, the other end resting on the hearth. Underneath this stick was a bed of hot sinders, and the pitch pine took fire at once and sent a glaring light through the house and the smoke from the same up the chimney. One could see to read in most any part of the room. When one stick was consumed another was laid on and the light was continuous and cheerful. During our conversation the wife asked me if we had plenty of pine in Illinois. When I told her we had none, only what little was used for ornamental trees she asked, "What on earth to you'uns do for lights in the evenin's?" I told her we used candles (kerosene was not then used to any extent).

"Candles! What do they look like? What are they made of?"

After a long description of the material used, of how they were made, the length, and "how big around" the wife then recollected that once in her life of having seen something about that length and color laying in a box at a store and she never knew what they were nor what they were for, but supposed it was something to eat sent down from the North, and she had a notion to buy one just to see how it tasted.

"I'll bet anything that them was candles I saw in the box."

After a two days' travel along the railroad, keeping with the patrols, I reached camp with my lame horse, having led him all the way. My horse was practically worthless, but my fondness for him blinded my reason and I clung to him and went to work to restore him to a condition of usefulness again.

AUGUST 7, 1864, SAND TOWN, GEORGIA

While lying in camp on the battlefield at Resaca, during the month of July 1864, one of those peculiar laughable incidents occurred, such as can only occur in the army. The regiment lay in camp on the gentle slope of a side hill, just back of where the heavy lines of rebel infantry had stood during the battle of Resaca, where the heaviest of the fighting had been done. For two days our armies had poured the shot and shell into those rebel lines, and the ground on which we were camped had been plowed all up with cannon balls, and shells of all descriptions lay buried beneath our feet. Some shells had gone deep into the ground and exploded, tearing great holes in the earth, while others had gone in and the fuse gone out, and the shells lay beneath the ground unexploded. When a camp fire was built no one thought or cared whether he was building it over an unexploded shell or not. If the camp fire was continued day after day over the same spot, the heat would gradually work down and explode the shell if one chanced to be beneath the fire.

One afternoon Mr. Hawkins,[2] one of the boys of Co. G, concluded to have some pork and beans cooked well done for supper. Accordingly he put a kettle of pork and beans cooking over the camp fire, and stayed by them nearly all the afternoon attending them to see that the fire was neither too hot nor too cold. All of a sudden there came an earthquake shock, the pot went up and the fire went out and Hawkins turned a back double somersault. And the beans, oh where were they? Ask of the ashes that were far around and of Hawkins, who could not say. His eyes, his mouth, his ears, and his hair were filled with ashes and the air was filled with smoke. There was not a bean to be seen. Hawkins supposed that he was very badly hurt until he got the ashes out of his eyes and found the boys all laughing, when he too laughed and thought it was a fine joke. Had Hawkins been killed in the explosion the idea of beans going up to heaven from the wicked State of Georgia would have brought the laugh and smile to the face of the most sedate. Hawkins ate no beans for supper that night.

On the 21st of July General Kilpatrick returned and took command of our division again, having recovered from his wound.[3] We knew now that we would soon go to the front, as Kilpatrick was of such a restless spirit that Sherman could not sleep nights until Kilpatrick should have some active work for his division.[4]

Captain Woodcock was promoted to major and Lieutenant Horace C. Scoville, of Co. K, was promoted to captaincy to fill the vacancy caused by the promotion of Major Woodcock. Lieutenant Scoville was at the same time a prisoner of war in the hands of rebels, captured at Nickojack.

On the 26th the regiment passed recommendatory resolutions as a compliment to Dr. Winston, who had resigned. The doctor was loved by the men of the regiment. He was a skillful physician and a kind-hearted conscientious doctor, who performed his whole duty.

On the 22d I was on picket and a stench filled the air all about us and our position was almost unendurable. A stench had filled the air for many days and no one knew from where it came as the country round about was thickly studded with underbrush. One of the boys came to the conclusion to find the source of the nuisance. He hunted about in the thick under-brush for a time when he came upon the rotting remains of a dead rebel. He probably had been wounded at the battle of Resaca, and crawled off to a place of safety and lay down and died of his wounds alone in his solitude, and his body made food for insects, beasts of the field, and fowls of the air.

On the 22d, 23d and 24th of July a great battle, or series of battles, was fought in front of Atlanta, and the telegrams that came to us were of such a conflicting nature that we could get no head nor tail to the results.

On the 23d, however, agreeable to our expectations, Kilpatrick started with the cavalry command for the front. It was not, however, until August 3 that the whole division of cavalry was concentrated and started together for the front, and the first night we camped near the Altoona Pass. Here the whole division was together and Kilpatrick at its head. We were across the Etawa River and were making for the front. We traveled in the direction of Sand Town [Sandtown], a village of two houses, a barn, strawstack, and sand. This peculiar village was on the south bank of the Chattahoochee River, about ten miles west of Atlanta. The rebels held it, sand and all. The rebels were on the south bank and we went to the north bank and wanted to cross, but they were determined we should not and we were determined to cross. This made trouble and a fight ensued, which was kept up on a skirmishing plan for two or three days. Rebels were prowling all about our camps, especially nights, stealing horses and gobbling up a single man when they could catch one alone. Our men had all heard of the bad treatment at Andersonville,[5] and nearly every man regarded it as about equivalent to death to be taken prisoner and held. Every man would fight as long as there was a possible show for escape before ever surrendering, and if caught would leave no hair's breadth chance of escape pass without trying when the opportunity was offered.

David Boyle,[6] of Co. H, was carrying a dispatch from Colonel Atkins' headquarters to General Kilpatrick's. The road on which he was galloping was thickly studded with a dense undergrowth of young timber, when all of a sudden rebels stepped from the underbrush just in front of him. Dave was wiry, quick, and active. Quick as thought his Spencer pumped a couple of balls at the men in front and he wheeled his horse to run back, when to his surprise several guns were at his breath [*sic*] from the road over which he had just come. David had only one chance left, to die or surrender, and very quick at that. Of course he surrendered. David's restless, active nature did not make him the right kind of a man to hold as a prisoner, even after he was caught, but the rebels did not know that and David was as cunning as a fox. They led him away off into a dense swamp timber and there hid away and waited for the darkness of night when they would again return to the 92d camp, crawl into our lines, and steal horses. There were five rebels in the band, and when it was sufficiently dark four of the number started out for their prowling, horse-stealing raid, and left one of their number to guard over David. At proper bed time David lay down upon the ground and apparently went to sleep. He pulled his handkerchief over his face to keep the mosquitoes from biting, but as he did so he quietly punched a small hole through with his finger just large enough to peep through when he was sound asleep. David's sleep that night was like that of a weasel. He snored like a sound sleeper, but an eye was peeping out of that hole in his handkerchief. The guard sat upon a log and for a time was wide awake, but as the still night hours came and went the guard began to gape, stretch, nod, fell asleep, and snored. David sprang upon his guard with the lightning speed of a panther, snatched the gun from his hands, and with one quick power-ful blow the gun was smashed to splinters and the rebel's brains were scat-tered about on the leaves. David then picked up his own trusty Spencer and got on his own horse and rode away. But his trouble had not yet ended for he had not gone far when he met the other four rebels on four white horses that they had stolen that night of our band boys, and were returning to their place of concealment. To be captured again would be certain death for David. He abandoned his horse and took to the timber hotly pursued. He ran and skulked about until he eluded his pursuers and then returned to the regiment minus hat, coat, shoes, shirt, and the very picture of hard times.

SEPTEMBER 6, 1864, SANDTOWN, GEORGIA

While lying in camp on the river opposite Sandtown the rebels continued to prowl about our camp and picket lines, killing and capturing a man whenever the opportunity offered. The surrounding country was more or less covered with a thick growth of young timber. Nate Davis,[7] of Co. K was captured while carrying the mail to the regiment. One of our pickets was shot through the head and instantly killed; while standing on vidette post, some rebel had crawled near enough in broad daylight, to take delib-erate aim, and the vidette never knew what hurt him.

There is something remarkably unpleasant about standing on a vidette post in the dead hours of the night midst the extra darkness occasioned by the growth of underbrush, especially when a prowling bushwhacker is known to be on the lookout to shoot the vidette.

On the night of the 25th of August I was connected with a picket post around which bushwhackers were prowling and trying to shoot the vidette. Lieutenant P. R. Walker had charge of the whole picket line, and my business was to change the videttes every two hours, on a post where the bushwhackers commenced to prowl around. The vidette stood in a bad place, nearly a half mile away from any field or opening, into a dark second-growth forest, on a road not frequently traveled. Everything passed off quietly till about midnight, when I went out with fresh men to take the positions of those who had stood two hours. Although everything had been still and quiet, yet when we reached the first vidette, there was a tremulous tone to the command, "halt," when we reached the post; "Who comes there?" was given in the same excited tone. "Relief guard" was returned with as much mildness and easiness as I could command given purposely in a mild voice, to allay excitement. I knew the voice well, being that of "Si" Shores,[8] a member of Co. B. "Advance one, and give the countersign," was obeyed, and then I told the guards with me to ride up. "Si" then told us in a low whisper that a bushwhacker had been crawling upon Charley Rowley,[9] who stood twenty rods farther out in the road, and was trying to shoot him. That Charley heard him walking and crawling on the leaves until he was as close as he dare let him come. He was afraid to shoot with no show of precision. If he shot, the rebel could get a tolerable fair bearing from the flash of his gun, and would have the advantage. Charley turned his horse, and rode carefully and slowly back on the dirt road, making as little noise as possible, back to where Si stood, and the two together went still farther back to the open country and there awaited our approach. When they heard us coming they rode just ahead of us back to their positions. We listened to Charley's story given in detail in a very low whisper. The man to take Charley's place was A. B. Sechler,[10] of Co. H. This was a position to try a man's pluck. For several men to be there together, all mounted and well armed, was not much of a strain upon the nerve, but to be left there, solitary and alone, under the circumstances, was more of a draft upon one's courage, than many might suppose, while sitting under their own vine and fig tree, either no one to molest or make them afraid. If the rebel should kill the vidette before morning, it would be of no particular importance, as a national affair, or of military importance to the whole army. But to the individual vidette, it was of as much importance as the whole nation, and even more. The mettle of which Abe was made, would soon be put to its greatest test. Should he utterly refuse to stand there alone, I should not have blamed him. But Abe never faltered; the only thing he requested was the privilege of having the position established a little farther back, at the junction of the two roads. Charley showed us where there was another unpicketed road, that led into the one we were on, and entered it back of the post. If rebels should come down that, the vidette would be cut off, with little or no chance of escape. I moved the post to the junction of the two roads, and Abe took his post without a murmur. I reported to Lieutenant Walker, who kept everything in "readiness" to fly with the quickest possible speed to any point that might be attacked or fired upon. We had no further trouble that night.

SEPTEMBER 19, 1864, FAIRBURN, GEORGIA

It was the aim and desire of General Kilpatrick to cross the Chattahoochee River with the cavalry, but the question was, how could that be done when the rebels were on the other side of the river manifesting a stubborn determination to prevent us from such a move? If the rebels would only all get into some convenient place to be shot we could shoot them all and then the crossing would be made easy; but on the contrary they always were in the very worst place to shoot, and they had loop holes and concealed places to shoot from, and they would send bullets whizzing past our ears, whenever we approached too close to the river bank, that made a very disagreeable sound. Several feints were made to approach the river as if we were going to take the river by storm and build a bridge across, and as we failed to cross the rebels seemed to feel a sort of contentment or satisfaction that we could not get across. But Yankee ingenuity was at work in secret behind it all. The river could not be forded and a bridge must be built to cross on.

On the morning of the 15th of August, at one o'clock at night, we all saddled our horses, fell into column, and marched quietly down the river to a point where there never had been any attempts made to cross. A few pontoon boats were hastily placed into the river and strong picket forces paddled across the stream and formed in line on the opposite bank and there quietly held their position while the pontooners lay in their floating bridge across the stream. At daylight the rebels were hustled from their beds of encampment by the Yankee cavalry marching into their midst with no river between. Kilpatrick was in his glory. A strong force of his men were across and the balance were crossing. It seemed to do him good to see the rebels flutter and skedaddle, firing only now and then a stray shot to save themselves. Sandtown with all its nothingness and sand was ours. We were now in a position where we could harass the rebel left flank to a considerable degree.

In the city of Atlanta, the rebel stronghold which they still held, were four railroads centering there, one from the north, one from the east, one from the south, and one from the west. Sherman's infantry had possession of the ones from the north and east and from the other two, the south and west, the rebel army were daily supplied with provisions and munitions of war.

As soon as the cavalry were all across Kilpatrick dashed out with his whole force in the direction of a little station on the railroad running west from Atlanta. The cavalry moved at a rapid pace, the rebels flying in our front, and long before night we reached the depot and burned the ties, twisted the rails, and retreated a few miles and encamped for the night.

While dashing upon this station I met with an accident that cost me the life of my horse—the horse I prized so highly. We were riding by column; four men side by side, stringing out into a column miles in length, all riding on a run. My horse had not wholly recovered from the injury received on picket. He was still a little weak in one leg, but well enough for ordinary service. I was one of the middle files with two men on the right and one man off my left. All of a sudden my horse stepped upon a rolling stone in such a way as to bring all the strain upon the weak leg, which gave away, and he fell flat upon his side right in the midst of the ranks of that rushing cavalcade. Just what I did at that moment and how I did it I don't know, but the first thing I remembered I was standing erect outside the running column, looking in past the running horses that dashed by me, and there lay my horse at the bottom. The next horse that was behind lay on top with Charles Ames, the rider, fast between the two. By hard work I got the column to turn and bow around on one side, and then I went up and rolled the top horse to a position where he got up and let Charlie loose. Charlie was considerably squeezed and bruised, but not seriously injured. My own horse appeared to be all right, but when he went to rise up I discovered that his sound leg was broken square off near the body. He tried hard to regain his feet, not seeming to realize his condition. He made many attempts before he would desist, but it was an utter impossibility. Now came the hardest part of all. What must I do with him? We were only on a dash and would soon desert the country. If I left him there he would starve to death while writhing with pain from his broken limb. Must I leave him in such a condition or dispatch him with a ball from my own gun? It was but an easy matter to shoot at rebels whenever in sight, but to shoot one's own trusty and true horse was like committing murder. I halted between two opinions when an officer rode up who had charge of the supply of horses, and gave me very positive orders and I was sworn to obey.

We returned to camp the next day and began to prepare for a long march, fixing up our guns, saddles, and other equipment.

At sunset Tuesday evening, August 18, 1864, Kilpatrick's whole cavalry command started on the most remarkable and hazardous raids that it probably ever undertook.[11] Our horses were fed, our supper eaten, and we were in our saddles in time to see the last rays of the evening sun sinking behind the western hills as we rode down and again crossed the pontoon bridge to the south side. We had been told that we were going on a long scout but no man knew where except those in command.

The 10th Ohio Cavalry had the advance that night and everything passed off quietly as we jogged along the dark road through the timber until about nine o'clock, when the advance was fired on. A charge was made by the advance guard and one rebel killed and one captured. On we went, the advance guard clearing the road for a time.

By ten or eleven o'clock at night the rebels became more bold, stubborn, and obstinate. The column was frequently halted and the rebels were constantly firing into the advance guard from the dark shadows of overhanging trees and thickets, and they would retreat when pressed. Kilpatrick became impetuous and restive at this slow progress, and with one of his characteristic oaths ordered up three companies of the 92d with their Spencers for advance guard, and let them try to keep the road clear. Co. B was selected as one of the three companies to be placed on the extreme advance with the other two for supporters. When we got to the line of the 10th Ohio boys to relieve them, they told us that the rebels were only a little way in advance ready to shoot us as soon as we advanced. It was all timber and dark beneath its foliage, but above it was moonlight.

Our regiment had a good reputation among the men of the cavalry division as good fighters, and for the first time as I rode into that "outer darkness" to be shot at I was sorry we had such a reputation. To tell the truth, for the first five minutes I felt more like going back than going ahead, but go ahead was the order and we were sworn to obey. Not a man of us would ride in the road, as the rebels always took a centre shot down the road. We had not gone far when sure enough slam bang came shot after shot from the darkness; nothing seen except flashes, and we pumped a half-dozen or a dozen shots at every flash, and never halted, but rode straight ahead. After a few shots and none of us being hit and the bushes had scratched our faces and torn our clothes and hung our horses in grape vines, the first flush of timidity departed, the scratching of brush aroused a little ire, and a spirit of recklessness seemed to take possession of every man, and we rode boldly and defiantly ahead, shooting at every flash, shadow, or doubtful object we saw, never allowing the column to halt a single moment. The rebels selected a spot and threw a large force in line as they had with the 10th Ohio boys, and then fired a volley at us and drew their revolvers and kept up a continued fire from them. Quick as a flash the whole three companies of the advance were in line and we pumped such a continued deadly volley into that line that they broke, and we could hear their horses run for more than a mile. They never tried that trick again that night. After that at nearly every crook or turn in the road two or three rebels would halt, wait till we were near enough and shoot down the centre of the road, then wheel and run as fast as their horses could carry them. We soon discovered that they shot pretty accurately down the centre of the road. It was really dangerous to ride in the road on horseback and several of our men must certainly get shot before morning.

Ed Webb[12] was a boy that knew no fear and was always glad at any scheme or arrangement to get a good shot at a rebel regardless of the danger surrounding it. Ed and I entered into an agreement whereby we should dismount and give our horses to the orderly to bed further back and out of danger and we would take to the advance on foot, keeping on the outside of the wagon track so that the rebels would shoot between us every time; and then we would carry our guns cocked ready to "shoot on the fly." This would give us several quick shots at short range at every batch of rebels. The plan was a success. The balls passed between us every time and we got five or six shots at every batch. We forgot all about danger, and I think I can truthfully say we really enjoyed it.

The column behind was nearly two miles in length and about three o'clock in the morning we heard fighting about a mile back or half way down the column. Word came to us to halt. We did so and stood at the foot of a little hill. We had stood but a moment when a man in our front rode in sight at the top of the hill. I knew he was a rebel and I believed we could get him alive. I sang out: "Halt!" He stopped. "Advance one and give the countersign." He rode directly down to us and as he approached he said: "Wall boys, it's a right pleasant evening."

We both leveled our guns on him and told him to give us that gun of his but foremost or he was a dead man. He handed it down as instructed. We ordered him off his horse, took a revolver out of his belt, a kit of fine tools out of his pocket enclosed in an awl handle. He was a Texas Ranger; stood six feet in his stockings, and was an active swarthy fellow. He had been sent out with a dispatch and was returning from a southwest direction, and had heard none of the fighting and supposed we were some of their own pickets.

There was some hard fighting back down the road. The rebels had cut our cavalry columns in two and it took some hard fighting to get them together again. It was long after daylight before the command got under way again.

EPILOGUE

The following is a portion of an account of the battles of the 92d Illinois Volunteers as related by Gen. Smith D. Atkins, dedicated to the memory of John M. King, Richard King, and all the soldiers in the 92d Illinois Regiment at a reunion five years after the Civil War. The text begins where King's diary ends.

Do you recollect your review of General Sherman, the smoking ruins of Marietta, and the destroying of the railroad, and the commencement of our march, leading Sherman's columns southward, while Hood was marching north? Do you remember the brilliant charge of the first brigade at the old Rebel earthworks at Lovejoy's when the brigade took back again the two pieces of artillery the Rebels had taken from Stoneman? And the night marching across the Ocmulgee on the pontoons, and into a country where horses and turkeys and sweet potatoes were plenty. And from Clinton to Macon where Captain Becker, with a battalion so handsomely repulsed the charge of Crew's brigade; and do you recollect how that Rebel brigade scattered in utter confusion in every direction through the woods and fields, leaving us an open road up to the Rebel earthworks east of Macon? Can you not now even hear the cannon thunder, and the bursting shells from the nine pieces of artillery with which the enemy opened on us—and can't you see the long line of burning railroad ties, with the iron rails heating for bending? The cutting to that railroad put Wheeler in our rear, and cut off the Rebel General Cobb with his Georgia "Melish" and gave Sherman uninterrupted roads as he wheeled his grand army to the left and held his course for Savannah. And then that rainy night when we retired on the Clinton Road, and buried our dead, and amputated the limbs of the wounded. And the next morning when the boys, under that cool, intrepid officer, Colonel Ban Buskirk, who honored the silver leaves he wore, and had doubly earned the eagles he would have honored, so handsomely repelled the four heavy columns charging against you, and achieved as brilliant a little victory as the history of the war can furnish. I give the credit to the skill of your command and your cool bravery; but you, I knew, will give the credit to your trusty "Spencers" that served you so well and faithfully on many a trying occasion.

And then away through Milledgeville to the left flank of the army, feinting on Augusta, and turning short off for Miller. Do you remember the day when Wheeler came up in our rear, joined by Wade Hampton and his Potomac cavalry, and you so steadily and ably held the rear guard while Kilpatrick's column, uninterrupted, continued its march all day long? I seldom have seen the cool bravery and courage of the Ninety-Second put to a severer test, or more evenly and squarely vindicated. After they had charged one or two of the rail barricades and found them full of Spencers, they became very shy of charging and the remark I made to Kilpatrick was true, that there was no danger to his Division as long as the Ninety-Second was between it and the enemy. Kilpatrick thought the next day that he would superintend the rear guard in person, and came very near getting his precious little person into a Rebel prison, and he himself confessed if it had not been for one of the regiments of my Brigade, the 9th Michigan Cavalry, with their Spencer Rifles, he would have been captured.

Do you recollect Buckhead Creek Church, when an orderly came to tell us that General Kilpatrick was captured, and we waited for the first brigade to pass through ours? And the fight on the Chavish plantation, a little farther on, where we all sat down in the road and gave Wheeler and Hampton, with their combined force far outnumbering ours, an opportunity to run over us if they could, and how they couldn't!

The only mistake of that engagement was that Kilpatrick did not have a couple of regiments ready to charge the confused ranks of the enemy, after we had given them so handsome a repulse! But that was lacking a great many times.

And then there was the fight at Waynesboro. Do you recollect your night on picket, when the enemy brought up his artillery and Erb and Merrill were mustered out honorably? And the next morning, when you were double-quicked into the fight without breakfast. How proud I was of the old Regiment that morning! How coolly you charged the enemy's long line of barricades, capturing eighty-seven of the "Johnnies" and grinding out the shot from your coffee-mill guns on the backs of the fleeing mass that attempted to retreat. How soldierly you behaved, scorning to leave your ranks to take charge of the prisoners your valor had captured, leaving them to be picked up by the cavalry following, and yourselves pressing forward, shoulder to shoulder, and repulsing, with the deadly fire of your death dealing Spencers the heavy charge of Rebel cavalry by which they attempted to regain their lost ground!

That was a brilliant victory, but brilliant as it was, we paid dearly for it. Brave "Gedee" Scott and his no less brave comrades who sleep today in their narrow little beds on that victory-crowned field was part of the price paid for that victory. And on to Savannah, where the dashing waves of the Atlantic sounded welcome to the brave Western men who had marched from the heart of the Continent, over mountain barrier, through rocky defile and dismal swamps, to plant the eagle-surmounted shot and shell-torn standards of the old Republic on the ocean-beat shore! Have you forgotten foraging after rice in the straw for your horses, your trip to the Altamaha River, your foraging expedition to Taylor's Creek after corn, sweet potatoes, honey, turkeys, and chickens? How did you like your oysters gathered up from the neglected oyster beds, on New Year's Day 1865 at King's Bridge? Do you remember our second review by General Sherman, in the streets of the captured city of Savannah, where we passed in review before the Secretary of War? And away again through rain and swamps on to the "sacred soil" of South Carolina? Do you remember how you put your cartridge boxes on your heads and held your guns up over them and waded the Salkehatchie River under fire of the enemy, and charged up the steep hill opposite, and drove them out of their earthworks. When will you forget Narmwel wrapped in flames or Blacksville Station, with its miles of burning railroad ties? When will you forget Aiken? Wheeler and Hampton had there prepared a trap for you, and Kilpatrick's dare-devil dash drove you squarely into the jaws of the trap, but when they sprung it and thought they had you nicely, they found they had caught a tartar!

APPENDIX

The following letters salvaged by the family were written by John M. King and his brother Richard.

⊳—⋅—O—⋅—⊲

Triune, Tennessee, June 1863

Dear Parents,

I once more sit down to write you a few lines to let you know that we are well and hope these few lines find you enjoying the same blessing. We have had a number of letters from you—these all stated that you had not heard from us for a long time. I have answered every letter I have had from you. We got a letter a week or so ago. We would have answered it then but John had written the day before. John has sent $60 to you and to S. Smith to be distributed. I sent my overcoat there a long time ago along with a lot of others. You never have said whether you got it or not. We got two months' pay on the ninth. John made out, got his back pay.

We left Franklin on the second. We are only nine miles from Franklin now. We have thought all the time till lately that we should have to move on the enemy before long but since old Rosa [General Rosecrans] has had to send reinforcements to General Grant we will likely hold our own for the present. We have begun felling trees already for a stronger defence here.

We dare not leave camp; if we are absent from one drill without leave we are liable to a fine from two to ten dollars according to the nature of the offence. This is calculated to bring all shirks to limric. If one man can do his duty another can. So you see it is all right.

We have had two little scares since we came here. The last time they [the Confederates] made believe that they had come in earnest, they managed to bring two pieces of artillery to bear on our camp and we managed to bring four to bear on them which caused the Rebs to beat a retreat. The artillery was brought up on our right. When it commenced firing the Rebs of course fired them then they sent several shells over our heads which caused the boys all to lie down. We had a small grave behind us and the battery. One of the shells struck a tree and glanced off and fell about a rod in front of where I lay. The picket firing lasted from eight until about 2 P.M. Our pickets held well their ground. They were not driven but a short distance. They were only reinforced by two companies of infantry and some cavalry.

I suppose you will get tired reading this miserable letter. Besides, I believe John has written since that little scare. I believe this is all, so good-bye, write soon.

From your sons,
Richard and John King

If I have written anything that makes you think I am homesick you need not credit it for I never felt better since I left home. We have got that box that Henry sent.

⊳–⬦–O–⬦–⊲

Huntsville, Alabama, January 19, 1864

Dear Father,

I received your kind letter of Jan 1. I was glad to hear from you as I always am.

You said it was the coldest weather there that you ever knew in Illinois. The citizens say it was the coldest weather here they ever knew. The ground was froze about two or three inches deep here and up at Polaski where we were on the ninth the thermometer stood 10 degree below zero. Some of these Southerners nearly froze to death, by the way, there is a great deal of suffering among the children of the poor class. New Year's day our Company scouted for horses and mules and one of our boys [James Foster] went into a house where a woman and two or three children were actually starving, this was in the backwoods near the south line of Tennessee. He gave them all the meat and hard bread he had.

Our Company captured sixteen horses and mules that day. It makes the old planters look "blue" to take their stock from them. We receipt them for their animals but they must prove themselves loyal before they get their pay.

Father, I have often thought of the old stories I have heard you tell but could not appreciate the merit of them at the time. We travel most all the time, we have been here four days, I expect to leave tomorrow. I have a very good knowledge of all the country about here. I have kept a diary and have all our travels day and date. By the way, if you go to Rockford soon I wish you would buy me a pocket map of Kentucky and Tennessee, Georgia, Alabama, and Mississippi. It would be of much value. The lighter it is the better, for you know a soldier don't like heavy articles. Everything in the South is very dull. I have seen several towns in one day along the Memphis and Charleston R.R. that would not average three families a piece and each town was as large as Byron and some larger. I will name a few, Belfont, Bigwood Station, Littlewood, and Brownsborough.

Huntsville occupies about ⅙ of its original inhabitants, large and nice brick buildings are entirely deserted and are used for our troops' winter quarters and their stores are used by Yankee sutlers, and their first-class depot used for stables. There is one of the finest depots here that I have seen this side of Louisville.

The Rebs have paid dear for their rebellion. I have often been back where the army had passed over and everything was complete desolation. I have often heard it remarked when I was home that they would like to see the old battle fields and the country where the army had moved.

But I would rather take a dose of Herick pills than to see anymore for beauty's sake. I used to like to hear the boom of cannon. But the scream of a shell at Triune, Ringold, and Chicamauga spoiled all that beauty. I have seen all the blood I care about and felt the sting of one ball (a graze) and that's enough unless necessary. Richard and I are well and fat. I was never more fleshy now than I ever was. Give my love to the family.

Yours Truly

John

>-!-◆>-•O-•◆•!-◄

Camp at Concord, North Carolina, June 13, 1865

It has been so long since I have heard from you. I have been looking for a letter every day for a long time from you and in doing so I made up my mind not to forget to write to you. Of course I don't owe you a letter but then at present I suppose I have more time to write than you have. We have had some excitement here about getting home. I did think some time ago that we would be home before long but our officers did not go the right way to work and the whole has to be done over again. It does seem as though our officers are acting thus on purpose to prolong our stay in the service because when we are out of the service those poor fellows will not get their one and two hundred dollars a month any longer and will have to go back to their old occupation again of standing behind the counter or searching over old law books. I do not wish to speak disrespectful of our officers in the least, but I think I will be safe in saying that if they had done as becomes officers who look to the interest of their men we would have been on our road home now if not already there.

The weather here is very pleasant with an occasional shower. The farmers here have nearly finished their harvest but the crop is light. Flour is worth 86 cents per cut. This town is as large as Oregon [Illinois;] it has a court house and jail and three churches. The soil here is baked very hard by the sun. Wheat doesn't yield more than half as much to the acre as it does in Illinois.

I want you to write when you get this even if we are on the road home. I will get the letter no matter where we are, the mail most always finds us. Tell Ma she must not worry about Johnny. I think he is doing well. At least he was when Thomas Austin left him. If you don't know where to send a letter I think one would reach him if sent to Bedlows Island, General Hospital. His descriptive roll came to Co. A a short time ago. I had thought before that he would soon be discharged . Tell Lucy I have not got any answer to my letters yet. She must not forget to write. Well, Father I must close my letter. I expect to see you soon and I look forward to that time with pleasure and delight. I know you will forgive me for leaving home for I feel that I have done my country good service for which either of us ought never to forget.

Richard

NOTES

CHAPTER 1
EVERYONE SEEMED TO BE ENLISTING

1. The previous statement begins King's memoirs and is also transcribed directly from his diary.

2. Mount Morris Seminary, first established in 1853 by the Methodist Church, was once the centerpiece of the town of Mount Morris. The old "Sandstone," as it is known today, still stands with several fellow historic college halls to compose the town square. The buildings are now home to local businesses.

3. Eugene Evarts of Marion, Illinois, enlisted August 5, 1862, and died at New Albany, Indiana, April 17, 1863.

4. The second battle at Manassas, known also as the Battle of Bull Run, had devastating results for the Union army. In late August Union general George McClellan led his men against the Confederates, who had broken through Bull Run Gap and were poised to take control of precious ground immediately south of Washington D.C. In five days of fighting the Union lost 16,000 men of a total force of 65,000 and behind Union lines all was confusion. See James M. McPherson, *Battle Cry of Freedom: The Civil War Era* (New York: Oxford University Press, 1988), pp. 533–34.

5. Wilber W. Dennis of Byron, Illinois, was replaced by Horace Smith after the former officially resigned his captaincy January 23, 1863. See Adjutant General's Report, Ninety-second Infantry.

6. Temperance was at this time much in vogue with the more "upstanding" young men of Illinois small towns.

7. Chief Black Hawk (1767–1838) was a renowned Native-American chief of the Fox and Sauk in the Black Hawk War of 1832.

8. Albert Woodcock of Oregon, Illinois, was appointed major of the 92d Infantry on April 21, 1864. See Adjutant General's Report.

9. Major Dutcher does not appear in the Adjutant General's Report.

10. Captain Weld does not appear in the Adjutant General's Report.

11. First Lieutenant William H. Crowell was a resident of Marion, Illinois. He enlisted September 4, 1862, and resigned February 19, 1863.

12. No record is found of these men.

13. Smith D. Atkins of Freeport, Illinois, was mustered in September 4, 1862, and appointed colonel. He was mustered out June 21, 1865, as brigadier general. See Adjutant General's Report.

14. Benjamin F. Sheets of Oregon, Illinois, was appointed lieutenant colonel after his enlistment in September 1862. He resigned April 21, 1864. See Adjutant General's Report.

15. Major John H. Bohn joined in September 1862. He was a resident of Mount Carroll, Illinois, and resigned April 21, 1864.

16. This common expression used by Union soldiers refers to escaped or released slaves.

17. This performance would have been a form of what we know today as tap dancing. The barn door acted as a stage for dancers.

18. James R. Tobin of Leaf River, Illinois, enlisted in August 1862. See Adjutant General's Report.

19. Lake Michigan.

20. Robert Lockwood was a resident of Byron, Illinois. He enlisted in August 1862 and transferred to the 65th Illinois Infantry on an unrecorded date. See Adjutant General's Report.

21. Clinton Helm of Byron was the chief surgeon for the 92d throughout the infantry's existence. He was mustered out June 21, 1864. See Adjutant General's Report.

22. No record remains of Dick McCann.

23. This is probably a reference to the assassin bug of the Reduviidae family, known for its powerful, short, curved beak adapted for sucking blood and capable of inflicting a painful bite. Also known as the kissing bug, it often bites the lips of sleeping victims.

24. Cumberland Gap was the center of repeated struggles between the North and South. The most well-known maneuvering there, however, took place during the time noted by King.

25. Juba was a dance popular among the plantation slaves of the eighteenth and nineteenth centuries and is based on complex rhythmic clapping and body movements. The dance is of West African origin.
26. James Tobin was listed as a deserter as of October 1862. See Adjutant General's Report.
27. Information about Colonel Cockran not available.
28. Both Elias Barrack and Michael Crowley of Byron enlisted August 15, 1862, and were mustered out June 21, 1865. See Adjutant General's Report.

CHAPTER 2
IN THE HANDS OF A BRAINLESS COMMANDER

1. Major General Absalon Baird.
2. The following document was included with the diary:

> Order for delivery of property. To the Sheriff of Fayette County: You are commanded to take the slave Sylvester, about 38 years old and of black complexion and of the value of Five hundred dollars, from the possession of the Defendant [Colonel] Smith D. Atkins and deliver him to the Plaintiff, William Hickman, upon his giving the Bond required by law; and you will make due return of this Order of the first day of the next January Term of the Fayette Circuit Court. Witness John B. Norton, Clerk of said Court, this 18th day of November, 1862.

3. Camp Dick Robinson was situated in bluegrass country near the position where the pike for Lancaster and Crab Orchard leaves the Lexington and Danville Pike, between Dick's River and the Kentucky. It was the gathering point for four full Kentucky regiments and nearly 2,000 east-Tennesseeans. Brigadier General George Thomas took command there for the Union army in October after the Union had resecured Kentucky.
4. Reuben Edgar of White Rock, Illinois, enlisted August 12, 1862, and was mustered out June 21, 1865. See Adjutant General's Report.
5. Second Lieutenant Ephraim F. Bander of Leaf River appears several times in King's memoirs under different spellings. He spells the name in some sections as "Beander." In this passage, King is implying some

kind of indiscretionary behavior that cannot be substantiated anywhere. Bander served from September 4, 1862, to January 23, 1863, when he resigned. See Adjutant General's Report.

6. Unable to verify this statistic.

7. No record is found of the attacker or the victim in the stabbing incident on the *Tempest*.

8. Earl Van Dorn was a diminutive but hard-bitten Mississippian who was wounded five times in the Mexican War and in frontier Indian fighting. He had put together a motley force numbering 16,000 consisting of divisions who had fought and won at Wilson's Creek as well as Indians from the Five Civilized Nations in Indian Territory, mostly Cherokee. Joseph Wheeler was a twenty-six-year-old cavalry commander who came from hard fighting at the Yankee lines two miles northwest of Murfreesboro, where General Bragg's division had drawn up astride Stones River. The February 3 offensive that King refers to is not listed in the books I researched. See McPherson, *Battle Cry of Freedom*, p. 579.

9. The battle King had just missed was the second battle over the stockade, which was not really a fort at all. Johnston sent 12,000 men to the area just as Grant was sending 15,000 Yankees. Ten thousand Union reinforcements arrived on February 14, and Grant ordered the navy to shell the fort while his troops closed the ring to prevent the garrison's escape. But the naval ships were overwhelmed and each took some forty or more hits. Heavy fighting continued at the fort and by nightfall nearly a thousand Union and Confederate men had been killed. Under the cloud of inevitable defeat, some Confederate officers escaped, including slave-trader Nathan Bedford Forrest, head of a cavalry battalion that fought with distinction that day. On February 17 Forrest led 700 troopers out of Fort Donelson across an icy stream too deep for infantry to ford. Some 12,000 Rebel fighters were forced to surrender. See McPherson, *Battle Cry of Freedom*, pp. 400–402.

10. First Lieutenant Alexander M. York was a resident of Lanark, Illinois. He joined in September 4, 1862, and later was promoted, although the records do not determine to what rank. See Adjutant General's Report.

11. Stone River is King's allusion to Stones River, where General Rosecrans defended Murfreesboro against Rebel general John Bell Hood. Granger's 4,000 troops, including King, had been sent directly across the Tennessee River from Decatur, some thirty miles down the Chattanooga & Nashville from capital headquarters.

12. Quinine was used extensively by both armies as a cure for fevers.
13. First Lieutenant Horace J. Smith of Co. K was an Oregon, Illinois, resident. He received his commission September 4, 1862, and was later promoted to captain of Co. B.

CHAPTER 3
WE WERE ALL ANXIOUS FOR THE FRAY

1. Charles Ames of Byron enlisted August 12, 1862, and was mustered out June 21, 1865.
2. The Copperhead movement begun in the North by mostly Democrats opposed military action against the Confederates. This group opposed the transformation of the Civil War into a total war—a war to destroy the old South instead of to restore the old Union. The title "copperhead" originated as an epithet used by Ohio Republicans to liken the group to the venomous snake of that name. By 1863 some Democrats proudly accepted the label and began wearing badges bearing likenesses of the Goddess of Liberty from the copper penny to symbolize their opposition to Republican "tyranny." See McPherson, *Battle Cry of Freedom*, pp. 493–94.
3. Many Civil War historians note that Granger was a difficult and obstinate man, devoted to protocol, and for that reason unpopular among his men. But he is also cited as being an effective leader and even commended for several tactical maneuvers he made. Those include the stubbornly hard training of his midwestern troops, who had their own reputation as being tough and gritty fighters, possibly in part thanks to the gruelling campaigning under Granger. See Shelby Foote, *The Civil War: A Narrative* (New York: Random House, 1974), pp. 496–97, 506–7.
4. There is no written verification of this invitation.
5. Major General Philip Henry Sheridan.
6. It is difficult to imagine, with our knowledge of modern medicine, just what exactly afflicted King. His reference to "scorpute" may be a misspelling of scorbutus, another name for scurvy. It is unlikely, however, that scurvy alone would cause the symptoms he describes, including numbness and discoloration of the legs.
7. There is no written record of Henry Middlekoff of Co. K.
8. Brigadier General Felix K. Zollicoffer was killed in battle at Mill Springs, January 19, 1862.

CHAPTER 4
THE REBELS SEEMED DETERMINED TO FIGHT

1. Barton H. Cartwright enlisted April 20, 1863, and was mustered out June 21, 1865. There is no listing of his place of residence. See Adjutant General's Report.

2. Earl Van Dorn was known as a ladies' man. The general's frequent riding companion while at Spring Hill was Jessie McKissack Peters, the young wife of Dr. James Bodley Peters, a man in his late forties. On May 7, 1863, Dr. Peters called on the general in his quarters in the Martin Cheairs house and shot and killed Van Dorn as he sat at his desk. Peters fled to Union-held Franklin. He justified the killing, testifying that Van Dorn had "violated the sanctity of his home." See William C. Davis, *The Confederate Generals* vol. 6 (Harrisburg, Pa.: National Historical Society, 1991), p. 75.

3. In an infantry regiment the colonel, lieutenant colonel, major, three doctors, and chaplain are entitled to ride on horseback.

4. Confederate general Nathan Bedford Forrest was a Tennessee native. He led a force of 2,500 men living off the friendly countryside and fading into the hills like guerrillas—they could strike at times and places of their own choosing, wreaking havoc among the much larger Union forces. See McPherson, *Battle Cry of Freedom*, pp. 513–14.

5. Also called "all fours" and "pitch," seven-up is a card game originally requiring seven points to win.

6. On June 23, the 92d Volunteer Infantry marched to participate in the movements of Rosecrans's army that resulted in the evacuation of Murfreesboro and Shelbyville by Bragg's army. The boys of the 92d then participated in the engagement at Guy's Gap and in the capture and taking charge of 505 rebel prisoners, and took post at Shelbyville. See Report of the Headquarters Twenty-third Army Corps in *History of 92d Volunteer Infantry, Mounted*.

7. J. G. Wilder was directed to make an advance through Confederate pickets, opening a gap where Thomas and Granger would follow with their men. Wilder took his order literally. His mounted men, armed with Spencer rifles, drove Southerners back through heavy and deadly fighting. See Robert Underwood Johnson and Clarence Clough Buel, *Battles and Leaders of the Civil War* (Secaucus, N.J.: Century Magazine, 1983), p. 143.

8. John Hunt Morgan led a raid across the Ohio River into the North in July 1863. After a long chase through southern Indiana and Ohio, Union cavalry captured Morgan and most of his men. In November 1863 he made a spectacular tunnel escape from an Ohio penitentiary and returned to the Confederacy after more daring feats against the North. See McPherson, *Battle Cry of Freedom*, pp. 513–14, 515–16, 628.

9. No listing for Patterson is found.

10. Major General Robert H. Minty, 4th Michigan Cavalry; Brigadier General George Wagner, 15th Indiana.

11. James Mullarkey is not listed as a Co. B private.

12. Collins Willey of Lane Station, Illinois, enlisted August 6, 1862, and was mustered out June 21, 1865.

13. Alabama is dotted with many dramatic caverns that have been since preserved for the public. Judging from its proximity to Bridgeport, the cave King explored most likely is Sequoyah Caverns, now a public park.

14. Captain Robert M. A. Hawk of Lanark joined September 4, 1862, and was promoted from first lieutenant in January 1863. He was a member of Co. C. See Adjutant General's Report.

15. Not surprisingly, there is no historical record of this interaction with Major General Thomas L. Crittenden.

CHAPTER 5
I BELIEVED MY TIME HAD COME

1. Major Geneneral McCook was later retired from field service as a result of his poor showing at Chickamauga. See Foote, *The Civil War*, pp. 486–88.

2. General George H. Thomas, commander of the Army of the Cumberland in the Tennessee and Georgia campaigns, was commonly known as the "Rock of Chickamauga." His holding of the left wing of the army during the Chickamauga battle was considered one of the most glorious feats of the war. With the right wing of the army routed and in utter confusion, Thomas kept his position against the whole of Bragg's army until ordered to withdraw. He declined the brevet of lieutenant general, which President Johnson offered him in 1868. This anecdote of King's reinforces the enormous popularity "Old Pap" enjoyed among the fighting soldiers.

3. This famed Confederate prison housed thousands of Union men during the Civil War. In a report by Thomas Thatcher Graves, aide-de-camp on the staff of General Weitzel, the Northern troops "liberated" the prison after capturing Richmond. "As we entered the suburbs the general ordered me to take half a dozen cavalry men and go to Libby Prison, for our thoughts were upon the wretched men whom we supposed were still confined within its walls. . . . Not a guard, not an inmate remained; the doors were wide open and only a few negroes greeted us with "Day's all gone, Massa!" See Johnson and Buel, *Battles and Leaders of the Civil War*, p. 725.

CHAPTER 6
HALF THE WINTER IN THE SADDLE

1. There is no official reference to Captain Becher based on my research.
2. Lieutenant Skinner is not listed as a member of Co. B.
3. John E. Bond of Rockville, Illinois, enlisted August 1, 1862, and was mustered out June 21, 1865. William C. Murtfelt was a resident of Marion, Illinois, who enlisted August 9, 1862, and mustered out June 21, 1865. See Adjutant General's Report.
4. A line guard is a prison wall surrounding an enclosure, beyond which no soldier can go either night or day.

CHAPTER 7
BANG UP AGAINST A WHOLE BRIGADE

1. The general referred to here is John B. Turchin, leader of the XIV Corps of the Army of the Cumberland.
2. Brigadier General Phillip D. Roddy.
3. Horace Smith's injury is not listed in official documents and he was mustered out with his fellow soldiers on June 21, 1865. See Adjutant General's Report.
4. This Confederate officer is listed killed in January 1864.
5. John F. Miller, colonel of the 29th Indiana.
6. Jesse J. Phillips, lieutenant colonel of the 9th Illinois, was killed May 9 at Snake Creek Gap.
7. A Unionist guerrilla. The term originates from free-soil guerrillas in Kansas or Missouri during the border disputes of 1857–59.

CHAPTER 8
WE SUFFERED A TERRIBLE SLAUGHTER

1. General Washington Elliott was chief of cavalry under General Thomas.
2. General Judson Kilpatrick of the Army of the Potomac.
3. Probably a misspelling of Brigadier General Kenner Garrard.
4. R. Joural O'Conner enlisted August 13, 1862. Interestingly, his death, at the hands of Lieutenant C. S. Pointer, while a prisoner of war is in written record. He died April 23, 1864. William Cattarach (also listed as Wm. Castana) enlisted November 10, 1863, and also was shot by Pointer while a prisoner. He died May 7, 1864.
5. According to King's memoirs, Elliott was taken to Andersonville, where he eventually starved to death. This is verified in official documents with a date of death of September 7, 1864. See Adjutant General's Report.
6. While Lieutenant Point has become infamous in the 92d's history, his first name does not appear listed. Accounts of the affair are garbled and contradictory, according to Lee Kennett in *Marching Through Georgia: The Story of Soldiers and Civilians During Sherman's Campaign* (New York: HarperCollins, 1995), p. 76, but the version the 92d men believed was that the Rebels headed to their own lines with their dismounted prisoners in tow, and when the prisoners couldn't or wouldn't move fast enough, the guards began to shoot them.
7. Robert M. A. Hawk, a native of Lanark, Illinois, was captain of Co. C. See Adjutant General's Report.
8. The Army of the Cumberland had been hard hit by losses at Chickamauga, and the Confederates had planted artillery on Lookout Mountain south of Chattanooga, threatening Rosecrans's supply routes. President Lincoln, fearing Rosecrans was unequal to the impending crisis, activated Joe Hooker to command an expeditionary force of 20,000 men from the Army of the Potomac. It was reported to be the longest and fastest movement of such a large body of troops before the twentieth century. See McPherson, *Battle Cry of Freedom*, pp. 677–78.
9. The Union army had cut the Confederates off from supplies and reinforcements and they had no choice but to flee. Bridges across Oostanaula were destroyed by Union forces. Upon hearing the news, Sherman was said to have banged on his table so emphatically that the

dishes rattled, shouting, "I've got Joe Johnston dead!" See Foote, *The Civil War*, p. 335.

CHAPTER 9
WHERE NO MAN OUGHT TO GO

1. Edwin A. Irvine of Rockvale, Illinois, was enlisted August 11, 1862 and discharged July 31, 1864, to accept a commission in the U.S. Colored Troops. Julius Norton of Co. B of Byron died at Florence, Alabama, November 19, 1864, as prisoner of war. There is no William Doty listed. See Adjutant General's Report.
2. George and William Hawkins, both of Waddams, Illinois, were recruited August 9, 1862, and mustered out June 21, 1865. See Adjutant General's Report.
3. Kilpatrick spent ten weeks recuperating from his injury sustained in the Resaca Battlefield. In his new role, still weakened from his injury, he was advised by Sherman to "fight but not to work." See Foote, *The Civil War*, p. 520.
4. In fact, Sherman had great faith in "Little Kil," who had a reputation as a fighter, unlike his colleague Garrard, whom Sherman said "would flinch if he spotted a horseman in the distance with a spyglass." See Foote, *The Civil War*, p. 409.
5. This infamous prisoner-of-war camp was established by the Confederates in Georgia. Overcrowding and lack of food led to the deaths of thousands. At one time more than 30,000 Federal prisoners were held at the camp. See Foote, *The Civil War*, pp. 416–17.
6. David Boyle of Co. H was a resident of Lane Station, Illinois. He enlisted August 11, 1862, and was mustered out June 21, 1865. See Adjutant General's Report.
7. Nathaniel Davis of Co. K was a resident of Marion, Illinois. He enlisted August 15, 1862, and was mustered out as a prisoner of war on June 14, 1865. See Adjutant General's Report.
8. Josiah Shores of Co. B was a resident of Rockvale, Illinois. He was mustered out June 21, 1865, as a corporal.
9. James (Charley) Rowley of Lane, Illinois, enlisted August 11, 1862. His termination in the service is unlisted. See Adjutant General's Report.
10. A. B. Sichler of White Rock, Illinois, enlisted August 11, 1862, and was mustered out June 21, 1865. See Adjutant General's Report.

11. Reinforced by two brigades from Garrard, Kilpatrick headed southeast under orders to break up the Macon railroad around Jonesboro.

12. Edwin W. Webb of Leaf River, Illinois, enlisted August 14, 1862. He was mustered out June 21, 1865. See Adjutant General's Report.

BIBLIOGRAPHY

Abbazia, Patrick. *The Chickamauga Campaign*. New York: Combined Books, 1988.

Adjutant General's Report, Ninety-second Infantry

Davis, William C. *The Confederate Generals*. Harrisburg, Pa.: The National Historical Society, 1991.

Foote, Shelby. *The Civil War: A Narrative*. New York: Random House, 1974.

Johnson, Robert Underwood and Buel, Clarence Clough. *Battles and Leaders of the Civil War*. Secaucus, N.J.: Century Magazine, 1983.

Kennett, Lee. *Marching Through Georgia: The Story of Soldiers and Civilians During Sherman's Campaign*. New York: HarperCollins, 1995.

McPherson, James M. *Battle Cry of Freedom: The Civil War Era*. New York: Oxford University Press, 1988.

Miller, Francis Trevelyan. *The Armies and the Leaders*. New York: Castle Books, 1957.

Mitchell, Joseph B. *Military Leaders in the Civil War*. New York: G. P. Putnam's Sons, 1972.

Nevins, Allan. *The War for the Union*. New York: Charles Scribner's Sons, 1959.

INDEX

Dennis, Capt. Wilbur W., 2–3, 11, 25, 36, 241n.5
  and drinking, 4–6, 12–13, 22–23, 35; elected to captain, 6; and fighting, 12–13, 22–23; resignation of, 35
Diver River, 102
Doty, William, 217
Dover, battle of, 47, 48
Dress parade, description of, 34
drilling, description of, 9, 61
drinking, 2–4, 38, 44
Duck River, 66, 93, 100
  description of, 98; bathing in, 98–99

E

Edgar, Reuben, 30, 127, 200, 243n.4
83d Illinois Infantry, 48, 48, 49
Elk River, 163
Elkhorn River, 22
Elkmont Springs, TN, 162
Elliott, E. M., 193, 194, 196, 249n.5
Elliott, Brig. Gen. Washington, 189, 191, 249n.1
Enfield rifles, 11
enlisted soldiers,
  treatment of, 33–34, 40, 57; pay, 36, 65, 100–101, 146; comparison with officers, 41–42, 45; fighting, 44, 151
Etowa River, 217, 225
Evarts, Eugene, 2, 241n.3
exams, physical, 7–8

F

4th Alabama Cavalry (CSA), 173
14th Kentucky Infantry, 24, 27
40th Ohio, 80
49th Michigan, 63
false alarms, 25–26
Forrest, Nathan B., 63, 64, 85
Fort Donelson, 46
  description of, 49
Fort Donelson, battle of, 46, 47, 48, 94
fox hunting, 183
Franklin, TN, 61, 63, 64, 65, 67, 68, 69, 71, 87
  raid of, 80
Fredericksburg, battle of, 30
furlough, description of, 10

G

gambling, 101, 146–47
Garrard, Brig.Gen. Kenner, 191
Good Templars Society, 3
Gordon's Gap, 206
Grant, Gen. Ulysses S., 97, 99
Granger, Maj. Gen. Gordon, ix, 32–33, 37, 63, 67, 69, 92, 245n.3
  description of, 32–33, 64; forbids fires on picket, 68, 70; as butt of jokes, 70, 83; body guards of, 78–79; calls temporary truce, 82; and drinking, 82, 87;